THE LAST FRENCH
AND INDIAN WAR

BY THE SAME AUTHOR

L'Union des deux Canadas (1791-1840). Trois-Rivières: Éditions du Bien public, 1962.

Les Juifs et la Nouvelle-France. Trois-Rivières: Boréal Express, 1968.

L'Assemblée nationale en devenir. Pour un meilleur équilibre de nos institutions. Quebec City: Assemblée nationale du Québec, 1982.

Québec 1792. Les auteurs, les institutions et les frontières. Montreal: Fides, 1992.

IN COLLABORATION

Journal Boréal Express. Vol. I (1534-1760); vol. II (1763-1810); vol. III (1810-1841).

With Jacques Lacoursière and Jean Provencher. *Canada-Québec, synthèse historique*. Montreal: Renouveau pédagogique, 1968.

With Louise Côté and Louis Tardivel. *L'Indien généreux. Ce que le monde doit aux Amériques*. Montreal: Boréal/Septentrion, 1992.

Denis Vaugeois

THE LAST FRENCH AND INDIAN WAR

An Inquiry into a Safe-Conduct Issued in 1760
that Acquired the Value of a Treaty in 1990

Translated by Käthe Roth

McGILL-QUEEN'S UNIVERSITY PRESS · SEPTENTRION

ABBREVIATIONS

ANQ   Archives nationales du Québec
CD   Constitutional Documents
DCB   *Dictionary of Canadian Biography*
MAS   Microfilm: "Arret Sioui"
NAC   National Archives of Canada
RCA   Report of Canadian Archives
RJQ   Recueils de jurisprudence du Québec
SCR   Supreme Court Records

Les éditions du Septentrion wishes to thank the Canada Council for the Arts and the Société de développement des entreprises culturelles du Québec (SODEC) for support of its publishing program, as well as the Government of Quebec for its tax credit program for book publishing. We are also grateful for financial support received from the Government of Canada through the Book Publishing Industry Development Program (BPIDP).

Graphic Design: Gianni Caccia and Folio infographie

Cover: View of Oswegatchie and Fort de la Présentation (1760) by Thomas Davies. National Gallery of Canada, 6271

Copy editing: Joan Irving

Original French edition
© 1995 Les éditions du Septentrion/Les éditions du Boréal

English edition co-published by
Les éditions du Septentrion
        and
McGill-Queen's University Press
© 2002 Les éditions du Septentrion

ISBN 2-89448-311-2

Legal Deposit – 1st quarter 2002
National Library of Canada

Table of Contents

III
THE MURRAY DOCUMENT AND THE HISTORIANS

Introduction

IN CANADA, 1990 was the year of the Indians. Following two decisions in the Supreme Court, the *Sparrow* and *Sioui* rulings, the Oka crisis dominated the news. An Aboriginal member of the provincial legislature in Manitoba, Elijah Harper, drew attention for his opposition to ratification of the Meech Lake Accord. All of these events took place from May to August, 1990. Pure coincidence? No. They are closely connected.

We have to return to 1969 to find one of the starting points. In that year, the prime minister, Pierre Elliott Trudeau, had to beat a retreat from his White Paper proposing "the repeal of the Indian Act" and the abolition of Indians' special rights. The document, published with the "authorization" of Jean Chrétien, at the time minister of Indian and Northern Affairs, proposed to extinguish special status for Indians in favour of "true equality" and offered measures to encourage their participation in the cultural, social, economic, and political affairs of Canada. These proposals backfired. The Indians wanted nothing to do with them. Trudeau had to pull back. For their part, the Indians became more united and determined than ever before.

Trudeau went on to other things.

At the beginning of 1980, Trudeau returned to the prime-ministership after a short stint in the position by Joe Clark. In May, the Parti Québécois, in power inQuebec since November, 1976, held its referendum on the independence of Quebec.

Quebec had devised strict referendum rules. The YES and NO camps had to account for all of their expenditures and respect

These Elliotts were not Trudeau's ancestors, according to the genealogist Alexandre Alemann. In fact, Trudeau never claimed that they were.

well-established limits. The federal authorities derailed the plans of the *indépendantistes* and bought advertising time and space to broadcast messages of all sorts, many of them with a double meaning, such as "No, thank you." Theoretically, the YES camp should have been able to use the resources of the Quebec government, but the fight quickly proved to be unequal.

The premier of Quebec, René Lévesque, led the YES camp. The polls did not support his position, and the federal offensive, which he hadn't foreseen, threw him off track. Trudeau's confidence – not to mention arrogance – exasperated him.

On May 8, Lévesque snapped. "His name is Pierre Elliott! Don't forget that. He has chosen the Anglo-Saxon side of his heritage!" he remarked to a man who accosted him in a reception centre for senior citizens.

"They've told me . . . Mr. Lévesque said that part of my name is Elliott," Trudeau retorted, six days later, to an audience won over to his cause. "Since Elliott is an English name, it is perfectly understandable that I speak out for the NO side," Trudeau insisted, referring to the premier of Quebec. Trudeau savoured the moment. "Quebecers who will vote 'no' are not as good Quebecers as the others. One or two drops of foreign blood might flow in their veins . . . . Yes, Elliott is my mother's name, you see, it is the name of the Elliotts who came to Canada more than two hundred years ago. It's the name of the Elliotts who settled in Saint-Gabriel-de-Brandon . . . more than one hundred years ago. You can see their graves in the cemetery."

The crowd was delirious. Everyone realized that Lévesque had made a huge gaffe by attacking Trudeau's ancestry. It was an even more regrettable faux-pas since it had come from someone who was normally given to tolerance and openness.

The damage was done. Quebec wanted change. It would have change, Trudeau said. "I personally solemnly undertake that after a NO victory, we will take immediate measures to update the constitution." Although he was angry, he seemed also to be fiercely determined.

During the same flight of oratory, Trudeau pointed at his face and said, "I ask you if this face is that of a pure European." The allusion to his Aboriginal roots was obvious.

Like most French Canadians, Trudeau had many ethnic roots. Whichever were dominant, he had the same discourse for "French Canadians" and for Indians, self-styled "of pure blood": "Take your place. Fight, impose yourselves, but don't live apart, on the margins." The subtext: "Be like me!"□

On June 25, 1980, just over a month after the NO victory (May 20), Trudeau paid a visit to his British counterpart, Margaret Thatcher, to inform her of his intention to repatriate the Canadian constitution.

Quebecers wanted changes, and they weren't long in coming. In October, the Canadian prime minister announced that he would submit to Parliament an amendment formula and a charter of rights. Very much a realist, Trudeau knew that it was difficult to change the distribution of powers between the federal and provincial governments or to make any constitutional changes. But he was ready to confront the recalcitrant provinces, especially Quebec. The re-election of the Parti Québécois on April 13, 1981, only increased his determination.

In London, where they made their fears known, Quebecers received unexpected help. Indian demonstrations and demands were multiplying. Repatriation of the constitution? Yes, and then? Trudeau made fun of Quebec's opposition, but the Indians' opposition gave him pause. He knew the hearing that they would get in Europe. Their colourful demonstrations could wreak havoc. He decided to soften their impact and sent Jean Chrétien to the front.

He brought out the three sections (25, 35, and 37) of the Constitution Act, 1982, that made explicit reference to the rights of Indians. Section 35 says, "The existing aboriginal and treaty rights of the aboriginal peoples of Canada are hereby recognized and affirmed." What were these aboriginal and treaty rights? Subsequent conferences were planned to attempt to specify them. On March 15–16, 1983, the prime minister held a constitutional conference to begin, as promised, a process aimed at responding to the expectations of Natives.

At the opening session, an Aboriginal leader reminded participants that the Creator had given North America to the Indians. "If the Creator truly had reserved North America for the

□ *See Clarkson and McCall,* Trudeau and Our Times, *vol. 1,* The Magnificent Obsession. *See also Graham Fraser,* René Lévesque and the Parti Québécois in Power *(Toronto: Macmillan, 1984).*

"Just say no." Montage by David Neel, a Native artist from British Columbia. Elijah Harper is "surrounded with symbols: four pieces of copper, which represent the cultural and monetary wealth of a country; ten paddles for the ten provinces of Canada; and eagle feathers, which symbolize the discord between Anglophones and Francophones, and between aboriginals and non-aboriginals." (Eva Major-Marothy, *L'Archiviste*, vol. 20, no. 1 [1993], p. 6. Translation.)

Indians," Trudeau retorted, "He would never have allowed Europeans to learn how to make ships to cross the Atlantic."

The 1983 conference was followed by a number of other meetings over the next few years. On April 30, 1987, prime minister Brian Mulroney's efforts led to the signing of the Meech Lake Accord. The Indians, however, were opposed to its ratification. An Aboriginal member of the Manitoba legislature, Elijah Harper, sticking to positions that he had taken in 1981–82, rallied the opposition camp and, in June, 1990, blocked his province from ratifying the accord. This contributed to the failure of the entire lengthy and difficult process.

In parallel to this tortuous political process, another process was quietly playing out in the courts. The Constitution Act, 1982, had given treaties a legal standing. So, at the same time as the failure of the Meech Lake Accord was in the works, the Supreme Court delivered two major, consequential decisions: *Sparrow* and *Sioui*.

The first dealt with ancestral rights; the other, with rights issuing from treaties. Section 35 of the Constitution Act, 1982, now took on its full significance.

An Indian from British Columbia, Ronald Edward Sparrow, had invoked his ancestral rights to avoid an arrest related to fishing.

The Sioui brothers, descendants of refugee Hurons who had settled near Quebec City in the mid-seventeenth century, had a harder time basing their case on ancestral rights. They had the wits to look for a treaty. That is how a safe-conduct signed by Brigadier James Murray on September 5, 1760, in Longueuil, near Montreal, acquired the value of a treaty in the sense of section 88 of the Indian Act.

This is the content of the document, according to the version of the Supreme Court; see Appendix B:

> THESE are to certify that the CHIEF of the HURON Tribe of Indians, having come to me in the name of His Nation, to submit to His BRITANNICK MAJESTY, and make Peace, has been received under my Protection, with his whole Tribe; and henceforth no English Officer or party is to molest, or interrupt them in returning to their Settlement at LORETTE; and they are received upon the same terms with the Canadians, being allowed the free Exercise of their Religion, their Customs, and Liberty of trading with the English: — recommending it to the Officers commanding the Posts, to treat them kindly.
>
> Given under my hand at Longueuil this 5th day of September, 1760
> By the Genl's Command,
> JOHN COSNAN   Ja. MURRAY
> Adjut Genl.

What happened in Longueuil in September of 1760? Strangely, historians have neglected the period from the surrender of Quebec City (September, 1759) to the surrender of Montreal. And they have written nothing on the role of the Indians. Clearly, the claims by Aboriginals in the 1970s and 1980s triggered the first research.

Of course, the Franco-Indian alliances were known, but had they been accorded the importance they deserved? And had anyone examined the promises that the British made to end them?

On September 5 and 6, 1760, three armies – those of Haviland, Murray, and Amherst – converged around Montreal. More than twenty thousand British soldiers appeared as if by magic and took up positions from Longueuil to Lachine. History in the large sense is not interested in their march and their progress, just as it overlooks the Indian presence and neglects to cite the articles of the Act of Capitulation of Montreal that refer to them.

After the surrender of Quebec City, Murray was charged with the occupation of the city and the surrounding region. What were his relations with the Indians, in particular the Hurons? What were his contacts with Amherst? What strategy did Amherst, commander-in-chief, use to deliver the final blow to New France? He led an army of eleven thousand men from Lake Ontario to Montreal: Oswegatchie was on his route. The French attempted to block the three attack routes to Montreal by reinforcing the Jacques-Cartier fort east of Quebec City, the Saint-Jean fort on the Richelieu River, and the Lévis fort more or less facing Oswegatchie. These three sites were under the charge of very skilled French officers: Jean-Daniel Dumas, Louis-Antoine de Bougainville, and Pierre Pouchot.

Little by little, from the above, the structure of this book emerged.

First, the events. For the Europeans, the war that ended with the Treaty of Paris in February, 1763, was called, simply, the Seven-Years' War: it had lasted from 1756 to 1763. For the Canadiens, it was the war of the Conquest. For the Americans, it was the third – if not the fourth – French and Indian War. This name has significance, though attention has not been paid to it. An examination of the Sioui arrest will lead us to an extraordinary network of Franco-Indian alliances.

If some seventy thousand French and Canadiens were able to keep one and a half million Americans at bay, and even strike fear into their hearts, it was thanks essentially to their many Indian allies. William Johnson understood the need to break these alliances and engage the Indians at least in a form of neutrality. As "superintendant" of Indian affairs appointed by London, almost at the suggestion of the Iroquois, how did he act? What promises did he make to the allies of the French to convince them to change sides?

An examination of the "Murray treaty" leads to another treaty, the "Swegatchy treaty," "regularly concluded in August 1760 between the British and the Algonquins," according to a judgment rendered on May 17, 1993, by Judge Jean-Louis Baudoin of the Quebec Court of Appeal.

Second: the role of the courts. Examining the "Murray treaty" in detail might seem to be a waste of time. After all, a Supreme Court decision cannot be appealed. However, it is important to establish the significance and scope of a "treaty" – that is, the rights that arise for the Indians – since the Constitution Act, 1982, forces governments to "recognize and affirm" them.

In fact, the Supreme Court was not as careful as it should have been, either in its reconstruction of the events of 1759 and 1760 or in the acceptance of various proposed versions of the safe-conduct given by James Murray to the Hurons of Lorette. It did not examine the document in question, and it also took dangerous shortcuts with the facts.

Third: And what do today's historian think? Since they don't agree on the significance of the events, it is an interesting exercise to examine their respective points of view. History is a demanding discipline, as we shall see.

In *Love in the Time of Cholera*, Gabriel Garcia Marquez tells the same story five or six times. You will permit me this comparison, since – with a lesser talent, of course – I will proceed in somewhat the same manner. I will also tell the same story: first the bare (or almost bare) facts, then the facts as seen by the courts, then those facts as seen by the historians. Of course, the procedure involves some repetition, but I think that each time the circle will broaden and more light will be cast on the subject.

Readers will find themselves involved in an inquiry. I had to find clues, identify the actors, locate and learn how to decode documents, compare points of view, and listen to the experts.

The question of Indian treaties is an important one. In British Columbia, Quebec, and the Maritimes, there are no territorial treaties, as there are in Ontario, or "numbered" treaties, as in Manitoba, Saskatchewan, and Alberta. At least for the moment, treaties arising from the depths of the past date from the 1760s, such as the one signed in May, 1760, in Halifax between Governor Charles Lawrence and the Mi'kmaq chief, Paul Laurent (*Marshall* ruling, September, 1999). By all evidence, Aboriginal claims are nowhere near ending, so it may be a good thing to take the time to get a clearer view of them.

I myself went from question to question, from surprise to surprise while writing this book. I did so freely, refusing to serve a cause or be "politically correct." I hope that this book will be read in the spirit in which it was written!

DENIS VAUGEOIS

I

IN THE CROSSFIRE

This Indian warrior carries metal objects. At his feet is a tomahawk adorned with trade objects, as are his hair and his ear. His sack is beaded, and his body is tattooed in the style of Indians of the ***pays d'en haut***. (Bougainville, 1993, p. 346.)

THE DEATH OF JAMES WOLFE ON THE PLAINS OF ABRAHAM, SEPTEMBER 13, 1759.

The artist Benjamin West decided to portray the scene ten years after the event. This painting, controversial at the time, finally received the favour of the king, who had a copy made. Copies were also made for four other major clients. The publisher Richard Boydell sensed that the image was a money-maker and ordered reproductions from the engraver William Woollett. He made a profit of 15,000 pounds sterling, a fortune at the time. The engraver also received some 7,000 pounds. West, for his part, received glory and honours.

Nevertheless, the artist had taken some liberties with his subject. The composition is from his imagination. By placing a Ranger at the far left and an Indian prominently in the scene, West confirmed the American locale to counterbalance the flag that was the symbol of British power.

Wolfe had a rather low opinion of the Indians, considering them cruel and depraved. Above all, he had had to fight them, and his injuries were no doubt due to their way of waging war, and thus from the fire of several Canadien, or even Indian, marksmen (see p. 137), of whom there were several hundred on the French side.

In addition, West highlighted his contempt for the English general's prejudices by portraying the Indian in a pose worthy of the masterly painters of antiquity. While he did portray the tattoos on the Indian's body, he gave him a very dignified pose and a noble profile.

West was not of Wolfe's generation. He had had an opportunity to see the Iroquois as allies and to appreciate their pride. What had been seen as barbarous became virility and purity. The distance between Wolfe and West is less a question of time than of sensibilities.

* * *

Wolfe's victory, which was somewhat by default, marked the end of another French and Indian War – the last one. North America was no longer French. Nor would it be Indian. This book opens on the days after the Battle of the Plains of Abraham.

The Year 1760

From the Surrender of Quebec City to the Surrender of Montreal

T HE SURRENDER*f* OF QUEBEC CITY, on September 18, 1759, was the beginning of the end for New France. It was obvious that the other French posts would not be able to resist the English for long: ultimately, Montreal, then Detroit, would have no choice but to surrender in their turn. Time was on the side of the English.□

Although the war in North America would soon be a thing of the past for the French and the English, was it over for the Indians? The history books don't say. In fact, they say nothing about the winter of 1759–60. They mention Lévis's futile victory at Sainte-Foy in the spring of 1760, followed by the arrival of English reinforcements on the river, and, at the end of the summer, the surrender of Montreal and the protestations of Lévis, who finally burned his flags on St. Helen's Island. This is what schoolchildren learn about the year 1760.

The War with Three Names

The war that started in Europe in 1756 officially lasted seven years, ending with the cession of Canada to Great Britain in 1763. For the Europeans, it was the Seven Years' War; for Canadiens,○ the Conquest; for English Americans, the French and Indian War. It

□ *New France, which stretched from the Gulf of St. Lawrence to the mouth of the Mississippi, had only 70,000 inhabitants. The thirteen American colonies, concentrated on the Atlantic coast, had a population of more than 1.5 million. In January, 1759, Bougainville (1993, p. 65) asked, "With Quebec City taken, is Canada taken? Yes, no doubt, since there is no second-line fortified place, no place with a depot, war munitions, and food supplies."*

○ *People of French extraction living in Canada. The differences between the French and the Canadiens were very similar to those between the British and the Americans; see Gervais Carpin, Histoire d'un mot. L'ethnonyme "Canadien" de 1535 à 1691 (Septentrion, 1995).*

□ *This war (1689–97) was also known to Americans as King William's War, after William III, who opposed Louis XIV. When the European conflict broke out, in May, 1689, New England (population 200,000) and New France (population 15,000) also went to war. In spite of their much smaller numbers, the French and Canadiens held their own, thanks to their Indian allies. The English and Americans had the Iroquois, whom they set against Lachine at the beginning of August, 1689. The counterattack was horrific. The Canadiens and their allies – mostly Abenaki – spread terror in Schenectady, Salmon Falls, and Casco. Houses in Casco were still burning when a major attack was directed at Quebec City. William Phips struck in mid-October, 1690. Frontenac responded "with the mouths of his cannons" in another episode well known to Quebec schoolchildren.*

○ *Aside from the three wars mentioned here, other, smaller conflicts were also dubbed "French and Indian War."*

△ *Quoted in Pierre Margry (ed.), Découvertes et établissements des Français dans l'ouest et dans le sud de l'Amérique septentrionale, 6 vol. (Paris, 1876–88), vol. 4, pp. 308–32.*

was the third War to have the latter name. Previously, the Americans had used it for the War of the Augsburg Confederacy□ (which had sent William Phips to Quebec in 1690), which ended with the Treaty of Ryswick (1697), and then for the Spanish War of Succession, which ended with the Treaty of Utrecht (1713). The major event of this war in North America was the sinking of part of Admiral Walker's fleet. Why do American historians call these three conflicts "the French and Indian Wars"?○

For the Americans, the enemy was New France, whose territories formed an arc restricting them to east of the Allegheny Mountains, an arc that might have reminded them of the Indians' traditional weapon, the bow and arrow. In fact, the surrender of Montreal on September 8, 1760, ended a 150-year rivalry that had involved the constant threat of attacks by Canadiens and Indians.

For the first half-century after they settled in North America, the French and English managed to get along. The French saw the Iroquois – supported by the Dutch, and later by the English – as their enemy. But the Iroquois threat did not stop the French from exploring and taking possession of lands; they intended to become the masters of the continent by controlling its points of entry: the St. Lawrence and Mississippi rivers, Hudson Bay, and ultimately the Hudson River. They seemed unstoppable. In 1699, however, Canadien Pierre Le Moyne d'Iberville sounded an alarm: "If France does not seize this part of America [Louisiana] . . . the English colony, which is becoming very considerable in size, will grow to the point that, in less than a hundred years, it will be strong enough to take all of North America." Less than two years later, d'Iberville tried again: "The English on this continent," he stated, ". . . will be in a position, in league with the Savages, to raise sufficient forces by sea and by land to become masters of all of America."△ The future would bear him out.

In the early eighteenth century, the French compensated for their very small population in comparison with the English by forging alliances with the Indians – hence the expression "French

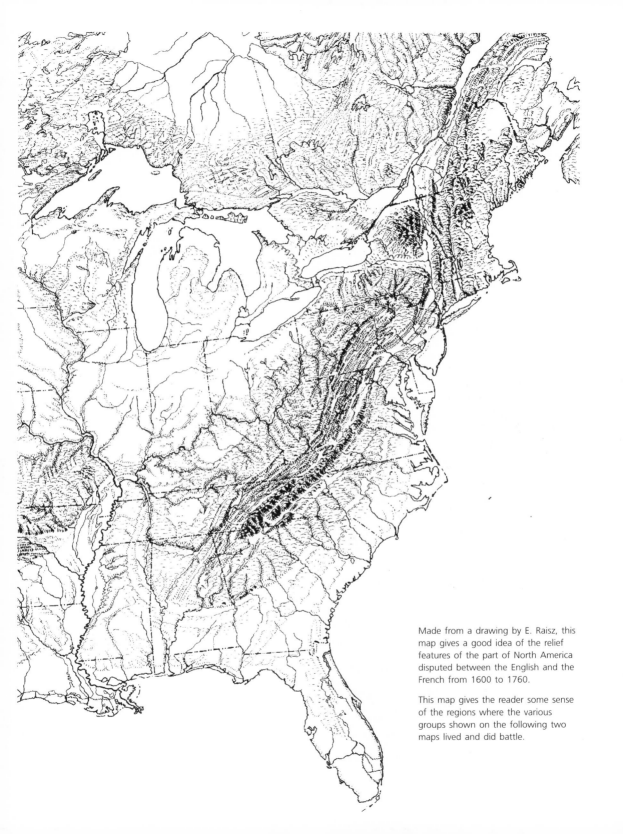

Made from a drawing by E. Raisz, this map gives a good idea of the relief features of the part of North America disputed between the English and the French from 1600 to 1760.

This map gives the reader some sense of the regions where the various groups shown on the following two maps lived and did battle.

CHIPE-
WAYAN

ESKIMO

Ft. Churchill

York Factory

CREE

MONTAGNAIS

Ft. Bourbon

ASSINIBOINE

Ft. Albany

Moose Factory

Ft. Maurepas

MICMAC

Kaministiquia

CHIPPEWA

ALGONQUIN

ABENAKI

MANDAN

Michilimackinac

Montreal

DAKOTA

Fort Oswego

Albany

FOX

Ft. Niagara

Detroit

KICKAPOO

MIAMI

IROQUOIS

Conestoga

ILLINOIS

SHAWNEE

Vincennes

Kaskaskia

OSAGE

Occaneechee

CHEROKEE

CHICKASAW

Arkansas Post

Augusta

CADDO

CREEK

Charles Town

CHOCTAW

Ft. Toulouse

Natchitoches

Los Adaes

Mobile

San Antonio

New Orleans

St. Augustine

SEMINOLE

**Zones of Encounter
c. 1750**

▨ CONQUEST AND
ENCAPSULATION

▲ INDIAN REMNANTS

▨ ARTICULATION AND
INTERDEPENDENCE

◉ MAJOR PIVOTS

▨ PARTICIPATION AND
REVERBERATION

This map, taken from geographer D. W. Meinig's *The Shaping of America*, shows two
European zones: the English zone on the Atlantic coast, and a rather small French zone in
the St. Lawrence Valley. Both are represented in dark grey on this map. The first has
peninsulas pushing toward the interior of the continent, one toward Lake Ontario via
Mohawk Valley, and a second extending toward the Great Lakes. Its zone of influence is
represented by the dotted light-grey area around Kaskaskia, at the mouth of the Mississippi
and stretching into northern Florida and Louisiana.

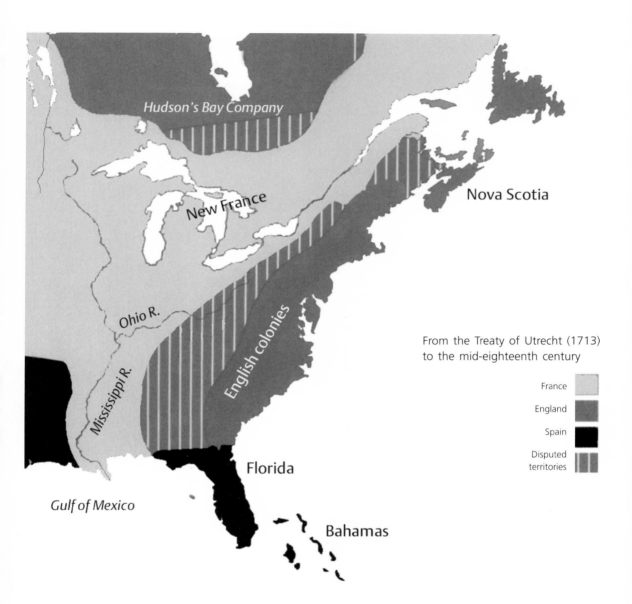

Hudson's Bay Company

New France

Nova Scotia

Ohio R.

Mississippi R.

English colonies

From the Treaty of Utrecht (1713)
to the mid-eighteenth century

France

England

Spain

Disputed
territories

Florida

Gulf of Mexico

Bahamas

This map, drawn from a representation by historians John A. Dickinson and Brian Young in *Diverse Pasts: History of Quebec and Canada* (Copp Clark, 1995, p. 105), shows a New France that controlled the St. Lawrence Valley, the Great Lakes, and the Ohio and Mississippi rivers.

The maps on pages 22 and 23 each have their good points. Meinig's map is useful in establishing the limits of the Thirteen Colonies and situating Native groups. But its author did not understand the strength of French America and its exceptional network of alliances with the Indians. The map does not take account of the British gains due to the Treaty of Utrecht (Acadia, Newfoundland, and Hudson Bay), no doubt because these territories were never integrated into the American union formed after the War of Independence.

□ *Together, the French and the Indians were clearly perceived as a common enemy that spread terror incessantly in the American colonies. For the American settlers, the "imperial" wars (King William's War, Queen Anne's War, the Great War for Empire) all meant the same thing: the enemy was constantly at their borders. The French and Canadiens had problems with the Natchez in 1729, the Chickasaws starting in 1732, and their on-going enemies the Foxes. In general, the Mohawks were the main – sometimes the only – ally of the British and English Americans. The other Iroquois tribes chose either neutrality or an alliance with the French. See Axelrod,* Chronicle of the Indian Wars.

and Indian Wars." □ And what an enemy the Indians were! For the real picture, one must go beyond historical analysis to the archival documents that contain the first-hand descriptions.

And these texts must be consulted in their entirety; "selected texts" and anthologies do not suffice. For example, in *Histoire du Canada par les textes*, a book by three excellent historians pub-

Wolfe and Montcalm: One Monument

1760: A rivalry that had lasted 150 years was drawing to an end. By all accounts, once Quebec City had fallen, the other French posts could not resist for long. New France was a fragile giant. The Thirteen Colonies concentrated on the Atlantic coast had an enormous numerical advantage.

In fact, France, more populous than England, had let many fewer immigrants cross the ocean. It was strongly unified, and it applied the same rules to all its colonies. If a Huguenot was banished from France, he was banished from the entire kingdom.

England, on the other hand, was living through a troubled era, shaken with revolutions and crises. America became a land of refuge. The settlers arrived in waves to build a land that suited them, and the Thirteen Colonies were born. They had the shortcoming of being divided, but over time they forgot their differences, first to fight against common enemies, the French and their allies the Indians, and later to separate from an overly greedy metropole.

The imbalance between French America and English America was considerable. Things could not stay this way indefinitely. In 1759, encouraged by major victories, the English and Americans were ready for the final stroke. They intended to avenge the defeats of Phips in 1690 and Walker in 1711, as well as the deaths of thousands of American settlers massacred in frontier posts. In the spring of 1759, Vice-Admiral Saunders set sail with 180 ships and some 30,000 sailors. James Wolfe led a fleet with 9,000 soldiers. The objective: to take Quebec City. After a 20-minute battle, Wolfe died without tasting victory. Montcalm, who commanded the French troops, was also mortally wounded.

Near Château Frontenac, in Quebec City.
Mortem virtus communem, famam historia, monumentum posteritas dedit (Their courage gave them the same death; history, the same renown; posterity, the same monument).

lished in 1952, only one text out of 105 mentions the Indians! Two other texts in the book could and should have referred to them: those on the surrender of Montreal in 1760 and the Royal Proclamation of 1763. In introducing the former, however, the authors do not cite the articles concerning the "Savages." From the latter, the authors include a brief passage that mentions the reservation of lands "for the use of said savages." This is very short shrift, especially since, in 1973, Justice Hall of the Supreme Court of Canada called the Proclamation a "declaration of Indian rights".☐

Nor does *Canada–Québec*, a historical analysis first published in 1968, give any details about the outcome of the Conquest for the Indians. Although the Indians are not completely absent from the text, with the exception of an introductory passage that mentions their "significant role," they are barely mentioned.○

A reading of documents of the time – letters, memoirs, personal diaries – reveals a very different picture: one has the impression that there was no issue *but* the Indians. Samuel de Champlain, the priest Gabriel Sagard, Father Louis Hennepin, Baron de Lahontan, Father Joseph-François Lafitau, and the explorer Nicolas Perrot wrote at length about the Indians in their accounts of their voyages. This was perfectly natural. Because they were portraying lands unknown to their European readers, they gave detailed descriptions of the inhabitants, the climate, and the fauna and flora. Europeans, fascinated, snapped up these works, making Lahontan's and Hennepin's books virtual bestsellers.

Gradually, however, such accounts were replaced by colonial administrators' reports, correspondence, and memoranda, and these are the documents that historians drew upon to formulate their analyses. This was, they believed, a tale of colonization. The texts detailed European exploration and trading activities, inter-colony rivalries, and so on. History is always written from the viewpoint of the author, and so these documents tended to gloss over the role, and even the existence, of the Indians. In their studies of the "French and Indian Wars,"

☐ *"Its legal strength," stated the judge, "is analogous to that of the statute of the Magna Carta." (SCR, 313: pp. 394–95. Calder ruling, 1973; translation.)*

○ *In the first edition, titled* Histoire 1534–1968 *(Montreal: ERPI, 1968), the authors had mentioned "what we owe the Indians" (p. 21). The second edition (1969), titled* Canada-Québec, synthèse historique, *had a slightly expanded chapter on Native peoples, but they remained more or less an afterthought in this book and in most similar works.*

Rare Book Collection. National Library of Canada

Henri-Raymond Casgrain (1831–1904) in his doctoral robes. A prolific author, he left useful transcriptions of a large number of eighteenth-century documents.

 Frégault, 1955, p. 382.

historians such as Groulx, Parkman, Frégault, and Eccles never speculated about how things had turned out for the Indians.

Garneau, Casgrain, and Chapais skipped lightly from the defeat on the Plains of Abraham to the surrender of Montreal, as did their English-speaking colleagues. Guy Frégault was a bit of an exception in this regard. In *La Guerre de la Conquête,* he devoted an entire chapter to the year 1760 – thirty-six solidly documented, marvellously written, perfectly clear pages describing the relentless strategy of General Jeffery Amherst, who was determined to force Montreal's surrender. "If the operations [of 1759] were shaped like gigantic pincers, the nature [of the 1760 campaign] resembled a vise," Frégault wrote.□

And, indeed, it was a vise, inexorably tightening. Murray was sailing up the St. Lawrence with 3,500 regular soldiers, followed by Lord Rollo at the head of the Louisbourg regiments. William Haviland was advancing via Lake Champlain and the Richelieu River at the head of 3,400 men, including 1,500 regular soldiers. And Amherst, the commander of all British troops in North America, was leading some 1,000 men down the St. Lawrence from Lake Ontario to Montreal.

The Indians and the "Balance of Power"

As we will see throughout this book, the Indians of North America were very much affected by the end of hostilities between the English and French in 1763. "In North America the Indian nations quickly came to realize, too late, that the French would have been the lesser of the two evils" wrote the Toronto historian John Eccles (1974, p. 185). For decades, in fact, they seemed to be on the road to assimilation or integration. Then, little by little, they underwent a remarkable reawakening. In Canada, constitutional conflicts once again placed them between two rival forces.

Paradoxically, the Quebec independence movement gave Native claims a new lease on life. For the federal authorities, the Native "card" was perhaps the last one that they had to play to counter Quebec's independence, both domestically and internationally. The Indians were once again holding the "balance of power" with respect to, beyond various privileges and rights, a fundamental issue: territory.

Frégault saw the English conquest as resulting from the convergence of these three armies. The conflict between the French and the English was drawing to a close – in North America, at any rate. This was Frégault's subject. When he described the beginning of the war, in 1754, 1755, and 1756, the Indians were part of the story. But little by little, he shuffled them aside to concentrate on the confrontation between the two metropoles. He showed how their respective colonial systems – the American and English system, on the one hand, and the Canadien and French system, on the other – evolved along parallel lines and had much in common, including a future in North America.□ From very similar homelands, the Americans and Canadiens coveted the same riches. Had their rivalry not preoccupied them, they no doubt would have noticed how different they were from people in their respective metropoles and distanced themselves from their native countries.○

It was normal for historians to study the role of the European powers in the "New World," to observe the birth of new nations. After all, the anthropologists were always there to study the disappearance of indigenous populations! Very quickly, the Indians were no longer of interest to historians.

It was not until more than two hundred years later, after a fresh outbreak of Native claims, helped along by renewed tensions between Quebec and Ottawa, that the "Indian question" resurfaced. Quebec Natives are heavily crossbred – they are more white than red – but

□ *"In truth," Bougainville wrote in 1759 (1993, p. 56), "New England must be sorely vexed by the wars that our Savages make with it. In its bosom are almost 4,000 families from its frontiers weeping for their relatives who have been massacred and whose goods have been sacked. They know that in taking Canada they will be delivered from the cruelty of the Savages and will enjoy forevermore the sweetness of peace."*

○ *These differences were due to adaptations to a new world, made necessary by a particular physical environment and facilitated by the Natives. No one contests this fact, but few experts are interested in it. After all, isn't Europe the centre of the world? Don't all great civilizations have their origins in the Mediterranean? And the history of the Americas, is it not the triumph of civilization over savagery?*

Jeffery Amherst (1717–97). He did not like North America, or the Indians, very much. An extremely prudent man, he adopted a steamroller strategy.

□ Governor Murray's Journal of Quebec – From 18th September, 1759, to 25th May, 1760. *See* Historical Documents published under the auspices of the Literary and Historical Society of Quebec, Quebec and Montreal *(1871), p. 3.*

tradition is tenaciously maintained. What interests us here has its roots in the Native community of Jeune-Lorette, near Quebec City. The Supreme Court ruling of May 24, 1990, the "Sioui decision," refers back to 1760, the year of the surrender of Montreal.

For a historian, this stunning judicial decision provides an opportunity to explore the true role played by the Indians, to try to uncover the exact nature of the meeting between the Lorette Hurons and Commander James Murray on September 5, 1760 – and, above all, to try to find out how the final "French and Indian War" ended for the Indians allied with the French.

After the Surrender of Quebec City

On September 13, 1759, Montcalm, mortally wounded, retreated before a dying Wolfe. On the 18th, Quebec City surrendered. The next day, Lieutenant-Colonel James Murray took possession of the city – "or, more precisely, of its ruins."□ On October 12, he was

JAMES MURRAY

At the Battle of the Plains of Abraham, he commanded the left wing of the army in combat formation. On October 12, 1759, he was appointed governor of the garrison of Quebec. About a year later, on October 27, 1760, after Montreal's surrender, he became governor of the District of Quebec; he was appointed governor of the New Colony or Province of Quebec on November 21, 1763.

appointed commanding officer of the garrison in Quebec City. On the 18th, the British fleet, under Admiral Saunders, set sail for England.

Murray organized his quarters for winter. He had already had extra wood laid in and ordered that a census be taken of the population in the surrounding area. He thought it prudent to require the settlers to turn their weapons in to his officers, and he established detachments at Sainte-Foy and Ancienne-Lorette to forestall surprise attacks. He warned the people to remain calm, reminding them that they could expect nothing in the way of support from a French army in retreat. He had the foresight to set down some regulations and establish a civil court, which was headed by Colonel Young. Noting that his troops were disorderly, he revoked all permits to sell alcohol and threatened a lashing to anyone caught drunk. Finally, he requisitioned the Jesuit college, first because he was in need of a warehouse, but also because he wanted the Jesuits, "who are in general remarkably [gifted for] intrigue,"□ removed from the area.

The snow soon came, and Murray had to equip his men with snowshoes. If he was concerned about who supplied them, he didn't mention it. He was told that a number of Indians were prowling the area, but he simply urged his men to be on guard. His true enemies, now, were the snow and the cold of winter. His men didn't have warm clothes, and he couldn't do anything about it. On the other hand, he ordered as many snowshoes as possible to be manufactured and ordered "the men to be practised walking in them."○

At the beginning of February, Murray sent his militia captains to requisition as many snowshoes as possible. "But this search produced only a few."△ The settlers' excuse was that they had lost theirs and had not been able to procure others.

Murray, however, had less difficulty dragging from them an oath of loyalty and a few guns. By the end of December, he controlled the region; in February, he found it appropriate to appoint two judges on the south shore of the river opposite the town.

□ Murray's Journal, *Nov. 14, 1759, p. 9.*

○ Murray's Journal, *Dec. 28, 1759, p. 15.*

△ *Ibid., p. 20.*

□ "In mid-October 1759, [Murray] had under his command almost 9,000 men, of whom 3,000 were not in a state to fight. The numbers of invalids kept growing. At the beginning of January, the hospitals were full of them, and two or three were buried every day. A month later, the rigours of winter had thinned the ranks even more. On March 19 [1760], fevers, dysentery, and scurvy had reduced the garrison to 4,000 men able to serve" (Frégault, 1955, pp. 374–75). And the winter wasn't over: "On the morning of April 28, Murray could call to action only somewhat fewer than 3,900 fighters, including officers and 129 artillerymen."

○ Murray's Journal, Dec. 28, 1760, p. 31.

He did his best to overlook the disease that was decimating his troops. Out of six thousand men who had been fit to take up arms, barely four thousand remained. Winter mowed down seven hundred; the rest were too ill to be pressed into service.□

When the opportunity presented itself, bands of Canadiens and Indians provided "distractions." There were some false alarms at the beginning of March, but when Murray was awoken, on Sunday, April 27, during a night of violent wind and heavy rain it was no false alarm. It was three in the morning. The enemy had landed the previous evening at Pointe-aux-Trembles (Neuville) and quickly taken up a position between Sainte-Foy and Ancienne-Lorette. "I resolved," Murray noted, "to give enemy battle before they could establish themselves."○ Lévis was in command of the French troops: seven thousand men, including three thousand militiamen. Flanking him were experienced officers: François-Charles de Bourlamaque, seconded by La Corne Saint-Luc, nicknamed "the Indians' general"; Jean d'Alquier; and Sieur de Lapause, who left to posterity a diary and memoirs on his adventures in Canada.

Count de Malartic, who took part in the battle of Sainte-Foy, also left an account, published in Dijon in 1890 as *Journal des campagnes au Canada de 1755 à 1760*, in which he evaluated the French losses at "seven or eight hundred killed or wounded." In fact, the French side had 193 dead and 640 wounded, while the English troops lost 259 men and had 829 wounded. Malartic himself was wounded in the chest: "I placed myself in the care of a surgeon who opened this contusion with twelve lan-

A Canadien militiaman, 1759. "When they [the Canadien militiamen] left for a campaign," wrote Bougainville (1993, p. 58), "the king gave them equipment: shirts, greatcoat, belt, leggings, and so on." But they had a bad habit of leaving these items at home, convinced that they wouldn't be away long. If they were, "Disgust would sweep over them; the desire for their fields, their seeds, their harvests would make them say they were ill. They had to be sent home or they deserted."

COUNT MAURÈS DE MALARTIC

Malartic wrote *Journal des campagnes au Canada de 1755 à 1760,* which was published by his great-grand-nephew, Count Gabriel de Maurès de Malatric, and Paul Gaffarel, a literature professor in Dijon.

cet blows." Since the battle had "lasted more than five hours," he estimated enemy losses to be considerable. "A number of carts," he recalled, "took away their dead and wounded." Later, he added, "The Savages, who were of no use during the action and pillaged the equipment and haversacks, returned once they saw us masters on the battlefield, to take scalps. They took those of many Frenchmen."□

English Reinforcements

After capturing Sainte-Foy, Lévis began a siege of Quebec City. Murray's fate now depended on which ships arrived first. If French reinforcements were to arrive sooner, he could be caught and cornered in their crossfire.

France was on the verge of bankruptcy. Berryer, the French minister of the navy and the colonies, begged for assistance for New France, to little avail.○ Finally, a small convoy left Bordeaux on April 10, 1760, but it had been preceded by a new English squadron. Lévis had to retreat to Montreal.

Murray now had some breathing room. He fraternized with his prisoners and saw to the "mission" with which Lévis had en-trusted him: "To take care of the sick and wounded that he left behind him."△ Malartic was one of them. One evening, in need of a confidant, Murray beckoned him to "a window-sill of his house" and asked him, "Do you believe that we will give Canada back to you?"

"I am not well enough versed in politics to see things from such a perspective."

"If we are wise, we will not keep it. New England must have a bit to nibble at, and by not keeping this country we will give New Englanders something to keep them occupied."◇

□ *Malartic, pp. 318–19.*

○ *According to Bougain-ville (1993), who was sent to France in the autumn of 1758 "to make an accoun-ting to the Court of the situation in Canada and solicit help" (p. 378), Berryer "never wanted to understand that Canada was the frontier of our other colonies." It makes no sense to save the barn, Berryer reasoned, when the house is on fire. For these "poor barns," Bougainville obtained just 400 men and recruits. He had wanted 8,000 (p. 54) and a good deal of trade merchandise to "keep" the favour of the Indians: "Saving the colony depends on it," he maintained (p. 83). Bougainville returned to New France in the spring of 1759, followed closely by Saunders's fleet carrying 9,000 soldiers under Wolfe's command! See Filteau,* Par la Bouche; *Lacoursière, "The Battlefield."*

△ *Murray's Journal, Dec. 28, 1760, p. 45.*

◇ *Malartic, p. 331.*

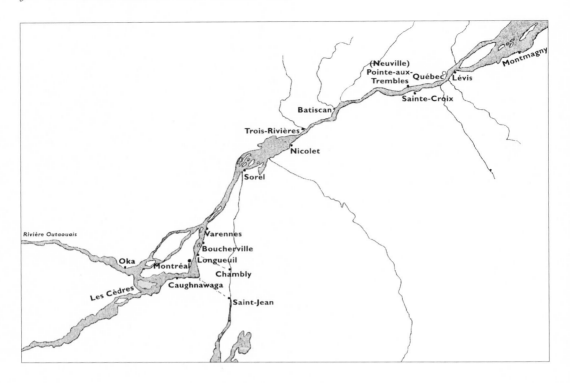

□ See the deposition by
Athanase La Plague in
Appendix G. See also
DCB, 4, pp. 596–98.

○ DCB, 4, p. 25.

Was this exchange really recorded in Malartic's journal? Yes, according to his publisher, his great-great-nephew, Count Gabriel de Maurès de Malartic. Murray's question was a bit premature; after all, Montreal was still in French hands. But it was an objective within his grasp. And he knew that he would not be fighting alone.

During Wolfe's siege of Quebec City, Jeffery Amherst had been doing battle in the Lake Champlain region. On October 18, he learned of the fall of Quebec City. A few weeks later, he received an emissary from Murray, the military engineer John Montresor, who had crossed the forests of Maine guided by a Huron from Jeune-Lorette, Athanase La Plague. Montresor no doubt handed over instructions regarding the 1760 offensive.□ In effect, Pitt, the British minister, was ordering Amherst to take Montreal – "according as you shall."○

There were three routes to Montreal. The first two were by the St. Lawrence River, from Quebec City to the east and Fort

Major-General Edward Braddock, the British top commander in North America, tried to lead his formidable army through 110 miles of forest and mountains, from Virginia to Fort Duquesne. Some 300 men preceded the troops to cut down trees.

A bullet pierced Braddock's lungs and killed him.

Braddock's body was interred. Two-thirds of his men were killed or wounded in the Battle of the Monongahela.

When he left Alexandria, Virginia, on April 20, 1775, Braddock intended to cross the Allegheny Mountains in May and reach Fort Duquesne in June. "No one believed that he would be able to get these pieces [massive ship's cannons and siege cannons], as formidable for their weight as for their firepower, through forests and over mountains, across land devoid of roads suitable for vehicles and cut off from watercourses," wrote Frégault (1955, p. 137). "He managed to do it, but at the cost of superhuman effort and to the detriment of the mobility of his corps. This monstrous war machine drew closer to the French fort [at the confluence of the Ohio and Monongahela rivers] inch by inch." On July 9, Liénard de Beaujeu and Jean-Daniel Dumas, at the head of a "detachment of seventy-two navy soldiers, 146 Canadiens, and 637 Indians," attacked Braddock's advance guard. Beaujeu was killed at the beginning of the battle, and the British commander had "five horses killed under him before he was mortally wounded."

Report of the Work of the Public Archives Branch for the Year 1918, Ottawa, 1920. Translation.

Oswego (on Lake Ontario) to the west; the third was by Lake Champlain and the Richelieu River. Amherst left nothing to chance: he used all three routes. In the spring of 1760, three armies began their marches. A total of almost twenty thousand men were to converge on Montreal.

Murray Begins the March to Montreal

Jean-Daniel Dumas, who had defeated Braddock, tried to slow Murray and his troops, who had left Quebec City on July 14, 1760. Murray's destination was Montreal; he wasn't going to bother with the posts dotting the shores of the St. Lawrence, for his strength was limited.

Dumas and his 1,500 men sighted Murray when they reached Pointe-aux-Trembles. Murray had chosen "to move his 2,800 men by boat," very stealthily, and his small fleet of eighty vessels was slowly making its way toward Montreal. Dumas's troops kept pace on the north shore and watched, powerless, as Murray stopped at Lotbinière on the south shore. Murray took his time. Before setting foot on land, he issued a proclamation to the settlers, no doubt similar to the one written in Quebec City soon before he left. In it he alternated threats and promises:

> Seduced by promises which never came to pass, Canadiens, you have always closed your ears to Our Remonstrances. Blind to your own Interests, you are the Victims of your Prejudices. For one instant, You are still Masters of Your Fate. Once this Instant has passed, a Bloody Vengeance will Punish Those who Dare take up arms. Their Land will be Ravaged, their Houses set Afire, and these will be the Least of their Misfortunes. Wise Colonists, on the Contrary, who, profiting from past Experience, remain calmly at home, enjoying their Religion, their Property, and, Under the Auspices of a Prince, Father of his country, Sustained and Protected by an Arm so Powerful, will become Rich and prosperous.

> [Signed] James Murray

Written in Quebec City on July 13, 1760
And Sealed with the Seal of Our Arms

Ja: Murray

Murray on His Way to Montreal

❏ "The battalion-detachments disembarked [on July 15], and the general went, with the rangers and a company of light infantry, several miles up the country: fifty-five men from St. Croix, and seventy-nine from the parish de Lobiniere, took the oath of neutrality. . . . 'At whose mercy are your habitations,' asked a threatening Murray, 'and that harvest which you expect to reap this summer . . . ? Therefore consider your own interest and provoke us no more.'" On the evening of July 15, the fleet moved off again. Near Deschambault, Murray "dispatched a flag of truce to M. Dumas" to denounce the actions of a band of Indians: "If these savages are not instantly recalled, or if any barbarities should be committed upon our troops, they shall have orders to give no quarter either to regulars, or others, that may fall into our hands; and that country shall undergo military execution, wherever we land." Knox, *The Siege of Quebec*, p. 265. I compared this edition with the one prepared for the Champlain Society by Arthur G. Doughty.

According to Knox, more than a hundred settlers, came to offer an oath of "neutrality."❏

Murray stuck to his plan. Once again, there was no question of confronting the French troops that were challenging him, even at Trois-Rivières. He simply kept sending out his messages: "A Bloody Vengeance will Punish Those who Dare take up arms. Their Land will be Ravaged, their Houses set Afire, and these will be the Least of their Misfortunes." The Canadiens needed no interpreters: the "Governor of Quebec and the Conquered Country" had written to them in French, and the message was clear! They had a choice: "Wise Colonists . . . will enjoy their Religion, their Property, [and] become Rich and prosperous."

At Sorel, Murray hardened his tone.○ He knew he was close to his goal – and to the other two British armies. On August 21, Haviland had reached the nearby fort on Île aux Noix. The fort was poorly defended by Bougainville, who had complained about the quality of his garrison: "Here, not a single gunner can take true aim."△ In addition, his Indian allies had abandoned him. This was the least of his worries in defending the site, but it deprived him of information on the enemy's movements and of the ability to communicate with Saint-Jean and Chambly. At least, his

○ *"The attached manifesto has been spread by my efforts in Canada; you cannot pretend to ignore it, Canadiens. Your stubbornness continues; you force me, in spite of my merciful nature, to carry out the threats that I made to you. It is time to begin. I warn you that from now on, I will treat harshly the Canadiens I take with weapons in hand, and I will burn all villages I find abandoned. James Murray. Written facing Sorel, August 21, 1760."* Quoted by Casgrain, Lettres et pièces militaires 1756–1760, p. 285. *It should be noted that Casgrain cites the above manifesto with slight variations and dates it July 23, 1760.*

△ *Casgrain,* Collection de manuscrits, *vol. 10, p. 144 (Bougainville to Lévis, Aug. 21, 1760).*

☐ Instructions from Montcalm to Bourlamaque, May 10, 1759. See Charbonneau, Les Fortifications de l'Île aux Noix, p. 54. Obviously, aim wasn't important for firing cannons; the number of shots fired corresponded to a code agreed to by Île aux Noix, Chambly, and Saint-Jean.

○ Casgrain, Collection de manuscrits, vol. 5, p. 105.

△ Ibid., p. 121. When Bourlamaque mentions the Indians' "discoveries," he is referring to the "reconnaissance missions" of the Indians charged with surveying the enemy and reporting its movements.

wretched gunners were able to fire the artillery effectively thanks to a code developed between the three garrisons.☐

The signals sent by Murray, on the other hand, were unequivocal. At Sorel, he landed two detachments one league apart with an order to march toward each other, burning "everything in their path" – or, at least, unoccupied houses, for the heads of the families to which they belonged were no doubt with the French troops.

The French and Canadiens in Retreat

Murray's method was effective. People came from all over to lay down their arms. Bourlamaque, trying to keep abreast of the British fleet on the south shore, reached Sorel too late. Exasperated by the number of Canadiens laying down their arms, he decided to burn down the houses of those who did. He had to reconsider this plan, however; as he explained, in a letter to Lévis on August 23, "I think . . . that I would have to destroy all of them."○

On the other hand, Bourlamaque realized that he would soon have no more men to execute his orders: the French-Canadian militiamen were deserting in large numbers. At first, just a few went to rejoin their families and protect their property. But in no time at all, the desertions multiplied. "The Canadiens will always offer an example of stability." "They will all go home," a skeptical Bourlamaque read between the lines. The regular soldiers began to follow suit; the desertion disease was contagious. On September 1, 1760, Bourlamaque wrote to Lévis, "I must tell you, my dear general, that soldiers in both battalions that I have here are deserting daily. . . . The officers say most of the soldiers have resolved not to return to France. . . . I am writing to Mr. de Roquemaure and asking him to hire Savages to arrest the soldiers that they meet in their discoveries, gone over to the enemy. I hope that they will provide me with the means to make an example of them."△

But Roquemaure was in a similar predicament. Lévis had met with the Indians at Laprairie "to convince them to support his plan." "While he was speaking," Roquemaure wrote in his journal

Louis-Antoine de Bougainville (1729-1811).

Montreal circa 1760.

□ *Casgrain,* Journal des campagnes du chevalier de Lévis, *p. 301. See also James Thomas Flexner,* Mohawk Baronet, *p. 219. In Casgrain,* Collection des manuscrits, *vol. 4, p. 303, there is an unsigned text titled "Follow-up on the Campaign in Canada": "On September 2, Marquis de Vaudreuil, believing the Savages in the most favourable frame of mind, brought them together at La Prairie, where Chevalier de Lévis had arrived. He proposed that they march with all the troops that were to the south to attack the English army. But at the moment when he thought he had convinced them to help us in this expedition, they received news that the English had accepted the peace proposed to them by the Savages of the Five Nations and left the camp for the second time. "Chevalier de Lévis learned at the same time that Fort Lévis had been taken after a battle lasting several days. . . ."*

○ *In February, 1756, Johnson had officially been named "sole agent and superintendent of the united Six Nations and their confederacies" (DCB, 4, p. 426).*

on September 2, "a deputy from their village came to tell them that they had made peace with the English, who were at Les Cèdres. At this point, they dispersed, leaving Chevalier de Lévis all alone with his officers."□

Like Lévis, all of the French forces lost their Indian allies.

Amherst's Hard March

Though they were allies of the French, the Indians did not present much of a problem to Haviland's and Murray's troops. But Amherst was in a much more vulnerable position on his march to Montreal.

Always extremely cautious, Amherst had lost some time in the summer of 1759, while Wolfe was besieging Quebec. He should have been marching on Montreal from Lake Champlain while Thomas Gage was coming down the St. Lawrence from Lake Ontario. But both Amherst and Gage were dragging their feet. In fact, they were barely creeping along.

At the end of July, 1759, Fort Niagara fell to the English. William Johnson,○ leading a thousand Indians, had defeated the reinforcements arriving from the Ohio Valley and forced Commander Pierre Pouchot out. The fall of Niagara isolated Detroit and cut the main westward route from Montreal.

□ *"The first post I will speak about is Oswegatchie, on the St. Lawrence River, about 150 miles above Montreal, at the mouth of the Black River. A hundred savages visit it from time to time. They are called the Indians of Oswegatchie, although they are one of the tribes of the Five Nations. The settlers of New England could easily transport merchandise to this fort to supply Mohawks, Cahnuagas [Kahnewahkes], Connecedagas [Kanesatekes], the Indians of St. Regis, and several Messesawger [Mississauga] haulers who live close to the strait. They supply goods more cheaply than they could be acquired from merchants in Quebec City or Montreal."* John Long (trader and interpreter of Indian languages), Voyages chez différentes nations sauvages de l'Amérique septentrionale, 1768–1787, p. 36.

Statue of William Johnson in Johnstown, near Johnson Hall.

Johnson met up with Gage near Oswego. In spite of Amherst's orders, Gage was reluctant to launch an attack on the small Fort Lévis at La Galette, near Oswegatchie,□ believing it to be an impossible mission. Johnson had other reasons to hesitate: his Indian allies had warned him not to attack this post, for fear of placing the "French Iroquois" who had settled there in danger. At least, that is what James Thomas Flexner, William Johnson's biographer, claims.○ Information garnered from prisoners confirmed that the Five Nations had approached the Oswegatchies.

The situation was complicated. Johnson was tempted to let Molly, his beloved Indian wife who was several months pregnant, come to Oswego, for she could give him insights into the Indians'

The Five Nations Court at Oswegatchie

○ "Since La Galette was near Oswegatchie," Flexner wrote, "any movement against the French fort would endanger French Iroquois. Although Warraghiyagey [Johnson] pretended to breathe fire, he had no real intention of hurting the Oswegatchies, the true objective being to frighten them into changing sides. He agreed at last that the attack should be delayed until the Iroquois could send their brethren a warning."

William Amherst reported in his journal that prisoners had told them about the pressure the Five Nations were putting on their Oswegatchie brothers to go over to the British side. See Webster, *Journal of William Amherst*, p. 39.

William Johnson (ca. 1715–74).

This engraving often decorated the commissions that William Johnson liked to give to Indian chiefs. It portrays an Englishman offering a medal to an Indian before the council fire. In the background is the Iroquois Tree of Peace, from which the Covenant Chain is hanging.

A rather approximate portrayal of Fort Johnson, built on the Mohawk River a few kilometres from Albany. William Johnson thus found himself at the crossroads of two important routes: the one from Montreal to New York and the one from Albany to Oswego and Niagara. Around 1761, he moved about 15 kilometres inland, to what is today Johnstown.

This wampum, according to Hiawatha, recalls the formation of the Five Nations Confederacy around 1500. In the centre is a pine tree; the rectangles on either side represent the Iroquois nations: the Agniers (Mohawks), the Oneyouts or Onneiouts (Oneidas), the Onontagués (Onondagas), the Goyogouins (Cayugas), and the Senecas (Tsonnontouans). One or two rectangles are missing from this very old wampum (see note at Appendix D).

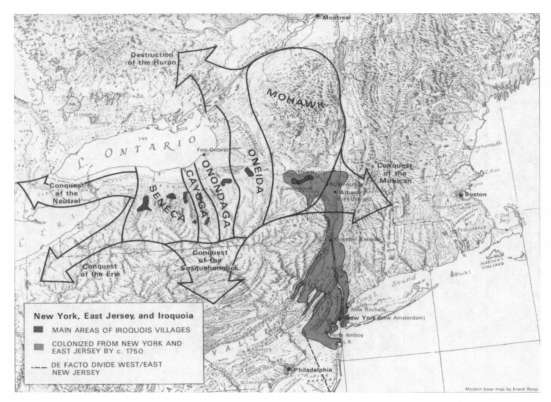

New York, East Jersey, and Iroquoia

MAIN AREAS OF IROQUOIS VILLAGES

COLONIZED FROM NEW YORK AND EAST JERSEY BY c. 1750

DE FACTO DIVIDE WEST/EAST NEW JERSEY

In the Five Nations Confederacy, the Iroquois were very active and sought to extend their influence in all directions. D. W. Meinig, geography professor at the University of Syracuse, provides an illustration of this in *The Shaping of America, vol. 1, Atlantic America, 1492–1800* (Yale University Press, 1986).

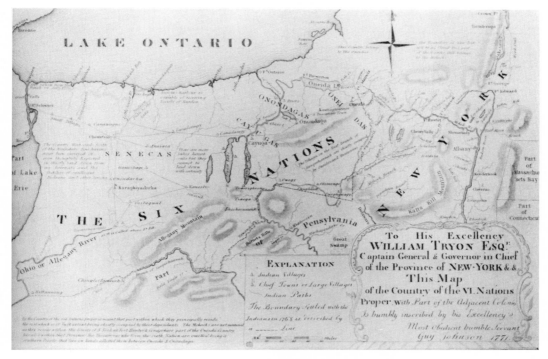

The Tuscaroras joined the Five Nations Confederacy in 1722. At this point, the Five Nations became the Six Nations, as shown in this map prepared on the order of Guy Johnson in 1771. In the documents of the time, both names were found.

□ *Flexner, 1959, p. 213. In April, 1759, at Canajoharie, William Johnson had warned the Oswegatchies and other Canadian Indians "to withdraw themselves from the French otherwise they may repent it when too late." The Oswegatchies, for their part, told him (or relayed the message) that they would "keep out of your way when the English army comes, [that] none of us shall join the French"* (Journal of William Johnson's proceedings with the Confederate nations of Indians at a conference at Canajoharie, *Apr. 1759, quoted in* Sawaya, Les Sept Nations du Canada, *pp. 115, 151).*

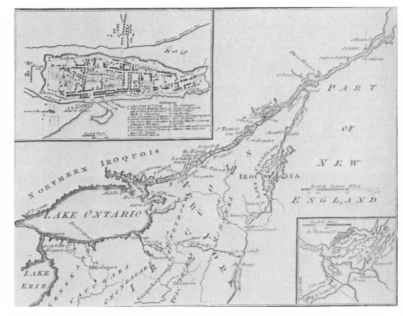

This map was published in *Gentleman Magazine* (London, England) during the period. It was intended to illustrate Amherst's march to Montreal. The upper-left inset shows a plan of the city; the lower-right inset, a view of the archipelago.

strategies. But imagining how discomfited Gage would be in the presence of his beautiful Aboriginal wife, Johnson decided that it would be wise for her to stay put. Instead, he joined her in the Mohawk Valley to attend the birth of his son, Peter Warren Johnson.

Having learned "in the most solemn manner" that the Oswegatchies "would not only quit the French but on our approach meet and join us, and show us the way to attack the enemy,"□ Johnson sent word to Gage, who held his position.

In early October – the 8th, according to Flexner – news of the defeat of Montcalm on the Plains of Abraham reached Oswego. The Mohawks were fairly agitated, but winter was coming – a propitious time for a truce. And Johnson had to take care of his large Fort Johnson family.

During the summer of 1760, Johnson rejoined Amherst at Oswego, accompanied by seven hundred fierce warriors, most of

William Johnson's crest, *Deo regique debeo.*

MOLLY BRANT (Kowatsi' Tsiaienni) was Sir William Johnson's spirit, soul, and inspiration. Tradition has it that she was a descendant of King Hendrick, one of the four Sachems taken to England in 1710 and killed in combat at Lac Saint-Sacrement in 1755.

She and Johnson got together in 1759 and had their first son, Peter Warren, that year. She then took charge of running Fort Johnson, on the bank of the Mohawk River, a few kilometres from Schenectady, on a site where the Six Nations Indians and their allies liked to meet. Molly was a remarkable hostess and skilfully directed her little army of domestics always to be attentive to the comfort of her guests.

Her influence was legendary: "One word from her goes farther with them than a Thousd. from any White Man." At ease both with her Indian kin and with Europeans, she played a decisive political role. A vital link between her husband and his various partners, she was also an irreplaceable companion and a generous mother. When Sir William died, she took care of their eight children, whom she left with teachers in Montreal during the War of Independence in the United States. She remained faithful to the British and suffered the lot of many Loyalists, being exiled to Kingston after the Americans won the war.

There is no known portrait of Molly Brant. When the Canadian government wanted to commemorate her by issuing a stamp (1986), the artist Sara Tyson reconstructed the features of this heroine, known for her intelligence and beauty, from various accounts. Tyson wanted to portray three facets of this notable person: her links with the Iroquois and with the Europeans and her loyalty to the Crown. A fervent Anglican, Molly Brant reconciled her two cultures by remaining faithful to her Native origins as well as to the British authorities. She was the sister of Joseph Brant (Thayendanegea), who accompanied Johnson from Oswego to Montreal in 1760.

□ "The Savages of this nation, called the Praying Indians because their chiefs wear crucifixes and walk the streets of Montreal saying their rosaries and begging, separated themselves many years ago from the Mohawk Indians and River Indians. Long after their separation, they continued a fraudulent trade between Albany and Montreal. The village contains about two hundred houses. Although built mainly in stone, they look dirty and miserable. There are about eight hundred inhabitants. . . . This village is regarded as the most respectable of all the Indian villages" (Long, 1980, p. 30).

○ Geoffrey R. Matthews, Harris Cole, Deryck Holdsworth, Donald P. Kerr, and Louis Gentilcore, Historical Atlas of Canada (Toronto: University of Toronto Press, 1987–93), 3 vols.

them Mohawks, and, apparently, a few Oswegatchies and Caughnawagas,□ as the Iroquois who had settled at these two places were called. There were also some Abenakis.

At the head of eleven thousand men, Amherst finally began his march to Montreal. The progress of this impressive army march to Montreal has not been extensively studied. Even the marvellous first volume of the *Historical Atlas of Canada, From the Beginning to 1800,*○ does not contain a precise

map of the upper St. Lawrence. Fortunately, there is an extraordinary map drawn by Pierre Pouchot, the last French defender of Fort Lévis (see p. 45). Pouchot wrote, among other things, *Mémoires sur la dernière guerre de l'Amérique entre la France et l'Angleterre,* an exceptional source – but one that remains almost

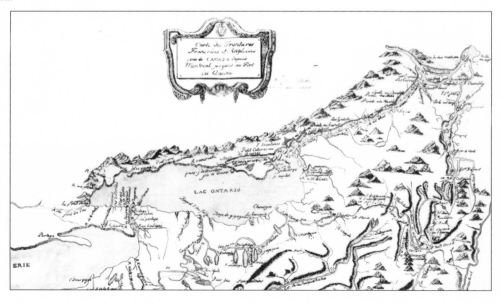

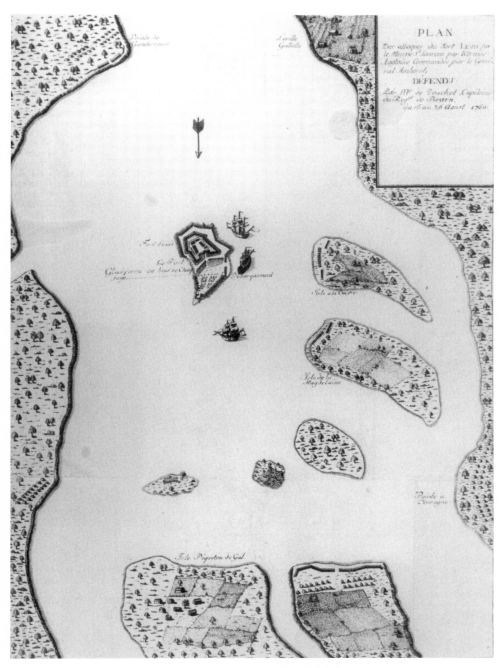

On pages 44 and 45, the maps that Amherst may have used. Copies are preserved in Amherst's papers. It should be noted that their author, Pierre Pouchot, captured at Niagara the preceding summer, was part of an exchange of prisoners.

□ *In fact, historians – and legal experts – are now discovering the 13,000 pages of what have been dubbed the* Johnson Papers. *To follow the path of Amherst's lumbering expedition, historians can also consult* The Journal of Jeffery Amherst *and the journal of his brother William, who served as his aide-de-camp in 1760.*

○ *They gave him the nickname Sategayogen, "the place of good business." See Bougainville, 1993, p. 188.*

completely untapped, even though there is currently great interest in clarifying a treaty that was concluded at Oswegatchie in August, 1760.□

Pouchot was a brilliant military man, an engineer by training, and he had a sense of humour. Fascinated by the Indians, he was loved and respected by them.○ He knew how to negotiate with them, as did many Canadiens but

Special row-galley ship built on Amherst's order.

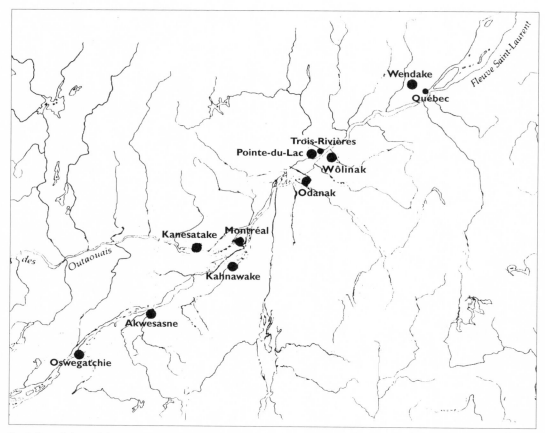

The Indian missions of the St. Lawrence Valley circa 1760.

few Frenchmen. He also knew the country between Montreal and Fort Niagara like the back of his hand, and he gives a long description of the difficulties of navigating between Oswego and Montreal.□ To understand the risks that Amherst's army ran, one must know the lay of the land. An attentive reading of Pouchot's *Mémoires* suggests that the choice of Sault-Saint-Louis, Saint-Régis, and Oswegatchie as sites for posts was very deliberate, as these villages occupied extremely strategic positions along the upper St. Lawrence.○

The Indian "Missions"

All of the Indian "missions" in the St. Lawrence Valley played an important military role, except for Jeune-Lorette, near Quebec City. In my opinion, military imperatives dictated the choice of the above-mentioned sites and those of Lake of Two Mountains, Odanak on the Saint-François River, Wôlinak on the Bécancour River, and the short-lived Saint-François-de-Sales de la Chaudière on the Chaudière River. These posts were positioned, respectively, to protect Montreal, Trois-Rivières, and Quebec City. The "resident savages," as the French administrators called them, were valuable allies. Although they were far fewer in number than the Western Indians with whom the French had generally good relations, they had made it possible, or at least easier, for the French to form "side by side," or aligned, settlements in the areas between Montreal and Quebec City, while the Americans, who had long felt terrorized – justifiably – by Indian and French-Canadian incursions, had formed "grouped" settlements.△

From this perspective, William Johnson's role takes on new significance: he tipped the balance. Thanks to his ties with the Six Nations and his knowledge of the Indians' way of thinking, he neutralized the French alliances and ultimately derailed the French strategy.

Were the Indians aware of the stakes? Pouchot's comments are extremely revealing. In his exchanges with allies and visitors, he constantly refers to Johnson: "You know that he is the enemy of your father Onontio [the king of France]"◇ – and thus the

□ *Pouchot, 1781, vol. 1, pp. 70–127.*

○ *Sault-Saint-Louis faced the rapids that travellers "regarded as the worst on this river, up to La Présentation [Oswegatchie]" (Pouchot, vol. 3, p. 71); Saint-Régis was "the side one always follows" and "where one must use toboggans" (Pouchot, vol. 3, p. 83); Oswegatchie was at the mouth of the river of the same name, which led "very far inland" (ibid., p. 95), and faced the island of Orakointon on which Fort Lévis was built.*

△ *Obviously, this is a hypothesis. To my knowledge, it has never really been examined, but the current renewed interest in the history of the First Nations will no doubt provide new opportunities. One thing is sure, however: for the Americans, the French and Indian Wars were extremely distressing. Lasting a century, they could not fail to leave their mark – even, perhaps, on how settlements were configured.*

◇ *"They call French officers Onontio, which means mountain," Pouchot wrote (vol. 3, p. 364), "because one of the first they knew was named Mont-Magny."*

□ *Pouchot, vol. 2, p. 183.*

○ *Ibid., p. 185.*

△ *Ibid., p. 187.*

◇ *Ibid., p. 234.*

□ *Pouchot, vol. 2,*
pp. 236–37.

○ *The DCB spells it Koua-*
tegeté or Ohquandageghte,
but I am following
Pouchot's spelling here.

△ *Pouchot, vol. 2, p. 253.*

◇ *DCB, vol. 4, p. 635.*

enemy of the Indians – he reminded an interlocutor.□ "I know very well the swamp into which Johnson and your dear English brother threw you. You, their nation's friends, they treat you worse than their dogs and their Negroes. You don't have permission to sleep in their forts. . . . You cannot deny this fact," he added. "All the children of Onontio are free and at peace in their country."○ "In the end, the French and the English will reconcile."△

At the time – spring, 1760 – there was war. But the Indians were only too aware that the French were in a poor position. There was much coming and going. News and rumours were travelling fast. Day after day, Pouchot and Johnson sent spies to keep an eye on each other.

On June 30, one of Pouchot's spies, Saoten, reported to him that "the Five Nations were threatening to rethink their position, and feared that as soon as the French were gone, the English would want to destroy them because at present they found themselves surrounded by all of their forts."◇ Pouchot's publisher added a footnote: "At all times, they [the Indians] were perfectly aware of the need to convince France and England to spare them, and in consequence to keep one from prevailing over the other."□

On August 8, one month before the surrender of Montreal, Pouchot received Kouatageté,○ who had been "sent on a mission to Chouaguen [Oswego]" on June 8. He brought back with him an Oneyut and an Agnier, "representatives of the Five Nations," whose mandate was to convince the Indians of Oswegatchie to remain neutral.○ Kouatageté, an erstwhile ally of the British, had slowly drawn closer to the French; he was baptised on April 27, 1760, and married soon after (May 10).◇ Although he made it known that he would no longer take up arms because of "religious scruples," he did not refuse to serve as Pouchot's informant.

One key role played by Indians during these wars was their constant "scouting" to observe the enemy. They served as guides, helped with transport, and formed part of the communications system. They did not like to fight in rank formation but excelled at ambushes. At Monongahela, the British admitted that they "had not seen a single enemy all day long." It was almost impossible for regular troops to react: "One might as well send a cow to chase a hare," wrote one observer at the time, "as to send our soldiers, weighed down as they are, after naked Indians and Canadiens in shirtsleeves!"□

But the Indians often refused to fight; they fled until they were just out of reach, then stopped. They were not eager to attack a fortified site. It was not unusual for them to sit by, almost as spectators, to watch how a battle "between the whites" unfolded.

This was basically what the "representatives from the Five Nations" proposed to the local Indians whom they met in council at Île Picquet on August 10. "They presented a very beautiful wampum belt," reported Pouchot, who was at the council but was not supposed to speak,

> on which were represented the English, the Five Nations, the three villages of our Iroquois missions, Chonegatchi, the lake, and St. Louis, with a man, and a beautiful road that connected them to each other, and they asked our Savages to take it, to remain neutral, to let the whites, who soon would have to make peace, fight, and to withdraw from their path, or to come without weapons. They assured them that they would be well received; that Johnson and they would precede the army only to watch the whites fight. . . . Then came General Amherst's subalterns, to urge them to pay attention to what these belts were saying, by which he was assuring them that in five or ten days he [Amherst] would be at Chuegatchi, that he would fight the French again, and that the Giver of Life alone knew what would happen.○

This sheds light on what may have happened in Oswegatchie in August, 1760, and on the links between the groups of "resident Indians."

The "representatives of the Five Nations" were in fact led astray by the response of the Oswegatchie Indians, who asked them to take their message to Montreal. It was their duty to do so, "since their father and the Iroquois of the Sault had agreed that the talks that went on between the Five Nations would go directly to Mont-Réal, without stopping at their town."△ In other words,

□ *Frégault, 1955, p. 139.*

○ *Pouchot, vol. 2, pp. 255, 256.*

△ *Ibid., p. 256.*

the Indians of Oswegatchie were making known their alliances with other "resident Indians": "After thinking long and hard about this response," the representatives realized "that they had to return" to Johnson and his Indians.

This was when Pouchot exploded. Of course, one might argue that he aggrandized his own role in his memoirs, but he is as credible as his contemporaries, who are quoted so heavily in the *Johnson Papers*. And he presents a different, no doubt useful point of view.

"If you were going to Mont-Réal, I would have nothing to say to you," Pouchot said, "and I would let your father talk; but since you are turning back, I must tell you what is on my mind. . . . Simply assure . . . your brothers the Iroquois that their spirit is lost, that by dispensing a bit of firewater Johnson will have them following where he wants, that they should look at the precipice toward which he is leading them."□ No doubt, the Indians present, both Five Nations representatives and Oswegatchie, were transfixed by this well-respected orator.

Pouchot spoke at length. He reminded his interlocutors of their past defeats at Johnson's side and his big promises. He evoked his own defeat at Niagara the preceding year, in which he had carefully avoided involving his Indian allies: "You listened to me then and retreated to let us fight." He turned the knife in the wound, evoking the forces that the French – with a little luck – might bring into the region. (In reality, Pitt's policy had been effective and the French reinforcements had been blocked in the Atlantic.) "The English will soon be forced to go and hide in a corner of the country they stole from the Abenakis."○ He dwelt on the tragedy of the Abenakis, who had been driven from Maine at the beginning of the seventeenth century:

> You can see the plight of the Abenakis in their own country. They go into the water and the woods to find something to eat & can no longer plant their corn. They are the dogs of the English, who hit them with sticks & hang them. The same thing will happen to you when the French have left you, & when you remind the English that they promised to give you what you need, they will laugh at you;

instead of when you had the French and the English for neighbours, and they tried to outdo each other.□

"Though they are friends of the English, the representatives were pleased that Mr. Pouchot . . . spoke the truth. . . . Those from Chouegatchi applauded this speech loudly." Although Pouchot wrote in the third person, he had no need to be modest.

The Fate of Fort Lévis

On August 16, 1760, Amherst's troops set up camp "at Pointe au Baril & across from La Présentation." La Broquerie, on his ship the *Outaouaise*, was observing them.○ "He shot his cannon three times. M. Pouchot sent two Frenchmen & two savages in a canoe to his ship, to find out what was going on." On the 17th came manoeuvres, the capture of the *Outaouaise*, and a dispatch to Vaudreuil.△ On the 18th, a few English ships sailed by Fort Lévis, in the *Outaouaise*, "not quite within range of the cannons, to protect themselves." On the 19th, fresh troops overran the fort without causing much damage and went to "camp at Pointe de l'Ivrogne." For three days, Pouchot observed constant movement between the ships and military preparations. On the 22nd, the attack took place: a conventional cannonade.

"One thing that amused the garrison at such serious times," recalled Pouchot,◇

was that the Savages, who had climbed up on the trenches and batteries to watch the combat between these vessels, which they regarded as theirs, because of the names that they had given them, and because they bore a painted Savage on their great flags, gave terrible cries, seeing them so mistreated. The English had persuaded them that with these ships alone they would drive us away. When these Savages saw them drifting in irons and running aground, they redoubled their cries and jeered at the English,

□ *Ibid.*, p. 260.

○ *See John Knox's journal, The Siege of Quebec (p. 284). According to Knox, Amherst set up camp at Oswegatchie on August 17, after the Outaouaise was captured.*

△ *In a letter dated August 26, 1760, Amherst reported to his superiors, "This day [the 17th] I took possession of Swegatchi and encamped there" (NAC, C.O. 5 B-2173, vol. 59, part 1, p. 6).*

◇ *Pouchot, vol. 2, p. 275.*

FRANÇOIS DE LÉVIS (1718–87), OR CHEVALIER DE LÉVIS.

He reached the height of his career in 1783 and was made a duke the following year. He is known mainly for preferring to burn his regiment's flags rather than surrender them. He was unable to accept the humiliation dealt to Vaudreuil by Amherst and refused to meet with him. His name was known to and respected by the Indians. The last fort built west of Montreal, across the water from Oswegatchie on Île Royale, bore his name. It was heroically defended by Pierre Pouchot in 1760. After the surrender of Montreal, Lévis quickly returned to France.

□ Ibid., p. 279.

○ Journal of Jeffery Amherst, p. 239. On August 26, 1760, Amherst sent Minister Pitt a copy of the surrender signed by Pouchot and took this opportunity to report on what had occurred since his departure from Oswego. No negotiation with the Indians is mentioned. (NAC, C.O. 5, B-2173, vol. 59, part 1, p. 10.)

△ Flexner, 1959, p. 218.

◇ Journal of Jefferey Amherst, August 1760, p. 240.

"You did not want to kill our father [Pouchot], at Niagara; see that you capture him now. If you had listened to us, we would not have found him here. A handful of Frenchmen are putting you to shame."

Night and day, "the enemies continued to bombard and cannonade," until the 25th, when they "shot with hot cannonballs, firepots, and shells."□ The ruins of the fort caught fire. "A brave garrison does not deserve such treatment," generally reserved for "rebels," Pouchot protested in writing. His note was kept in Amherst's papers: "Sir, It has just come to my attention that the Place that I have the Honour of Commanding for the King my Master has been Attacked with red-hot cannonballs. I did not Believe that we merited such harsh treatment from Your Excellency." He had no choice but to surrender: "I hope to receive favourable treatment if I ask you for Conditions."

Amherst noted in his journal, "I immediately answered & sent him terms of Capitulation by Capt Prescott for him to sign & send back to me, which he did. I ordered Lt Col Massey with three Companys of Grenadiers to take Possession of the Fort, the Garrison being Prisonners of War. I did not permit an Indian to go in."○

Johnson was quite upset. His Indians, "agreeable to their customs," wanted the French to pay for their insults to the Indians' ancestors since the beginnings of their colonization, and Johnson had to intercede.△ Normally, they would have had the spoils of war, but Amherst had reserved all the booty for the regular soldiers. In spite of his orders, a few Indians sneaked inside, where they saw grenadiers "pillaging and looting." Amherst wanted to placate them with a few gifts. Disappointed, 506 of the 691 Indian warriors decided to leave – and they took, with Johnson's tacit approval, anything they could grab.

On the 27th, a laconic Amherst noted in his journal, "The Indians scratched up the dead bodys and scalped them as if it had been the greatest feast to them."◇ The previous evening, Pouchot had come for dinner. Meeting the Indians with whom he had been in contact, the French commandant reproached them, concluding, "Too bad for you," to which they responded, "Don't be angry, father, you are going to the other side of the great lake. We will get rid of the English."□

Obviously, Amherst had invited Pouchot out of more than mere courtesy; he hoped "to gain some insight on what remained to be done on the country." It must have been Pouchot's pleasure to tell him. The worst was yet to come: Galops, Rapide Plat, Long Sault, Coteau-du-Lac, Les Cèdres, Buisson, Cascades. Of course, each of these steps would provide a perfect opportunity for the enemy to pounce on the convoy. Chevalier de La Corne (Louis, the brother of La Corne Saint-Luc) was on the prowl in the environs. The English knew this. But his troops were greatly depleted, as he had suffered desertions of both militiamen and Indians. Powerless to intervene, he had to be content with watching Amherst struggle in the waters of the St. Lawrence and reporting to Governor Vaudreuil, who was no doubt preparing a plan of surrender. From all sides, the news was bad. Every hour, hopes of resistance faded.

The Oswegatchie Conference

What happened between August 28 and September 6? What do the journals of General Jeffery Amherst and his brother William, who was leading the Oswego Light Infantry toward Montreal in August, 1760, tell us?

On August 28, Johnson informed Jeffery Amherst of the arrival of three Indians who were refusing to speak until the small group of which they were the advance guard arrived.○ The next day, "Captain Jacobs . . . arrived with Indians from the French & brought me a letter from a Priest to offer Peace on the Indian side."△

Amherst, ever cautious, repaired Fort Lévis, newly renamed William Augustus, as best he could.◇

On the 30th, "Sir William Johnson all day in conference with the Indians."

On the 31st, the fleet began moving again. "I advanced the two Companys of Rangers & Gages Regt.," Amherst noted in his

□ *Pouchot, vol. 2, p. 284.*

○ *"Sr Wm Johnson acquainted me at night of three Indians were come with a message from about thirty who were coming up to joyn us. They would not tell their story till the others came, but Sr Wm picked up from one of them that the Vessels with Governor Murray's Army was arrived at Montreal"* (Journal of Jeffery Amherst, p. 240).

△ *On June 21, 1760, Amherst informed Johnson that the siege of Quebec City (by Lévis) had been lifted and that Vaudreuil had released the prisoners whom he had taken on April 28 (at the Battle of Sainte-Foy) and at other times – a total of 123 – "among whom the Eldest Captain Jacobs of the Indians is included"* (Johnson Papers, vol. 3, p. 259). Many Indians had this name at the time.

◇ *From the reduction of l'Isle Royale [on which Fort Lévis stood] to the 30th inclusive, the army may have been employed in repairing the fort"* (Knox, 1980, p. 286). In his diary, Jeffery Amherst reveals much more interest in the repair work at the fort than in the arrival of a band of Indians. As we recall, the previous autumn he had spent his time doing construction work in the Lake Champlain region; he had the idea to build a fortress at Crown Point (St. Frederic).

Was a treaty signed in Oswegatchie in August, 1760? Where was this place? What was located there at the time?

Artist Thomas Davies gives a good idea. An officer in the British army, he belonged to the Royal Artillery that accompanied Amherst in his march to Montreal in the summer of 1760.

In mid-August, he was present during the attack on a French warship facing Fort de la Présentation. He painted a vivid picture of the scene. On the left are magnificent sunflowers and a couple of Indians observing the attack by the small English ships.

On the cape jutting into the river is Fort La Galette, also called La Présentation. Behind the small fort are a few houses of the Oswegatchie mission, founded by the Sulpician priest François Picquet. Today, the site is called Ogdensburg.

□ Journal of Jeffery Amherst, *p. 242.*

journal.□ "The Indians that came forward were likewise advanced but Sir Wm Johnson complained of several having staid behind and he believed would return home."

Jeffery Amherst's brother William mentioned no Indian presence on August 31 or on the following days. In an army of eleven thousand men, evidently, much happened beyond the purview of the commander. Thus, Amherst learned only on September 2 that a number of Indians had deserted at Fort Lévis in whaleboats: "When I came away," he noted angrily, "I knew nothing of it till I was at the Isle au Chat or I would have sent to have taken their whaleboats away."

The Path Is Clear

Johnson, who had returned from "Asquesashne," where he had gone the previous day (September 1), consoled Amherst by telling him that he had met with the missionary and ten men, who had promised to remain calm.□ He had also learned that Chevalier de La Corne had promised not to intervene and had returned to Montreal.

The news was good, but the weather was terrible. The pilots, including the Canadiens captured at Fort Lévis, advised the English commandant to wait before crossing Lake St. Francis.

On September 3, Amherst was still pinned down by the violent winds. He questioned a prisoner, a "Royal Notary," who told him about the fall of Île aux Noix and confirmed that Chevalier de La Corne had retreated to Montreal.

On the 4th, the weather was good, but the water level in the river was unusually high. The falls at Les Cèdres (the "Hole") cost Amherst more than fifty boats and eighty-four men. That evening, he divided up his troops, and half advanced to Île Perrot. The

□ *We know that William Johnson spent the day of August 30 in conference with the Indians. His last comment of the 31st was, "I left Capt. Osborne with 200 men in the Fort & 215 sick in Hospital at La Galette."*

West of Montreal, the St. Lawrence River is extremely dangerous. Here, Thomas Davies shows a few boats of the Amherst expedition caught in the rapids.

The Vestiges of Amherst's Shipwreck

Bronze mortar dating from 1721 (10-inch calibre, 93-pound shell), found at Coteau-du-Lac on September 10, 1978. According to archaeologist Michel Gaumond, it is among the largest and best pieces found from the last French and Indian war.

On September 4, 1760, Amherst's convoy faced the Les Cèdres rapids west of Montreal. Some 50 boats were swept into the tumultuous waters. In recent years, members of the Société historique et archéologique de Coteau-du-Lac began to research the scope of the disaster. In March, 1980, Michel Cadieux reported on behalf of the society to the heritage division of the Quebec department of cultural affairs. An archaeological-research permit and a grant of $6,000 were issued, allowing for 360 hours of diving over 36 days in the summer of 1979. The results were stunning and added to the discoveries made in the summer of 1978.

Carriage (base) of a 10-inch mortar.

Almost a hundred mortar shells were found in calibres of 4 1/2 inches, 5 1/2 inches, and 10 inches. According to the archaeologist Michel Gaumond, who graciously lent us these photographs, the mortars were used to demolish batteries protected by fortifications. They were therefore shot vertically. Loaded with powder and armed with a fuse that remained lit during their flight, the shells caused major damage when they exploded.

Portable Coehorn mortar, weighing only 86 pounds.

□ Journal of Jeffery
Amherst, p. 244.

○ "At night Lt Elliot came
from St Johns with a letter
from Col Haviland. I wrote
to Gen Murray" (Journal
of Jeffery Amherst,
p. 245).

settlers slowly emerged from their hiding places: "They came in
by degrees & gave themselves up & not a soul was killed by our
Savages. Several from the Island of Montreal came in & I
assured them all of my Protection as long as they remained
quiet."□

Amherst, Haviland, Murray

On September 5, progress toward Montreal continued. That
evening, Amherst received a letter from Saint-Jean signed by
Colonel Haviland, and he wrote to General Murray.○ According
to Murray's journal, he received the letter on the 5th, at the same
time that he was receiving the peace treaty from the Hurons and
Iroquois. On the 5th or 6th, Knox gave a long account of a serious
quarrel:

> The van of his [Haviland's] corps arrived yesterday at Longueuil,
> and they report that Sir William Johnson with a large body of In-
> dians, computed at fourteen hundred, will be there this day from
> General Amherst's army. Eight Sachems, of different nations, lately
> in alliance with the enemy, have surrendered, for themselves and their
> tribes, to General Murray. . . . While these Chieftains were negotiat-
> ing a peace, two of our Mohawks entered the apartment where they
> were with the General and Colonel Burton.

Almost immediately, they made as if to throw themselves
upon the Indians who were present. Murray and Burton quickly
intervened to separate the "enemy brothers."

Once again face to face, the Indians challenged each other. "We
two Mohawks would scalp every man of you," they shouted. "It is
well for you that you surrendered – and that these generals are
here – it is they who protect you." And he added, "'Let the treaty
be as it will [or, according to the translation by Judge Lamer, "no
matter what the treaty says" (SCR, 1990, p. 1058)]. I tell you, we
will destroy you and your settlement – root and branch – ye are
all cowards – our squaws are better than you – they will stand and
fight like men – but ye skulk like dogs,' etc. etc. Between every
pause the French chief uttered, 'Heh! Heh!' and reworked the
notches on his stick, till at length," he signalled to his compan-

ions. Murray and Burton had to intervene once again and beg the Indians to stay calm or suffer more severe punishments.

Was this on the 5th or 6th? And what treaty were the Mohawk referring to?

On the 5th, Murray noted in his journal, "March'd with them myself and on the road, met the Inhabitants who were coming to deliver their arms, and take the oath, these two nations of Indians, of Hurons and Iroquois, came in and made their Pace." At the same time, "Three of Sir William Johnson's Indians came in, with a letter from General Amherst, which I immediately answer'd."

□ Knox's Historical Journal, *vol. 3, p. 515.*

○ *Knox mentions the sudden arrival of two "of our Mohawks," while Murray writes, "three of Sir William Johnson's Indians came in." Where was Murray? On the road? Or "in the apartment" with the chiefs who were surrendering? In any case, Murray makes no allusion to the argument between Johnson's Mohawks and the Indians who were ex-allies of the French. As well, he received a letter from Amherst, which, to date, has not been found, in which Amherst gives him accurate information on his position. Murray also learned, either by letter or from the Mohawks, that Johnson was ahead of Amherst's army on the march to Longueuil, where he was expected on the 6th, according to the chronology proposed by Doughty in his edition of Knox's journal. In short, there are divergences (see p. 174) between Knox's and Murray's journals, although they agree on the essentials. Finally, note that when he met with Hurons and Iroquois (the former from Lorette; the latter, no doubt, from Sault-Saint-Louis) at Longueuil, Murray knew that Johnson was on his way and would be there in a few hours. He also knew Johnson's mandate with regard to the Indians.*

△ *See next page.*

What letter was this? When was it sent? Either Amherst had written a letter to Murray on the 4th, upon receipt of a letter from Haviland, or he had written and sent it on the evening of the 5th – as he noted – in which case it could have reached Murray only on the 6th, the date given by the publisher of Knox's journal.□ In his journal, William Amherst mentioned the arrival of Haviland's letter "this afternoon" – on the 5th. As Amherst had had news about Murray through his prisoner on the 3rd, it is not impossible that he had sent a message on the evening of the 3rd or the 4th (which might have gotten to Murray on the 5th).○

When he received the "Pace" from the Hurons, Murray sent them a document that archivists call a "certificate." Dated September 5, it said,

> These are to certify that the chief of the Huron Tribe of Indians, having come to me in the name of his Nation to submit to His Britannick Majesty and make Peace, has been received under my protection with his whole Tribe, and henceforth no English officer or party is to molest or interrupt them in returning to their settlement at Lorette and they are received upon the same terms with the Canadians, being allowed the free Exercise of their Religion, their Customs and liberty of trading with the English Garrisons recommending it to the Officers commanding the posts to treat them kindly.
>
> Given under my hand at Longuil [sic] this 5th day of September, 1760
>
> sigd Ja. Murray

By the Generals Command
Sigd John Cosnand
Adjt Genl

On the back of the document, long preserved among Murray's papers in Bath, England, appeared the following inscription: "Copy of a certificate granted by Genl Murray to the Huron Indians, 5th Sept: 1760."△

Vaudreuil's Surrender

On the 6th, "a fine day," Amherst landed at Lachine. That very evening, Marquis de Vaudreuil, the governor of New France, held a council. "The general interest of the colony required, it was agreed, that things should not be pushed to ultimate extremes."□

Twenty-four hours later, the articles of the Act of Capitulation were finalized. Vaudreuil signed first. "I sent him a duplicate bearing my signature," Amherst wrote to Pitt on the same day.○

In reprisal for the "cruel and barbarous war" that they and their Indians had waged, Amherst refused military honours to the French troops.△ He did, however, agree to article 8, which specified that injured Indians would be treated like the other sick and injured of both camps, and article 40, which ensured that "the Savages or Indians Allied with his Very Christian Majesty Will be maintained on the Land that they live on if They Wish to stay . . . They will have Like the French, Freedom of Religion and will Keep their missionaries."◇

Amherst also refused to admit, even indirectly, that the Indians who had fought on the side of the English might have committed misdeeds. When he saw article 9, which called for him to

PIERRE DE RIGAUD DE VAUDREUIL DE CAVAGNAL, MARQUIS DE VAUDREUIL (1698–1778).

The last governor-general of New France, he prepared the terms of the capitulation of Montreal. He did so with intelligence and realism. Born in Canada, he was the great rival of the Marquis de Montcalm, who had been sent to New France as lieutenant-general of the armies in 1756.

◇ *This document is considered a certificate because, of course, it begins with the words: "These are to certify." Murray did not have the authority to sign anything but a "certificate of protection," as he had been doing for a number of days for the Canadiens who were surrendering, in conformity with the terms of the Act of Capitulation of Quebec City in the autumn of 1759. The text of Murray's document given here corresponds to that quoted in* Knox's Historical Journal *edited by A.G. Doughty (Champlain Society, vol. 3, p. 517). At the word "Huron" in the index to this edition are found the following references: "Not to be molested in returning to their settlement at Lorette, ii, 517; from a certificate granted to, by Murray, 517."*

□ *Quoted in Frégault, 1955, p. 389.*

○ Documents Relating to the Constitutional History of Canada, *vol. I, p. 4.*

△ *According to C.P. Stacey, DCB, vol. 5, p. 26.*

◇ *The text of articles 8, 33, and 40 is given in Appendix C.*

□ *Nevertheless, "I ordered our Indians home," he wrote in his journal on September 22. In a report to Pitt, he was more specific: "I gave our Indians, as a Reward for their behaviour, as many necessarys and blankets out of the stores, as Sir Wm Johnson thought necessary, and ordered them home." That morning, he had appointed Gage governor of Montreal (NAC, C.O. 5/59, B-2173, p. 131). Also in this message, he estimated the population of Canada at 76,172 spread over 108 parishes (Government of Montreal, 37,200; Government of Trois-Rivières, 6,388; Government of Quebec City, 32,584).*

send them away, he retorted, "There have been no Cruelties Committed by the Savages of Our Army: and good order will be maintained." To article 51, which returned to this question, he again responded, "We will Take Care that the Savages insult no Subjects of His Very Christian Majesty."□

Amherst was proud of himself. On the evening of the 8th, he wrote in his journal, "I believe never Three Armys, setting out from different & very distant Parts from each other joyned in the Center, as was intended, better than we did, and it could not fail of having the effect of which I have just now seen the consequence."

Murray was also very pleased with himself, although things might have been even better if Amherst had been delayed. Would he hesitate a while before joining his forces with Haviland's to attack Montreal? The idea had come to mind. But he hadn't had the time to stop; on this occasion, Amherst was on time.○

Murray could, however, declare that his mission had been accomplished. He had provoked desertions by hundreds, and he had therefore conquered the populace without firing a shot – only setting a few fires, for which he commiserated with "all those unfortunates." But he had no regrets about this "cruel necessity"; the "effects of the fire" had been immediate. He had intimidated not only the Canadien settlers, but also hundreds of regular soldiers, not to mention the "French Indians" – for, after all, both groups had surrendered on September 5. In addition, he had met with Johnson. When and where? This is what we must try to find out.

"Canadien" "French"

○ I write "on this occasion" because I think that Amherst had let Wolfe down the preceding year. But for the rendez-vous of his army with Murray's at Montreal in September, 1760, he kept strictly to the schedule. In an interesting message sent to Murray from New York on April 15, 1760 (NAC, C.O. 5/58, part 2), he ended his orders with this revealing comment: "I am confident, I need not mention to you, that a proper care, in [illegible] the Canadians, as much as you possibly can, from Joining the French, must tend greatly to dispirit them, and make Our Conquests the easier."

An Account by Johnson and Amherst

In a letter sent from Fort Johnson to minister William Pitt on October 24, 1760, Johnson summarized his position.

> As there were nine Severall Nats. & Tribes of Inds. inhabiting ye Country about Montreal consisting of above 800 fighting men, previous to our departure I judged it highly necessary to gain them if possible, at least to bring them to a Neutrality, being very sensible of the difficultys which an Army had to encounter in their way to Montreal where a few Indians Joined with other troops might act to great advantage. I therefore proposed to Gen Amherst the sending them offers of peace, & protection, which he agreed to, and on our Arrival at Fort Levi, deputies came from the before mentioned Nations on my Message to them from Oswego, who there ratified a Treaty with us, whereby they agreed to remain neuter on condition that we for the future treated them as friends, & forgot all former enmity.□

Amherst was well aware that he had been very lucky in his march toward Montreal, especially between Fort Lévis and Lachine. "Sir William Johnson had taken unwearied pains," he wrote to Pitt, "in keeping the Indians in human bounds, and I have the pleasure to assure you that not a peasant, woman, or child has been hurt by them, or a house burned, since I entered what was the enemy's country." In fact, Johnson had done much more than prevent a few little incidents by his Indians. Amherst was deliberately downplaying Johnson's contribution; he didn't like Indians, was not comfortable with them, and no doubt did not want to share the glory with a baronet running wild in Mohawk country.

In his report, Johnson was more appreciative of his own efforts. Without "the greatest pains taken to prevail on some [Indian] nations, to act, some to a neutrality, and to divide others in their councils," Canada, he opined, would never have fallen "under our dominion."○

In the following months and years, the Indians would frequently refer to the peace of Oswegatchie, which lends credibility to Johnson's report of October 24, 1760. But the documents available do not offer a very accurate account of what happened

□ The words "Treaty with" in the passage were not necessarily in the original document, which was partly destroyed by fire. The publisher relied upon a transcription in which he was not able to verify every single word, and he placed the unverified words in angle brackets. In at least one other letter (Aug. 25, 1763), Johnson identifies the "Canadian Nations" – the "Hurons near Quebec" among them Johnson added, "After taking Fort Levi many of our Indians, thro some disgust left us, but there still remained a sufficient number to answer our purpose and bring us constant Intelligence having none against us, and the Peace which I settled with the 9 Nations before mentioned, was productive of such good consequences that some of these Indians joined us, & and went upon Partys for prisoners & whilst the rest preserved so strict a neutrality that we passed all the dangerous Rapids, and the whole way without the least opposition, & by that means came so near to the other two Armies, that the Enemy could attempt nothing further without an imminent risque of the City & inhabitants. "Thus Sir we became Masters of the last place in the Enemy's possession on these parts and made those Indians our friends by a peace, who might otherwise have given us much trouble" (Johnson Papers, vol. 3, pp. 269–75).

○ See next page.

○ *These two quotations are taken from Flexner's interesting biography,* Mohawk Baronet. Sir William Johnson of New York, *p. 220. In April, 1761, Amherst sent silver medals to Johnson to give to 182 Indians who had served under him on his march against Montreal. Among these medals, one – a gold one – was for Johnson himself, of whom Amherst said, "No one has so good a right to it as yourself"* (Johnson Papers, *vol. 3, pp. 278–79).*

□ *On the 29th, as we have noted, Amherst wrote in his journal, "At night Capt Jacobs who was taken with Capt Kennedy came to me. He arrived with Indians from the French & brought me a letter from a Priest to offer Peace on the Indian side" (p. 241). The next day, concerned primarily with his work site – the repair work on the fort – Amherst noted, "Sr Wm Johnson all day in conference with the Indians."*

○ *"Camp at Fort William Augustus [formerly Fort Lévis three miles below the present city of Ogdensburg], 30th Augst 1760. Dear Sir [Sir William Johnson, Baronet] I Send You with this a Translation of the Letter I received last Night . . ." (*Johnson Papers, *vol. 10, p. 177).*

that August. Of course, the Indians were interested in having their neutrality recognized. Johnson, for his part, was interested in aggrandizing his own role.

As we have followed Amherst's movements day by day, we have seen no explicit indication that a peace was concluded at Oswegatchie. Could it have occurred during the siege of Fort Lévis? It is conceivable, but not likely. No one, to my knowledge, has made the slightest allusion to this possibility.

We do know that on August 30, William Johnson spent the entire day "in conference" with an Indian delegation brought by Captain Jacobs (perhaps the captain whom the French had released when they lifted the siege of Quebec City in May).□ Amherst was busy finishing the repairs to Fort Lévis when he sent Johnson, on the 30th, the translation of a letter received the previous day○ (no doubt from the Jesuit priest Roubaud), "by which you will See the Temper and Disposition of the Enemy's Indians. With this Intelligence, and the Talk You will have from their Sachems, You will be best able to Judge what will be the most likely means to hinder the Indians from Joining the Enemy, in which Case, they may be Assured of being permitted to live in Peace and Quiet, and of receiving all the protection, they can desire."

If there is any evidence at all of a treaty of Oswegatchie, here it is. Taking account of the work in progress in the fort, Johnson was no doubt on the south shore of the St. Lawrence, at Oswegatchie, offering peace and quiet, along with all the British protection they could wish for, to the Indian emissaries who had come to meet with him. No minutes or documents resulted from the encounter, but certainly an agreement of neutrality and promises of protection were given.

The Caughnawaga Conference

For the Indians previously allied with the French (and for Johnson as well!), a true peace – the treaty that, for them, ended the French and Indian Wars – was concluded at Caughnawaga on September 15 and 16, 1760. There, Johnson found old and new Indian allies. A sixteen-point set of minutes was found in the journal of Jelles

Fonda, one of Johnson's agents. It is kept in the archives of the New York Historical Society.□

The great Warraghiyagey, he "who does much business," Johnson himself, represented the British authorities, as was his duty. "We who are present here as Representatives of 8 Natˢ," explained the Indians' spokesman, "will bury the French hatchet we made Use of . . . ."

At the end of this meeting, Johnson indicated his desire to go home. Delegates from each of the nations accompanied him, "to try yᵉ goodness of the Road." "We are ready," the speaker continued, "whenever You go to accompany You."

With no further ado, the Indians thanked their brother Warraghiyagey: "For opening the Road from this to your Country we on our parts assure you to keep it clear of any Obstacles & use it in a friendly Manner."○ As well, the speaker recalled that mistrust of firewater, "the only thing wᶜʰ can turn our heads and prove fatal to us, we who now represent 8 Natˢ here present entreat you in the most earnest Manner not to suffer any of your People to sell or give any to us."

The same request was made by the Six Nations. The "French Indians" were very grateful to be able to keep their priest; in the same breath, they expressed their desire to see trade regulated.

At the end, the chief of the Caughnawaga Warriors returned to the question of firewater and used it to demand a new interpreter to replace Louis Perthuis, whom they no longer wanted present. In one last demand, the chief claimed "the peaceable Possession of yᵉ Spot of Ground we live now upon" from those "who have now the Possession of this Country"; after all, he said, "we have according to our desire kept out of the Way of your Army."

On September 16, 1760, the Eight Fires met with "the Chain of Friendship." "The old Covenant Chain" was re-established "for ever."

For the British, the Indian question was far from being settled. First, there was Pontiac's uprising. Then, the War of Independence, setting Americans against British, gave the Indians a respite. For some time yet, the Indians believed that they held the balance of power, this time between the British and the Americans.

□ *This important document was reproduced in volume 13, pp. 163–66, of* The Papers of William Johnson *(Albany, 1962). Co-editor Albert B. Corey explains in his introduction that the documents in the book were unearthed during a new search in various American and Canadian archives. The minutes in question are very intriguing. Were they a copy or a rough draft? Was Fonda in Caughnawaga in September, 1760? His journal is silent for the days around August 30 and September 15 and 16. But in spite of the questions raised, it is an important document for illuminating the conditions of the alliance between the Eight Nations and the new masters. It is reproduced in its entirety in Appendix D.*

○ *The word "road" often had a specific meaning in Indian speech. "From this to your Country" no doubt means from Caughnawaga to Albany.*

II

THE SUPREME COURT
AND THE *SIOUI* RULING

Left to right, first row: John Sopinka, Gérard V. La Forest, Antonio Lamer, Claire L'Heureux-Dubé, Charles Doherty Gonthier. Left to right, second row: Frank Iabobucci, Peter de Carteret Cory, Beverly McLachlin, John Major.

On May 24, 1990, the day when the *Sioui* ruling was given, Justice Dickson was still Chief Justice of the Supreme Court. He retired and Justice Lamer took over on July 1, 1990. This photograph was taken a few years later: Justice Bertha Wilson, present for the *Sioui* ruling, was no longer sitting on the Supreme Court, while Justices Frank Iacobucci and John Major had been added. Other changes have taken place since that time.

The Supreme Court of Canada has been increasingly present in Canadians' lives since the Constitution Act, 1982, and creation of the Charter of Rights and Freedoms. This representation of the Supreme Court emblem adorns the interior of the court building.

"Existing rights – ancestral or issuing from treaties – of Canada's aboriginal peoples are recognized and confirmed." What are these ancestral rights? From what treaties do they come?

Huge numbers of cases are brought before the courts. Some are appealed all the way to the Supreme Court. One of them became the *Sioui* ruling, by which a safe-conduct issued by Murray to the Hurons of Lorette on September 5, 1760, in Longueuil, acquired the value of a treaty.

Murray's "Treaty" and the Courts

Monsieur le prieur [...] prit la liberté
de lui demander de quel pays il était.
Je suis Huron, lui répondit le jeune homme.

VOLTAIRE, *L'Ingénue*

THE HURONS OF LORETTE are of very mixed blood. Although they have adapted well to the society around them, they are still fiercely attached to the memory of their Indian origins. In each generation, there is a nucleus of individuals ready to take up once again the claims so ardently pressed by their predecessors.

In the days immediately after the British conquest, the Hurons of Lorette laid claim to the Sillery seigneury. There were barely a hundred of them,□ but this did not keep them from constantly returning to their battle cry between 1791 and 1835.

□ "They have at present but 32 Warriors and the whole Village, Men, Women and Children are short of 100," wrote the governor of Quebec, James Murray, in his report of June 6, 1762. "Their number is decreased at least one half within these forty Years, and the Tribe would by this time have been almost extinguished but for the supplies they got by captures in War, and the sale of unhappy infants whose Parents chose to conceal their own shame at the expense of such iniquitous bargains" (CD, vol. 1, p. 73).

In the summer of 1789, Charles Inglis, bishop of Nova Scotia, visited Quebec, a territory under his jurisdiction (until Jacob Mountain was appointed in 1793). Accompanied by his son, John, who acted as his private secretary, he visited the Indian villages of Caughnawaga and Lorette. "About 130 Indians there," he noted. "They danced well. Their priest, Father Jearaux, seemed a plain, diligent man" (RCA, 1913, p. 241).

The Hurons of Lorette "cannot be considered, properly speaking, as Indians" (October, 1836)

The Hurons in Sagard's time (circa 1630).

Louis Franquet is often quoted on the question of mixed blood. The Montreal publisher Joseph Cohen reprinted the French engineer's account in 1974 (Élysée) as *Voyages et Mémoires sur le Canada*. A fine observer, with a curious mind, Franquet was not interested only in fortifications. The habits and customs of the Indians, mainly those living near French posts, including the Hurons of Lorette, drew his attention. In 1752, he noted that these Hurons had mixed blood due to the capture of English people and the adoption of natural children brought by Europeans. Franquet's sentence structures are a little unusual, but his observations are interesting enough to warrant an attentive reading.

"The blood they [the Hurons of Lorettes] share," he remarked, "is mixed today: there are as many men and women of English slaves taken prisoner during the wars and whom they adopted, who took the habits and married. There are even French women who marry savages; as well, it is not without precedent that bastards born and

Watercolour by an anonymous artist portraying a Huron couple of Lorette around 1760. While the woman wears only earrings and necklaces as jewellery, the man wears large earrings, glass-bead necklaces, a wampum belt, armbands, and metal bracelets.

raised in the savage ways take nothing away from those of our [French] nation."

The mixing of blood intensified after the English victory to the point that an official report of the Executive Council of Lower Canada (October, 1836) concluded that the Hurons of Lorette could not be truly considered Indians: "By the Intermixture of White Blood they have now so lost the original Purity of Race that they cannot properly be considered Indians" (quoted by Beaulieu in *Les Hurons de Lorette*, 1994, p. 26). In a request addressed to Governor Metcalfe in 1845, the 18 signatories mentioned "intermarriages" from which "more than three-quarters of the Village" had come.

On the left, two Hurons of Lorette (late eighteenth or early nineteenth century). In the centre, leaning on his gun and chatting with the Indian woman, no doubt a Canadien.

The American historian Francis Jennings was interested in the question of mixed blood. In his attempt to define "nation" and "tribe," he recalled that the members of a tribe recognized each other as a "distinct community cemented by genetic and/or fictive kinship and ritual and distinguished themselves from outsiders. This concept is cultural rather than racial. . . . Under this legal definition in force [in United States courts today], tribes such as the Iroquois, which depended heavily on adoption/naturalization to replace casualties, might have vanished entirely long ago. No one has the faintest idea of what proportion of the Iroquois gene pool today goes back to aboriginal Iroquois ancestors. The record is clear that it contains contributions from many other Indian and European sources. The obvious reason persons of such various degrees of synethnicity can constitute a tribe is that they did and do" (Jennings, *The Ambiguous Iroquois Empire*, p. 37).

Chief Philippe Vincent was photographed by J.-E. Livernois around 1880. He wears a strange hat, a brooch, medals, armbands, a *ceinture-fléchée*, and bead-embroidered moccasins.

Hurons of Lorette circa 1838.

□ See Gérin, La Seigneurie de Sillery, p. 106.

○ See page 75.

△ *Quoted in Gérin, La Seigneurie de Sillery, p. 107. Even though some Hurons knew how to read and write – Louis Vincent had a bachelor's degree from Dartmouth College (1781) – in my opinion, the tone of the petition suggests the influence (and hand) of a fierce enemy of the Jesuits.*

Their first important petition was submitted on July 22, 1791.□ The last Jesuit missionary had just left them to become the superior in Quebec City. Unable to satisfy their demands, he advised them to appeal to Governor Dorchester.

The Hurons took a rather aggrieved tone when they talked of the Jesuits. "They kept us in crass ignorance, and we admit this with shame," stated the four petitioners, Thomas Martin, Zacharie Otis,○ Étienne Petit, and Augustin Picard.

The response from the authorities was too slow in coming. On January 12, 1793, the Indians were more insistent – and angrier. To the four previous signatories were added François Vincent, Zacharie Thomas, Simon Hélène, Joseph Vincent, and Louis Monique. It seemed that someone was encouraging them to denounce "the Jesuits' ambition and deceit, which are well known in all parts of the world."△ Expressing themselves "jointly and in the name of the Seven Nations, our brothers and allies," they asked the British authorities to resettle them "on our own land" – "like our brothers in the Seven Nations," they specified.

This time, they received a response. "Now that the affair is settled," Governor Prescott wrote tersely on March 31, 1793, "you would do best to resign yourselves to it."

The Hurons, experts at guerrilla warfare, decided upon a course of harassment. Each new governor received a new petition: Shore Milnes, Craig, Prevost, Sherbrooke, Richmond.

A Peak of Activity: 1819–24

Over the years, the Hurons refined their methods of pressing their claims and gained some support. Around 1820, Andrew Stuart, a politician linked to Papineau's Parti Canadien; John Neilson, a printer and publisher and also a member of the Parti Canadien; and Vallières de Saint-Réal, a fierce litigant, became interested in the Hurons' cause. All three were very independent-minded, cultured men with interests in literature, history, and the sciences. Stuart had defended representative Pierre-Stanislas Bédard, whom Governor Craig had had thrown in prison, and the Saint-Sulpice seminary in a case brought by the Crown. Later, he defended an

The History of the Captives

Between two Indian warriors, one carrying scalps, is a bound Indian captive.

The Otises were in fact descendants of English captives. Some members of the Otis family of Dover, New Hampshire, had been taken prisoner during raids conducted by French Canadians and Indians in the seventeenth century. According to Benjamin Sulte, Zacharie Otis was the grandson of Joseph-Marie Otis (born Stephen and taken prisoner in June, 1689) and Louise Wabert (an American captive raised by the Indians). Sulte believed that Joseph-Marie settled among the Hurons at the same time as did other captives. However, Sulte did not trace Joseph-Marie back in the registers, where "Indian names" were used for the most part. Tradition has it that he was the father of Jean-Baptiste, who was Zacharie's father. On January 12, 1796, Zacharie married Marie-Louise Galarneau, daughter of Louis Galarneau and Marie-Angélique Grenier.

The arrival of these English captives was long ignored by official history, which said little about the bloody raids led against New England – more than seventy of them, according to Marcel Fournier, who published a compilation titled *De la Nouvelle-Angleterre à la Nouvelle-France. L'histoire des captifs anglo-américains au Canada entre 1675 et 1760* (1992). It was these raids that led the Americans to name the wars against New France the "French and Indian Wars." The names of a number of captives (Fournier listed 227) were "Canadianized" (Carter to Chartier, Cummings to Camane, Edmunds to Émond, Farnsworth to Phaneuf, and so on). Other captives were assimilated with the Hurons, the Abenakis, and the Iroquois of Caughnawaga, where they introduced the family names Tarbel, Rice, Williams, Jacobs, Hill, Stacey, and McGregor. Many of these captives – Canadianized or Indianized – refused to return to New England when they had the opportunity. Thus, Esther Wheelwright, for instance, became superior of the Ursulines of Quebec City in 1760 (DCB, vol. 4, pp. 764–66). The best reference on this issue is Coleman, *New England Captives;* a series of six programmes produced by Michel Audy at Radio-Québec in 1986, *L'étoffe d'un pays,* also deals with the issue.

□ *Appendix R, vol. 33, Journal of the House of Assembly, Lower Canada, 4th session of 11th Provincial Parliament (1824).*

○ *Translation. A reading of the correspondence exchanged between Stuart, Neilson, and Saint-Réal leads me to believe that they were not unaware that these petitions were being written. In November, 1824, Stuart reminded Neilson that Saint-Réal had promised him "to prepare a Petition from them [the Hurons] to the King" (Neilson Collection, NAC, MG24, B1, vol. 4, folios 459–462).*

△ *See Appendix R, vol. 33, Journal of the House of Assembly.*

Indian accused of murder. Neilson and Saint-Réal shared Stuart's passion for uphill battles.

The petition presented to Governor Richmond on January 26, 1819, was particularly well written.□ The thirty-six Huron petitioners contested the king of France's power "to grant to the Jesuits something he had already granted to the Savages." They pointed out that "the other Savages of this Country were not stripped of their Goods, and the Iroquois of Saint-Régis and Sault-Saint-Louis, and the Abenakis of Saint-François, are in peaceful possession of the Seigneuries that the French kings allowed them to retain in their Land." "In a Land where their ancestors were once the masters," they added, "they [the Hurons] have lost even the right to hunt." In conclusion, they "beg the Chamber to consider the justice of their request and the extent of the wrongs, and to take the measures it deems appropriate."○

Once again, the petition was lost in a political maze; finally, on December 24, 1823, a parliamentary committee received the mandate to study it. On February 26, 1824, Andrew Stuart, the committee's chairman, submitted a long report.△ He noted the testimony of Nicolas Vincent – "interpreted" by Michel Tsioui – and the submission to the committee of "papers and documents that they [the Hurons] might have in their possession and that

Portrait of Nicolas Vincent taken from the lithograph *Présentation d'un chef nouvellement élu au Conseil de la tribu huronne* (1841). After Henry Daniel Thielcke.

they feel would help to support their petition."

The Hurons were heard with more respect and attention in the years 1824 and 1825 than ever before.

The interesting testimony of Nicolas Vincent, chief of the Hurons, on Thursday, January 29, 1824, shows that the Hurons had two main concerns: ownership of the seigneury of Sillery and hunting and fishing rights. When, in a roundabout way, they were offered land to farm, Vincent responded, "It is my seigneury that I am demanding. . . . The income . . . will help me to earn a living with my hunting and fishing." Later, he insisted, "Since these noble Canadiens have land

The Seven or Eight Nations of Canada

In a very interesting pamphlet published in 1991, *Étude sur la présence des Mohawks au Québec méridional de 1534 à nos jours,* Maurice Ratelle described the "Seven Nations" that he felt were well known to the supervisor of Indian affairs, William Johnson. They were the Iroquois of Sault-Saint-Louis, the Iroquois-Algonquins of Oka, the Nipissings of Oka at Lake of Two Mountains, the Iroquois of Oswegatchie, the Abenakis of Odanak, the Algonquins of Pointe-du-Lac near Trois-Rivières, and the Hurons of Lorette. Sometimes, the Seven Nations, or Seven Fires (villages) might correspond to seven, eight, or even nine nations.

In September, 1993, Jean-Pierre Sawaya completed an important study titled *Les Sept Nations du Canada.* He wrote of a Federation of Seven Fires that grouped the Indians "resident" in the Catholic missions of the St. Lawrence Valley. "Each nation composing the federation corresponded to a particular village; as a consequence, the village and the nation were equivalent. Their political organization was articulated around a council; the fire is the symbolic representation of the council of a nation. The organization was a federation of 'fires'; the fire was thus the basic unit. However, this unit did not necessarily correspond to a village, since a fire could involve more than one village, and a village more than one fire." The villages probably were Kahnawake, Oswegatche, Akwesasne, Kanesatake, Odanak, Wôlinak, Wendake, Pointe-du-Lac, and perhaps Restigouche. According to the time, two fires could count as one – that would have been the case for Odanak and Wôlinak. The Micmacs of Restigouche may have joined the alliance of the Seven Fires in the nineteenth century. Finally, these "Seven Fires, "Seven or Eight Nations" may occasionally have made alliances with the Iroquois Six Nations. This was likely the case on September 15 and 16, 1760.

to farm, let them farm it, and leave to us our rights to hunt and fish." And he recalled that "the Huron nation once had as its limits for hunting and fishing a territory from the arms of the Chicoutimi River to the arms of the Chenaux: this nation also went hunting and fishing from the south shore of the St. Lawrence River to the St. John River. Before these times, the Hurons had no limits on hunting or fishing; they were masters of the country as far as the Great Lakes.

"By the tradition of our elders," Vincent added, it was known that "almost two hundred years ago, the Seven Nations made an alliance together to live in peace and in common." He then complained that "foreign savages" – the Abenakis of the St. John River, the Micmacs, and the Malecites – had "come to hunt on our land

□ *In an interesting sixty-nine-page report submitted to Superior Court on June 7, 1994, by lawyer Jacques Larochelle, historian Cornelius J. Jaenen recalls Nicolas Vincent's testimony. After quoting several passages, he adds, "Nicolas Vincent reminded the commissioners of the promises in the treaties of 1760 – the treaty of Oswegatchie, the Murray treaty of Longueuil, and the Kahnawake treaty" (p. 57; translation). The wording is careful. At first glance, one might think that Vincent actually mentioned these three "treaties." But he did not, according to the documents I am aware of.*

○ *On Friday, February 27, representatives John Neilson and Jean Bélanger were added to the committee chaired by Andrew Stuart, whose other members were Louis Bourdages, representative from Richelieu, and Denis-Benjamin Viger, representative from Kent.*

Stanislas Kotska

and destroy our hunt," without respecting the agreements they had made to preserve the species concerned.

Asked about the needs of his tribe, Vincent declared that they had stopped asking for anything at all. Why? "We are tired of being refused," he said. However, "the misery is great." Four families had been reduced to living off hand-outs. The village was, nevertheless, quite active and "manufactured" various objects: shoes, snowshoes, belts, baskets, Indian sleighs, caps and mittens, porcupine quill necklaces, bags and reticules, bows, arrows, paddles, and "small canoes with little figurines of savages." But when purchasers were found, they paid "half the price we would have sold them for before."

Before finishing, Vincent and his large delegation (of which he had introduced each member) stated once again that they "are convinced and have no doubt that the seigneury they claim belongs to them."□

A few days later, on February 18, Stanislas Kotska, "guardian of the papers, titles, and records concerning the savages of the Huron Nation at Lorette," submitted to the parliamentary committee fourteen documents that the "Council of Huron Savages" felt "could serve to support their petition."○ There were two letters from the authorities (one from Governor Prescott, the other from jurist Sewell), some documents relating to the land, and two others, which became very important much later: a "certificate of protection from General Murray to said nation, dated September 5, 1760" and "a notarized deed of the submission by the Chiefs of the Huron nation of General Murray's certificate of protection." At least, this is how the two documents submitted were described in the minutes of this session, which were probably taken by Georges-Barthélemi Faribault, who had been appointed "clerk of the committees and papers" in 1815.

The documents submitted by the Hurons are not among the rather sparse archives of the House of Assembly. A fire at the parliament buildings in April, 1849, started by rioters, resulted in the loss of the libraries and archives of both legislative bodies. Fortunately, Faribault was a collector at heart, and a copy of

□ The copy preserved at the Archives du Séminaire de Québec is classified among the "Documents Faribault" as document no. 256. It is a typeset version. The directors of the archives have no information on the history of the document. At the bottom of the document, one can read a handwritten note: "If the above should prove of any use, it is . . . ". The rest has been torn and is unreadable. This document was assigned no. D-7A in Superior Court. See the handwritten version on p. 92.

○ On January 27, Ignace Parent appeared before justice of the peace George Allsopp to complain about Joseph Vincent, who "this morning . . . pushed him back and kept him from entering his home and ejected him from the Village." "As a consequence of the complaint," an order was given to apprehend said Joseph Vincent and bring him before the court (ANQ, 3B23-3701A). According to François Vincent, the current archivist of the Huron village – or, as he likes to call himself, the "guardian of papers" – the judge told Ignace Parent, a White, to resign himself to accepting his wife's way of life (she was an Indian), for he who married a woman married her country. The clerk of the court, Joseph-François Perrault, wrote a summary of the facts that describes the village's customs. On Perrault, an extraordinary character, see the biography by Claude Galarneau (DCB, vol. 7).

"General Murray's certificate of protection" was later found in the Faribault collection in the Archives du Séminaire de Québec.□

Another document (no. 8) submitted by Kotska has rarely drawn attention: it was an "excerpt of a Ruling by the Court of Special Sessions of the Peace, dated January 28, 1804." It dealt with a minor family squabble○ that would have fallen into utter oblivion had it not provided Joseph Vincent with the opportunity to submit Murray's certificate, which he might have thought would influence the judge in the case, George Allsopp.

Stuart's Conclusions

The report of the parliamentary committee was signed by Andrew Stuart and dated February 26, 1824. "To understand these papers," Stuart explained, "our committee had to learn about the history of the Huron Nations of which the petitioners are a remnant."

Document No. 256 Escaped the Flames

1848. French had become one of the official languages. Ministerial responsibility was set up. An indemnity was to be paid to victims of the reprisals following the rebellions of 1837–38. This was too much! British merchants in Montreal denounced the threat of "French Domination." The *Montreal Gazette* encouraged its readers to show their dissatisfaction. Learning that the governor-general had given royal sanction to the Compensation Act, a crowd gathered outside the parliament buildings on April 25, 1849. Lord Elgin was "assaulted by thousands of stones, sticks, and fresh and rotten eggs," noted the merchant W.R. Seaver in a letter to his wife. "They are now shouting that the parliament buildings are in flames, and from the door of my store I can see the red flames lighting up the sky. I am going over. I will continue after I see what is happening." The next day, he wrote, "The deputies barely escaped death and the splendid library building that contained rare paintings, all the archives of the province since the beginning of the colony, all the parliamentary acts, a building that alone was worth 100,000 pounds sterling, was totally destroyed." However, the Murray document escaped this fate.

It has been said that the fire was started by accident. The account of a nun from the General Hospital leaves no doubt on the subject. The building from where she observed the riot, then the fire, was itself threatened by the flames. "Some armed with sticks," she wrote, "broke the frames . . . others finally set fire to all corners with lit torches. . . . This fire was doubly strong because this combustible material [on which water was being pumped, she had specified] was violently pushed directly toward the General Hospital by a very strong and steady wind. . . . Soon, the fence and the frames were on fire . . . the spectators' diabolical pleasure . . . Some cut the hoses. . . ." Letter of April 25, 1849, preserved in the Archives des Sulpiciens, Paris, MSS-1209, No. 15.

Following was an interesting essay that emphasized "the solid, judicious, and noble spirit of this people, who were the most sedentary and hardworking of all we knew at the time on this continent."

Stuart gave a long description of the Hurons' settling "in the area of Quebec City" and the zeal of the commander of "Sylleri," who had encouraged the construction of "buildings necessary for the new colony of savages."□ He mentioned the epidemic of 1638 and the destruction of Huronia by the Iroquois in 1649 and 1650, quoted a number of pertinent documents, then moved on to the various steps the Hurons had taken.

□ *Noël Brûlart (1577– 1640), of Sillery, abandoned his diplomatic and political career for the priesthood in 1634, when he was fifty-seven. Three years later, he agreed to finance the founding of a seminary for the Indians and placed the land that had been conceded to him near the Kamiskoua-Ouangachit cove at the disposal of the Jesuits, as the site for the future Sillery seigneury. Archaeological excavations in 1959 and 1960 revealed the presence of Indians at that site 4,500 to 5,000 years ago. See Gaumond, "Premiers résultats." For the beginnings of Sillery, see Dion-McKinnon, Sillery.*

> The question of whether they had been the owners of Sylleri could not come before the court, without discussing the previous issue of their legal existence as an incorporated body. To gain a remedy for this wrong, they presented petitions to various branches of the Legislature.

> *The Christian savages* residing in the Province of Lower Canada *are in all regards English subjects, governed by the same laws, having the same rights, and subject to the same obligations as other subjects of His Majesty.* The difference of colour and language is not a legitimate reason for distinction. By the laws of both England and France, corporations can be created only by the Legislature. It was entirely impossible, no matter what the notary did, to establish in a court of law the filiation of the current inhabitants of Lorette. (Emphasis in original.)

To conclude his report, Stuart "recommends that a humble address from this Chamber be presented to His Excellency the Governor-in-Chief, asking him to confirm to the descendants of the Christian savages settled at Sylleri in the year 1651, and now residing in the village of Lorette, [ownership of] the said seigneury of Sylleri."

No action was ever taken on this recommendation. Other petitions followed: to Governor James Kempt, to his successor, Lord Aylmer, once again to Parliament in 1834, and to Lord Gosford the following year.

□ *A biography of James Murray was written by Major-General R. H. Mahon, and published in London in 1921 by John Murray. In his preface, the author thanks his aunt, Mrs. James Murray, and his cousin, the Reverend James Arthur Murray, who lent him the Murray papers, known as the Bath Papers.*

○ *As this document had, above all, the value of a safe-conduct, a copy was no doubt given to the Hurons. Another copy was made for Murray. The military men took notes, kept journals, and regularly made reports. It is reasonable to believe that Doughty had in hand the copy prepared for Murray's "records." As for Le Moine's version, he indicates that he had transcribed it from a document produced by "Vincent of Lorette." All the variations are minor except for the dates. Today, it is impossible to verify Doughty's and Le Moine's versions, as the originals cannot be found.*

Le Moine's and Doughty's Transcriptions

The historian James MacPherson Le Moine had possession of the document submitted in court in 1804. He cited it during a lecture "read in Ottawa May 28, 1890" to the members of the Royal Society of Canada. "I am grateful," he said, "to the great-granddaughter of General Murray, Mrs. Mahon, widow of Colonel Mahon, of engineering, in garrison in Quebec City in 1864, for the certificate that follows."□

Le Moine declared that he had made his copy "from the original produced at a special session of the Peace by Vincent of Lorette, Saturday, 28th January 1804." Some of the documents relating to this court appearance are kept in the Archives nationales du Québec (3B23-3701A). Curiously, the document cited by Le Moine has disappeared. Therefore, we must refer to the version given by the meticulous Le Moine:

> These are to certify that the chief of the Huron tribe of Indians, having come to me in the name of his nation, to submit to His Britannic Majesty and make peace, has been received under my protection with his whole tribe and hence forth no English officer or party is to molest or interfere with them in returning to their settlement, at Lorette and they are received upon the same terms with the Canadians, being allowed the free exercise of their Religion, their Customs and liberty of trading with the English Garrisons recommending to the Officers commanding the posts to treat them kindly.
>
> Given under my hand at Longueuil this 9th day of September 1760, by the General's Command
> (Signed) Jas Murray
> (Signed) John Cosnand, adt-genl

James MacPherson Le Moine

If we compare this version to that provided by the archivist Arthur G. Doughty, from the document preserved in the Bath Papers in England, we note slight variations: "tribe" instead of "Tribe; "nation" instead of "Nation"; "Britannic" instead of "Britannick"; "peace" instead of "Peace"; "his whole tribe" instead of "his whole Tribe"; "hence forth" instead of "henceforth"; "interfere with them" instead of "interrupt them"; "to their settlement, at Lorette" instead of "to their settlement at Lorette"; "exercise" instead of "Exercise"; "the English Garrisons, recommending to the officers" instead of "the English Garrisons recommending it to the Officers"; "Longueuil" instead of "Longuil"; "this 9th day of September" instead of "this 5th day of September" and "(signed) Jas Murray" instead of "Sigᵈ Ja. Murray."

Some of these variations can be explained by the publisher of the *Mémoires de la Société royale du Canada* not respecting scrupulously the capital letters in some words or the punctuation, while others certainly correspond to differences between the two versions.○ This is no doubt the case for "interfere with them" instead of "interrupt them" and "recommending to" instead of "recommending it to." As for the date of September 9, this can only be an error. Murray's and Knox's journals are unclear as to whether the date was the 5th or the 6th, but the 9th is impossible. Murray was no longer in Longueuil at that time, and the surrender of Montreal had taken place on the 8th.

Arthur George Doughty was appointed archivist of the Dominion of Canada in 1904. In this capacity, he organized the collection of documents relating to the history of Canada in France and England. The results of his work were summarized in very useful annual reports. In the annual report for 1910, published in 1912, Doughty told about his visit to "Mrs. Murray, of Pultney Street, Bath": "I found eight bound volumes and one hundred and seventy-five loose papers. The entire collection will be copied for the Archives during the winter. . . . Among the loose papers is a certificate granted to the Hurons at Montreal on the 5th of September, 1760, three days before the capitulation of Montreal."

The Opinion of Sociologist Léon Gérin

Léon Gérin, who had just been elected to the Royal Society of Canada (1898) and was considered, justly, a pioneer of social sciences in Quebec, became interested in the Hurons of Lorette. In a speech he gave on May 30, 1900, he took up the story of their claims regarding the seigneury of Sillery. Although he noted "a number of serious errors of fact" in the Stuart report, he agreed with its conclusions and recognized that "the claim of the Lorette

○ *Gérin,* La Seigneurie
de Sillery, *p. 112.*

△ *Ibid., p. 114.*

The Huron village of Lorette.

Hurons to the seigneury of Sillery is founded on strict right and
on equity."□○

He did not believe, however, that the seigneury of Sillery could
be returned to the Hurons "after the cession of Canada to Great
Britain." Nor did he believe that it would have been in the British
interest to let them keep the "receipts arising from a seigneury
such as Sillery," which, at any rate, would have been "contrary to
the letter and spirit of the Act of Concession."△

Regarding Compensation

□ The surveyor Joseph Bouchette, who travelled to London in 1814, was a spokesman
for the Hurons. Before returning home, he sent the authorities a brief note, on May 15,
1816, in which he recognized that the Hurons had "a legal right to two and a half
leagues in depth of the seigniory of Saint-Gabriel (part of Sillery) . . . but for many
years they occupied only the neighbouring land of the village of Lorette." If it were
decided that "they have lost their rights to these possessions, one might ask whether it
would not be politic to accord them the equivalent in Crown land." London sent the
question back to the colonial authorities. From time to time, a bureaucrat would look
into it.

The Hurons had to wait a long time before receiving, little by little, some territorial
compensation. They finally muffled their claims regarding the Sillery seigniory, but
not to the immense hunting territories.

Gérin recognized that the Canadian government was gradually acquitting itself of "a part of the moral obligation that weighs upon it regarding the Hurons." But the government's assistance was insufficient. "It remains for it [the Canadian government] to return to these people [the Hurons] . . . the facilities for development of which proximity to and competition with whites has deprived them. . . . Here above all, any social reform should take as its starting point development of the aptitude for proper agriculture and ownership of the land."

In another little-known text,□ Gérin studied the Hurons of Lorette, their way of life, and their love of hunting. When he visited their village, the Hurons complained to him about the government's rules and the leases handed out to private clubs. "Just as Gros-Louis had done the evening previous," Gérin

□ *Gérin*, Les Hurons de Lorette, *pp. 69–92.*

The Huron village of Lorette around 1840.

Michel Tsioui

recalled, "the Tsiouis of the Reserve bitterly complained of interference with their hunting privileges."□

Thomas Tsioui, a Huron elder about eighty years old, had three sons who were trying to earn a living as hunters. He himself had spent a good part of his childhood in the woods. Once a well-known guide, he now lived with his mementos, including a portrait of King George IV, a gift brought back from England by his father, Michel Tsioui. "The old man's contention is that the Tsiouis are the only genuine Hurons, all others being descendants of French Canadians who stole their way into the Huron community. As I objected that the Tsiouis themselves could not claim pure Huron extraction, their mothers and grandmothers in most cases being French Canadian women, the old man argued heatedly, that man and not woman, the husband and not the wife, made the race."○ Gérin held the opposite opinion: among the Hurons the child belonged to the mother's clan, not the father's. His visits to Lorette led him to note "that the clan was no longer a live institution; and even the memory of it had become very dim." In his eyes, Thomas Tsioui was himself no longer a Huron "in respect to some of the fundamental traditions of this people."△

Georges E. Sioui Offers His Version

Memory can be selective. The descendants of Europeans, like the descendants of Aboriginal peoples, as well as those who resulted from the blending of the two, have created their own histories. In his work published in 1989 titled *Pour une autohistoire amérindienne* (translated as *For an Amerindian Autohistory* in 1992), Georges E. Sioui proposes his own history in reaction to that which he had been taught: "Your ancestors," the nun who had given him his first history lesson proclaimed, "were savages with no knowledge of God. They were ignorant and cared nothing about their salvation."◇

According to Sioui, "Amerindian cultural values have influenced the formation of the Euroamerican's character more than the latter's values have modified the Amerindian's cultural code,

□ *Ibid., p. 76.*

○ *Gérin, "Le Huron de Lorette," pp. 325–26.*

△ *Gérin,* The Hurons of Lorette, *p. 87.*

◇ *Sioui,* For an Amerindian Autohistory, *p. 1.*

since it was not the Amerindians who left their natural surroundings."□

One thing is certain: Columbus's arrival in America created the opportunity for an encounter between two "old worlds," a monumental encounter that laid the foundation for a new world. The Americas and their first inhabitants were transformed, as we know – it has been said often enough – but Europe and even Asia were transformed as well. Sioui was right to dwell not only on "the formation of the Euroamerican's character," but also on the universality and importance of Aboriginal values. He credited the Huron-Wendats with a central historical role, and he suggested that this major nation of the midwest benefited from a migration of Aboriginals from the St. Lawrence Valley.○

Georges E. Sioui

What the World Owes to the Americas

□ *Ibid., p. 21.*

○ *Ibid., pp. 84–5.*

See Côté, Tardivel, and Vaugeois, *L'Indien généreux*. Today, the expression "discovery of America" has come under attack. Whether or not they were known to the rest of the world, the Americas and their inhabitants existed long before they were "discovered." . . . The Mediterranean Sea had long been perceived as situated at the centre of the planet. The Phoenicians, Egyptians, Greeks, and Romans who lived on its shores, and later the Europeans, saw themselves as living at the centre of the world and in the cradle of civilization. Asia and then America were "discovered" by Europeans carrying the torch of Christian faith and the repositories of human knowledge: Europe's mission was to instruct the rest of humanity. At least, it was in this perspective that the history of the world, and that of America, has most often been written.

"The point of reference was European knowledge. . . . Columbus thought he had arrived in India; therefore, the people he found were 'Indians'. Because they were free, close to nature, living in the forest, they were dubbed savages. By European standards, they were 'primitive.' . . . (p. 11) Europeans were stunned to discover, woven into these accounts [by travellers of the sixteenth and seventeenth centuries], stories about human beings . . . who lived without a monarch, owned the land collectively, and could hunt and fish wherever they wished.

These images of America entered the minds of European philosophers, and the ideals of equality and liberty found fertile ground. Did the discovery of America lead to the French Revolution? Did the Hurons, Iroquois, Abenakis, and Montagnais change the history of France? Who would dare to claim such a thing?" (p. 9)

□ *Ibid., p. 42.*

○ *"The name 'Iroquoians' helped establish official theories aimed at eliminating from Quebec the reality and rights of the Wendat. I shall use instead the term 'Laurentian Nadoueks.' ... The disappareance of the Laurentian Nadoueks is easily explained. In my opinion, the survivors of that dispersal then sought and found refuge principally among the Wendat (Hurons) of Huronia, and their Wendat descendants were dispersed for the second time during the 1640's, still because of European epidemic diseases, of which the Iroquois wars were but a consequence."* Sioui, *For an Ameridian Autohistory, pp. 82–3.*

△ *Ibid., p. 82.*

◇ *Ibid., p. 83.*

□ *Ibid., p. 37.*

When he arrived, Champlain did not encounter the Indians whom Cartier had mentioned during his voyages of 1532–42. "It is likely," Sioui explains,□ "that the St Lawrence Wendat-Iroquois disappeared in the sixteenth century because of the epidemics that raged in the St Lawrence Valley before the beginning of the seventeenth century."○

Sioui and the Hurons of Lorette had a serious problem. Official history had them arriving in the Quebec City region after the French. If this was true, it would be difficult for them to invoke ancestral rights – in Quebec, anyway.

To avoid being considered "immigrants on Quebec land," the Huron nation, Sioui wrote, "had to prove that the Wendat who took refuge in Quebec in 1650 – whose descendants are the Wendat of Lorette – were ethnically related to the St Lawrence Iroquoians. After Jacques Cartier's visit, these people mysteriously disappeared from the regions of 'Quebec' that had been their country from time immemorial and that comprised the lands traditionally occupied and claimed by the Wendat of Lorette."△

"In my opinion," Sioui continued, "the survivors of this dispersal [the Indians of the St. Lawrence Valley] then sought and found refuge principally among the Wendat of Huronia," then were dispersed *for the second time*" (emphasis in original) before some of them returned to Quebec.◇

To support his hypothesis, Sioui appealed to archaeologists and anthropologists: Bruce G. Trigger, a well-known anthropologist, supplied a preface for Sioui's book. While emphasizing the real merits of Sioui's research and hypotheses – he was the first Indian, according to Trigger, to set out "the rules that should apply to studying the history of aboriginals" – Trigger states, "His conception of relations between Hurons, Iroquois, and Europeans in the seventeenth century differs considerably from all other interpretations I am aware of." In effect, Sioui seriously questions "the rivalry between the Hurons and the Iroquois in the sixteenth and seventeenth centuries."□

Elsewhere, Sioui attributes to Trigger, who in fact never mentions it in his preface, "the hypothesis of an exodus of the Laurentians to Huronia, a theory now confirmed by archaeology. According to Trigger, most survivors of the Laurentian Nadoueks merged with the nations of Huronia. In fact," Sioui continues, "vestiges of their material culture – mainly pottery – have been found on every Huron site excavated. The Wendat of Lorette, Trigger concludes, form the only historic 'Iroquoian' that can claim at this point to be the rightful heirs, ethnic and territorial, of the Laurentian Nadoueks."□

In spite of the archaeological "proof," there is no unanimity regarding the ancestral rights of the Hurons of Lorette. In fact, many still feel that they are "immigrants" to Quebec.

If this were the case, the Constitution Act, 1982, which recognizes and confirms the existing ancestral rights of Aboriginal peoples, would not be of great help to them. Nor would the rights that might flow from the Royal Proclamation of 1763, covered in the Charter's section 25, be of any use. On the contrary, it would limit them to the village that existed in 1763. According to Sioui, the Huron-Wendats had, however, been 'legally' dispossessed . . . by virtue of the sacrosanct Royal Proclamation of 1763."○

So, if they had no ancestral rights, did the Hurons of Lorette have "rights issuing from treaties"? Which treaties could they call upon? The 1609 and 1624 alliances with Champlain? The agreement of 1645? The 1701 'Great Peace of Montreal?'△ (Of course, the French had a very different approach to the Indians than the English. The latter signed a multitude of treaties through which they forced the Indians to cede vast territories, while the former usually chose cohabitation, involving many intermarriages and innumerable alliances.)

Always seeking to protect the "traditional role" that he attributes to the Huron-Wendats "in Amerindian geo-politics," Sioui evokes certain actions by James Murray, as governor of Quebec,◇ but ignores others, such as Murray's confiscation of Athanase La Plague's trading permit.□ "The diplomatic English," Sioui

□ *Ibid., p. 84. Sioui is referring to a "recent interview" that he had with Trigger at McGill University. On this subject, see Beaulieu,* Les traités; *Blouin,* Histoire; *Falardeau,* Ce qu'il est advenu; *Gérin,* "Le Huron," The Hurons, La Seigneurie de Sillery; *Lindsay,* Notre-Dame de la Jeune-Lorette; *Morissonneau,* Huron of Lorette; *Trigger,* Children of Aataentsic: A History of the Huron People to 1660.

○ *Sioui, For an Amerindian Autohistory, p. 110.*

△ *On all treaties signed in Canada, see Boudreault,* "Réflexions."

◇ *Sioui, For an Amerindian Autohistory, p. 93.*

□ *See Appendix G.*

○ *Sioui,* For an Amerindian
Autohistory, *pp. 93–4.*

writes, "were well informed about Amerindian geo-politics and
dealt with the strategic nations for 'trading' purposes. They did so
in Montreal on 5 September 1760, the very day of the capitulation of that city, by signing a separate treaty with the Wendat, □
which for that people both then and now constitutes recognition
of a sovereignty they had never ceded or sold."○

The Siouis Spring into Action

Most Quebecers are almost completely unaware of the Constitution Act, 1982, for it has very little to do with them. Quebec has
never ratified it, or even accepted it. For the Indians, the situation
is very different. As we have seen, this law has the effect of recognizing a range of specific rights – both ancestral and arising from
treaties.

The Constitution Act was promulgated on April 17, 1982. Six
weeks later, on May 29, 1982, at around 6:10 p.m., Park Officer
Claude Noël, on patrol in Parc de la Jacques-Cartier in the
Laurentians, noted the presence of two tents. One was occupied

Montreal Surrendered on the 8th, Not the 5th, of September, 1760

□ "A separate agreement with the Wendat," an obvious allusion to the meeting with
General James Murray in Longueuil, was indeed made on September 5, but this was
three days before the surrender of Montreal. Georges Sioui makes more than one error
of date, among them this one placing the surrender of the Hurons and that of Montreal
on the same day! In his view, it was less a surrender than an agreement (he does not
dare use the word "treaty") between the British, the conquerors, and the Hurons, who
constituted a "strategic nation."

For his part, Alain Beaulieu (1994) attributes to the Hurons of Lorette "a marginal
economic and military role." "When they came to settle in proximity to the French, in
the Quebec City region," he writes, "the Hurons were only a pale reflection of what
they had once been" (translation).

The surrender of Montreal was signed on September 8, 1760. In his journal for
that day, Jeffery Amherst, commander in chief of British forces in North America, noted
(pp. 246–47), "At twelve the proposals came, which I altered and sent back and wrote
to Mons de Vaudreuil." The next day, "at day break I received a letter from Mons
Vaudreuil. He was determined to sign the Articles I had offered to him. . . . It was the
Afternoon before the Capitulation was copied and that I signed it. I wrote to the
Marquis de Vaudreuil & sent the Capitulation. Col. Haldimand took possession."

by a group of children accompanied by adults. Among them was Régent Sioui, who later explained to the court that "the reason for the presence of his family . . . was to teach the children the Indian customs." He showed three documents issued by the Band Council that constituted an authorization.□ In the end, he was found guilty of violating two articles of the rules of Parc de la Jacques-Cartier: having "felled and mutilated trees" and having "camped and made a fire . . . in sites not designated and prepared for this purpose" (translation).

Régent Sioui was accompanied by, among others, his brothers Conrad, Georges, and Hugues. In the Court of the Sessions of the Peace, all four were found guilty.

On July 12, 1983, they launched an appeal. The grounds were quite obscure: they alleged that the decree cited in their conviction was not a law of general application "therefore applicable to Indians."

In this regard, Judge Gaston Desjardins of Superior Court announced that he shared "the views expressed by the first judge," "unless the latter [the Siouis] can prove the existence of a treaty in the sense laid out in section 88 of the Indian Act (SCR, 1970, C. I-6) and section 35(1) of the Canadian Charter of Rights and Freedoms (Constitution Act, 1982, U.K. 1982, C-11, appendix B, part 1)."○

In his particularly careful ruling, Judge Desjardins re-examined the facts of the first trial and, in general, concurred with the views expressed by the "first judge." The trial notes have been preserved. They show that the appellants did not present their case very well, and that the judge's conclusions were predictable.△

Submission of a Mysterious Document

On the morning of May 18, 1984, the Siouis' lawyer, Michel Pouliot, made a daring move: he had Régent Sioui submit "a new document that has never been produced."◇ The judge was stunned. The lawyer for the Crown, Jean-Paul Drolet, admitted that he had "difficulty reading it." Obviously nervous, Mr. Pouliot

□ *These three documents are cited in their entirety by Judge Desjardins in the notes that accompany his ruling. See his note 1. The first document was an "authorization issued to hunt small animals"; the second was a permit giving "the right to the holder to circulate in the forest and fish for his personal use"; and the third authorized its holder, Régent Sioui, "to hunt and kill game for his food and usage." The three documents had been issued by the "Band Council of the Indian Reserve of Village des Hurons." The accused, for his part, stated that he had "gathered plants for medicinal purposes . . . following the traditions that he had inherited from his ancestors" (translation).*

○ *Ruling rendered by the Honourable Gaston Desjardins of Superior Court, September 6, 1985 (translation). In the Court of the Sessions of the Peace, the ruling was rendered by Judge André Bilodeau on June 9, 1983.*

△ *The appellants' and defendants' evidence was presented on May 18, 1984.*

◇ *Here I use the transcript of the evidence presented in Superior Court on May 18, 1984 (translation). Source: Supreme Court microfilm file titled "Arrêt Sioui." I shall cite it here as "MAS" and all quotations are translations.*

□ *MAS, p. 41.*

○ *Ibid., p. 42.*

explained, "It is an authentic document. It is a treaty that was made between General Murray, who was the first general representing British Columbia [*sic*] after the conquest of 1760."□

The judge was skeptical. He asked about the document, which seemed to him to resemble a "photocopy": "It must be contained somewhere, in the *Volumes d'autorité*, the statutes, so what is the reference?"○

"It is an authentic document preserved in the archives of Village des Hurons," Mr. Pouliot insisted.

The judge wanted to examine it more closely. "Even from a distance, I doubt that I will accept it as evidence," he remarked. "First we must establish the authenticity of this document, please," he added after glancing at what he called a "peace document."

"I have spent days looking at the constitutional documents of Canada," Mr. Pouliot admitted, "and I was not able to find the

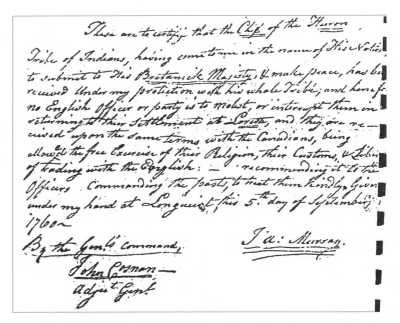

The document submitted to Superior Court was no doubt given back to the Siouis. I was not able to see it. The photocopy reproduced here was drawn from a collection of documents submitted to the Supreme Court during examination of the case that led to the *Sioui* ruling. (This document received the number D-7 in Superior Court.)

document. . . . All I can do is have my client testify, and he will testify to the content and provenance of the document, which is a certified true copy, but subject to being able to produce for you the authentic document very shortly."□

Georges Sioui, the historian, followed his brother to the witness stand. The judge questioned him: "Where is the original?"

"The original is in the possession of the Council of Members of Village des Hurons; it is kept there. Now it is preserved in Brantford, Ontario,○ in the absence of a museum. It is very easy to obtain the document."

"But we are proceeding today," the judge retorted, "and I want to see the original."

Uneasily, Mr. Pouliot asked for "a delay of perhaps a few days so we can produce the original."

□ *Ibid., p. 50.*

○ Brantford is a major Indian cultural centre. Once named Mohawk Village (Ohsweken) or Brant's Ford, this town, situated on the Grand River west of Lake Ontario, was founded by the Mohawk chief Joseph Brant. A meeting and gathering place, Brantford is known for its Brant County Museum. Later in his testimony, Georges Sioui said, "It [the original] is in the Museum of the Six Nations Indians, in Brantford, Ontario. . . . In the Woodland Cultural Centre." In effect, he was trying to explain to Judge Desjardins that, not having a safe place for preservation of ancient documents, the Lorette Band Council had deemed it preferable to entrust the Murray document temporarily to the management of the Brantford museum. "These documents will be returned," he explained, "when we have a museum capable of holding them."

□ *On the value of oral tradition, see the submission by historian Marcel Trudel, Jan. 10, 1991, in* Procureur général du Québec v. Meloche *(1 mb.64-1 mb.68) and his "Historical Report on the Mohawks." See also Ratelle,* Le "Two Row Wampum," *pp. 2–7.*

○ *MAS, p. 58.*

△ *Before being offered to the Huron Band Council, the Murray document had been offered to the National Archives of Canada twice: in 1972 and 1976. On page 115 is a summary of the evaluation made by NA archivists.*

It was obvious that the judge wanted to go on immediately. Addressing the witness, he asked, "So, have you seen the original?" Receiving an affirmative response, he said, "So, tell me about the original."

Georges Sioui tried to evoke tradition, but the judge wanted to hear about the document itself. A brief, rambling exchange followed, then the judge asked who had signed the document in question. "The chiefs, both the civil chief and the peace chief of the Hurons," Georges Sioui answered. It sounded as if he hadn't even seen the document in question! This was, in fact, the document of September 5, 1760, in which Murray received the surrender of the Hurons of Lorette, and only Murray's and his adjutant's names were mentioned on it.

Surprised, Judge Desjardins asked Sioui, "When you speak of the civil chief, whom are you referring to?"

Sioui launched into a complicated explanation.

"But," the judge asked, "where do you see this information on the document in question?"

"I take it from my tradition."□

"Fine! So, none of this appears in the document?"

"Nor is there any need." And Georges Sioui launched again into a variety of explanations involving a description of wampum and the "significance of the belt."○

The judge interrupted and asked once again for the original. Mr. Sioui was not listening; instead, he was insisting that the words "religion" and "customs" were in the document.

"When you saw this document for the first time, it was in the museum?"

"No, it was in the possession of the curator himself, the original curator, Mr. François Vincent."

If it couldn't have the original document, the Court could have access to the original curator! Except that he no longer had much to curate, since he had "sold his collection of documents to the Council . . . which is now the owner," Sioui explained.△

Pouliot asked François Vincent, who just happened to be in the courtroom, to take the witness stand. The judge was not very

return to Lorette without being molested, while preserving their freedom of religion and customs. In fact, they were placed under the protection of Murray – that is, of the English army.

Document D-7 thus constitutes both an act of surrender – "These are to certify that the *Chief* of the Huron Tribe of Indians, *having come to me* in the name of His Nation, *to submit* to His Britannick Majesty, and make Peace . . ." – and a certificate of protection – ". . . has been received under my protection . . ."

It therefore constituted a safe-conduct that allowed the Indians to return to Lorette without being molested by English garrisons that they might meet on their way.

This document was designated a "certificate" a number of times.

The chiefs of the Huron nation submitted it themselves, as a "certificate of protection from General Murray" to the Chamber of Assembly, on February 18, 1824 (D-10; 5 George IV appendix (R.), A. 1824). The archivist François Vincent, member of the Huron band of Lorette, used the same expression during his testimony when he submitted the above-mentioned document.

The expression "copy of a certificate" is used by the Champlain Society of Toronto in its work.[3] We note the same term in the report by national archivist Doughty.[4]

. . .

In conclusion, the Court is of the opinion that although the Huron nation held the power to sign a treaty at that time, this was not true for Murray. The latter did not have the intention of making a treaty. This statement flows both from the text of D-7 and from the context in which the document was written. In an affair of this nature, we must take account of the intention of the parties, its acceptance by third parties, and the juridical consequences that result from it.[5]

From this, I consider that Murray had neither the intention nor the power to give territorial rights to the Indians given that Great Britain had always denied such rights. In his capacity as a military man, all that he was concerned with was to make an alliance with the Indians in order to eliminate an enemy.

As well, D-7 was never considered a treaty either by the Huron nation itself or by the sovereign. In the *Calder* ruling[6], the Supreme

3. *Supra*, note 29b [*Champlain Society, Journal of John Knox, vol. 2*], p. 517.

4. *RCA, 1912*, p. 50: "Amongst the loose papers is a certificate granted to the Hurons at Montreal on the 5th of September, 1760, three days before the capitulation of Montreal."

5. *Supra*, note 25b [above-mentioned article by Green], p. 115: "What is important in cases of this kind is the intention of the parties at the time of the agreement, the recognition that they and others give to their agreement, and the legal consequences that they afford it during the years following its signature. Insofar as the Indians' treaties are concerned, there is little doubt, at the time of signing, that both parties were using terms that they thought covered their relationship, that they intended to create legal obligations of a permanent character and that they carried out the terms of the agreement for many years. These practices confirm that, whether or not they are treaties, they constitute mutually binding arrangements which have hardened into commitments that neither side can evade unilaterally."

6. Calder v. Attorney
General of British
Columbia (1973), SCR,
p. 313.

7. Supra, note 37 [Henri
Brun, Le Territoire du
Québec (Presses de
l'Université Laval, 1974),
p. 85].

□ Desjardins, 1985,
pp. 23–5.
○ Ibid., p. 31.

Court of Canada attached great importance to this aspect of the issue.

he authors breathed not a word of this paper when they made an inventory of historical juridical documents affecting the Indians: they cite the surrender of Montreal and the Royal Proclamation. Even in a document on the constitutional history of Canada (1759–91) published by the Public Archives, and in a document from the Department of Indian and Northern Affairs, they do not cite this paper of September 5, 1760. The Act of Capitulation of Montreal does not mention it.

For all of these reasons, the claim of the appellants to the effect that this document constitutes a treaty in the sense of section 88 of the Indian Act is rejected.□

The issue of ancestral rights remained. Guided mainly by jurist Henri Brun and referring to jurisprudence, Judge Desjardins noted that "the Indians did not possess, in fact, anything but a simple right of occupation on a certain territory." Evoking the Royal Proclamation of 1763, again through an analysis by Brun, then the report by the Commission d'étude sur l'intégrité du territoire du Québec, he noted that there existed

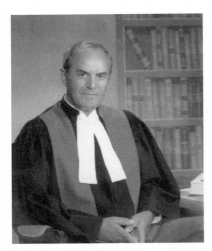

Judge Gaston Desjardins

an ancestral right to usufruct in favour of the Indians outside the territory of the Government of Quebec in 1763. This right consists of hunting and fishing for the subsistence of the Indians and their families. This right arose from the Royal Proclamation of 1763. It can be extinguished or altered, directly or indirectly, only by the federal government.[7] In this case, the territory covered was included within the borders of the Government of Quebec of 1763. It was not modified in any way afterward. Thus, the appellants cannot invoke the existence of an ancestral right to this part of the territory.○

Desjardins's conclusion was:

Thus, the reasons for appeal invoked by the appellants before this Court are all rejected.

The Parks Act and its rules constitute legislation of general application. The Indians must submit to it. The *Kruger* ruling dealt with this issue. This law denies no right to the appellants. It regulates activities, as it does for all other citizens, and this with the goal of protecting flora and fauna. Section 7 of the law authorizes the engagement in activities that are not expressly mentioned in it. The appellants did not avail themselves of this article.

□ *Ibid., p. 32.*

The infraction is one of strict responsibility. The evidence has, however, revealed, beyond a reasonable doubt, that the appellants acted in full knowledge of the facts.

. . .

The document of September 5, 1760, is not a treaty in the sense of section 88 of the Indian Act. According to the authors and the jurisprudence, a "treaty," under this section, is an agreement concluded between states that are sovereign or considered as such. History shows that the Indians have always benefited from this attribute. The Hurons of Lorette could thus make a treaty with Murray. However, the latter did not possess the powers required for this purpose. The war between the English and the French was not yet over. The text of D-7, the context in which it was written, and the authority that had been conferred upon him up to that day lead the Court to an ineluctable conclusion: D-7 is a certificate of protection or a safe-conduct that allowed Huron warriors to return to Lorette without fear of being attacked on the way by English garrisons.

The appellants have not proved the existence of an ancestral right to the territory under consideration. I refer here to the right to hunt and fish for their and their families' subsistence, which involves the right to circulate and set up their tent. As well, even if this claim had been accepted, the Indians would still be subject to generally applied provincial laws. In effect, the Parks Act does not repudiate any rights. It sets the modalities of their application, in the interest of the community. The Court considers that it is reasonable, in the context of a free and democratic society, to govern the right of an individual to circulate in the forest, in the general interest of the society.

For these reasons [which are not cited in their totality here], the Court: Rejects the appeal of the appellants, in each file, with costs.□

□ *The Superior Court rendered its ruling on September 6, 1985. On the 19th, Pouliot presented a "request for permission to appeal." The permission to proceed to the Appeal Court was given by Judge Yves Bernier on October 19, 1985. Two days later, Pouliot submitted a notice of appeal.*

○ RJQ, 1987, p. 1724.

△ Action through which one appeals in a higher jurisdiction the ruling of a lower court.

◇ See page 103.

A Defeat with the Scent of Victory

The Sioui brothers and their lawyer were not terribly surprised by Judge Desjardins's decision, nor were they concerned. They may have lost their case, but they had made an important point. The Superior Court had recognized that the Murray document "was *prima facie* proof." They decided to take their case higher.□

On September 8, 1987, Judge Claude Bisson of the Quebec Court of Appeal rendered his opinion, with Judge Paré agreeing and Judge Jacques dissenting. "After studying the dossier and the hearing, and upon deliberation, the Court has decided to accept the appeal, to set aside the ruling of the Superior Court, to cancel the declarations of guilt of June 9, 1983, to order the recording of verdicts of acquittal for each of the appellants, for the two chiefs [what are they charged with?], to sentence the defendant [the Crown] to pay to the appellants, in addition to the expenses made before all the courts, overall honoraria set as follows: Court of the Sessions of the Peace, $500, Superior Court, $700, Court of Appeal, $1,200."

This was essentially Judge Bisson's reasoning:○

The questions that this petition△ poses are the following:

1. When the Hurons, fighting up to then on the side of the French, gave themselves up to the victors, in Longueuil on September 5, 1760, three days before the surrender of Montreal, and obtained from governor Ja. Murray, the highest representative of the British government then in Canada◇, document D-7, had they thus concluded a treaty?

2. If no, the petition must be rejected; if yes, the additional question must be asked:

3. Was the treaty legally in force on May 29, 1982? If no, the petition must be rejected. If yes, the following question must be asked:

4. If document D-7 constitutes a treaty, to what point, always with respect to section 88 of the Indian Act, are the legislation and regulations at the basis of the complaints incompatible with the rights of the appellants with regard to the actions they took on May 28, 1982?

Was Murray the Highest Representative of the British Government Present in Canada at the Time?

As commander-in-chief of British troops in North America, Jeffery Amherst was obviously James Murray's superior. On September 4, 1760, Amherst's troops spent the day struggling against the rapids of the St. Lawrence. In the evening, they reached Île Perrot. "The Inhabitants of Isle Perrot," he noted in his journal, "had all run away & hid but they came in by degrees & gave themselves up & not a Soul was killed by our Savages.... I assured them all my Protection as long as they remained quiet" (*Journal of Jeffery Amherst*, p. 224). On September 5, the day that so interested Judge Bisson, Amherst received a letter from Haviland and himself sent a note to Murray. The three army corps were a few miles apart. The commanders were in contact and co-ordinating their movements. Here, Murray was called the "highest representative of the British authorities present in Canada at the time." One must understand the context of the period. At the beginning of September, 1760, Canada was still part of New France. It was not a political entity. It corresponded, for the most part, to the St. Lawrence Valley. After the Treaty of Paris and the reorganization of the conquered territory, the word "Canada" stopped being used officially. Historian Guy Frégault (1969, vol. 3, p. 15) wrote on the subject, "In 1763, there were still Canadiens, but there was no more Canada." To make things very clear, it is better to talk of British North America (especially after 1783), an expression that leads to the British North America Act, the constitution that gave rise to modern Canada.

To provide a proper context for his ruling, Judge Bisson cited section 11 of the Parks Act and sections 9 and 37 of the Regulation respecting the Parc de la Jacques-Cartier and summarized the text of the Murray document (D-7) and section 88 of the Indian Act.

Judge Bisson then aligned himself with the Chief Justice of the Supreme Court, Judge Dickson, who, in the *Simon* ruling (1985), had clearly shown his point of view by quoting a commentary by Judge Norris of the British Columbia Court of Appeal in the *Bob and White* ruling:

> The question [of the existence of a treaty] is, in my respectful opinion, to be resolved not by the application of rigid rules of construction without regard to the circumstances existing when the document was completed nor by the tests of modern day draftsmanship. ... In the section [88] "Treaty" is not a word of art and in my respectful opinion, it embraces such engagements made by persons in

□ *SCR, pp. 1035, 1041.*

○ *SCR, p. 1035.*

authority as may be brought within the term "the word of the white man" the sanctity of which was, at the time of British exploration and settlement, the most important means of gaining the goodwill and co-operation of native tribes and ensuring that the colonists would be protected from death and destruction.□

Judge Dickson added that the legislators wanted section 88 to be applied to all agreements concluded with the Indians by the Crown, and he recalled that "treaties and statutes relating to Indians should be liberally construed and uncertainties resolved in favour of the Indians."○

Guided by a "broad conception of what constitutes a treaty," Judge Bisson asked the following question: Is document D-7 "an agreement in which the contracting parties – the authority of whom is in question here – had the intention of creating reciprocal agreements to which they intended to conform solemnly"?

The response seems to be yes, as he writes:

– To the Hurons, it was surrender, with all of its implications: submission to the new authorities entailing a pact of nonaggression and peace "to submit . . . and make Peace"; they were ending the war;

– To the victors: protection "under my Protection" . . . safe-conduct for their return to Lorette, but above all "the free Exercise of their Religion, their Customs, and Liberty of trading with the English."△

The Court of Appeal Errs

△ It is curious, at least to a layman, that the Court of Appeal did not examine the two versions that the Superior Court had before it. Judge Desjardins, who had "discovered" the Doughty version, did not examine them either, but since he was ready to conclude that D-7 was not a treaty, he did not have much reason to do so. The Court of Appeal was in a very different position. It was ready to endow with the value of treaty a document for which it was verifying neither the provenance nor the authenticity. Judge Bisson wrote, "Two elements are no longer subject to debate before us: the authenticity of document D-7; the authority that Governor Murray had on September 5, 1760." How could the judge be so sure? We will never know.

I consider these last words decisive. A simple safe-conduct for a few days for the journey from Longueuil to Lorette would not necessitate discussion of religion and customs.□

I feel that as it constitutes a positive source of protection of fundamental rights, document D-7 is a true treaty.

The words "These are to certify . . ." are explained by the fact that the Hurons, not knowing how to write, could not sign,○ and that document D-7 was the recognition by General Murray of the verbal treaty that had just been concluded."△

What was the extent of the rights recognized by the Murray "treaty"? Judge Bisson refused to "limit the free exercise of customs of which document D-7 speaks to a precise location – that is, the territory of Lorette":

> I cannot rule upon a territorial limitation. In effect, all of the evidence tends to demonstrate that the Hurons circulated freely over the territories located north of the St. Lawrence River, including the territory currently within Parc de la Jacques-Cartier, a site where they practised their customs, among them hunting, fishing, gathering, extraction of medicinal plants and fruits, the building of shelters, and the capacity to make fires at sites of their choosing, to practise their religious rituals and other activities of a customary, religious, and commercial nature.◇

What were the customs cited by Murray in his document of September 5, 1760? Here again, Judge Bisson evokes Judge Dickson's admonition to use a "liberal interpretation." He concludes

□ *The judge's remark is understandable. But if he had examined the texts of the time, including Murray's journal, he would have noted how constantly this discourse flowed from Murray's mouth and pen. For instance, freedom of religion constitutes article 6 of the Act of Capitulation of Quebec City. The reference to customs is unusual, but can it be dissociated from the phrase "upon the same terms as the Canadians"?*

△ *RJQ, 1987, p. 1727.*

◇ *It must be remembered that there were fewer than one hundred people in Lorette in 1760. See Beaulieu,* Les Hurons de Lorette.

Totemic Signatures

○ This statement is stunning. The archives contain a number of "treaties" signed by Indians – for example, the treaty signed at Niagara on July 18, 1764, by William Johnson and the Hurons. There are a number of copies of this treaty. Even though they were prepared by a copyist, this person generally took care to transcribe the totems. Often, examination of these totems enabled order to be established among the various copies. The staff of the National Archives of Canada have made many studies of treaties concluded with Aboriginals. See Kennedy, "En quête," "Pour la conservation"; Patterson, "À la recherche"; Sylvain, "Sauvegarde des traités."

THE GREAT PEACE OF MONTREAL, 1701.

On the lower left is the signature of the Huron chief Kondiaronk, nicknamed the Rat. One of the crafters of the Great Peace of Montreal, he reconciled the Iroquois with other Natives allied with the French.

The signatures of Indians represented either their clan totem or their personal totem.

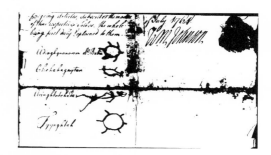

Peace, friendship, and alliance treaty signed by Sir William Johnson, July 18, 1764.

Another version of the treaty of July 18, 1764. The copyist placed the animal represented with the second signature in the wrong direction (see *L'Archiviste*, Nov.-Dec. 1990, p. 5). Although they sometimes made such small errors, the copyists generally tried to reproduce totemic signatures — where they existed, of course.

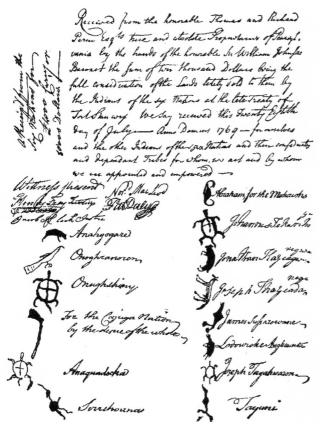

Treaty of Fort Stanwix (1768). In the right-hand column appears Joseph Brant's signature (fourth from the top) in three forms: his totem, his baptismal name, and his Mohawk name (Thayendanegea). With this treaty, the Iroquois ceded the land in the Ohio Valley.

□ *How could the judge state that the activities the Siouis were accused of were in the category of "customs" guaranteed by the treaty? He does not say.*

○ *RJQ, 1987, p. 1730.*

△ *The Siouis had been accused of having "cut down and mutilated trees in Parc de la Jacques-Cartier, thus coming into contravention of article 9 of Decree 3108-81," and of having "camped and made fires . . . in places not designated or set up for this purpose, thus coming into contravention of article 37 of Decree 3108-81." The rules regarding Parc de la Jacques-Cartier had been published in the Gazette officielle du Québec on November 25, 1981, in virtue of Decree 3108-81 of November 11, 1981. These rules specified the modalities of application of the Parks Act (LRQ, c. P-9). Without exception, the regulations were written by bureaucrats and not subject to public debate. This was called delegated legislation. See* Rapport de la Commission d'étude sur le contrôle parlementaire de la législation déléguée, Assemblée nationale du Québec, *July 1983.*

that "the treaty contains a guarantee of free exercise of the Hurons' customs that cannot be limited by a provincial legislative text; the activities that the appellants undertook on May 29, 1982, are within the framework of conditions guaranteed by the treaty; in virtue of section 88 of the Indian Act, the appellants cannot be sued."□

Whence Judge Bisson's ruling.

The Court of Appeal Is Divided

Judge Jacques saw things differently. He felt that the court was hearing a "territorial claim." "The same actions [a religious ceremony] performed elsewhere – e.g., within the Ancienne-Lorette reservation – would not constitute offences."

According to Judge Jacques, document D-7 did not recognize any territorial right, any more than did the Royal Proclamation, in the case of the Hurons of Lorette. The "depositions" of the witnesses did not shake his conviction. The words of Georges Sioui, who spoke of the forest as "a place of meditation, a place of interpretation where we are in the presence of the Master of Life," left him unmoved.

However, Sioui had given a spiritual meaning to the offence with which he was charged. "Our ancestors have always had their favourite spots to go and meditate," he had declared, "in particular to make their annual fast every spring, which we still do ourselves. In fact, it was at this time that I was arrested in the Parc des Laurentides."○

Given this testimony, one might wonder where the park conservation officers had been in previous springs. However, it must be noted that the decree under consideration was from November 11, 1981, △ the Constitution Act was dated April 17, 1982, and the infractions took place on May 29, 1982.

This Time, Quebec Appeals

The majority ruling by the Quebec Court of Appeal must have thrown the Quebec government, especially the justice department, into a commotion. This new treaty might well be invoked in a number of ways. Therefore, Quebec in turn asked for permission to appeal, on February 25, 1988. Less than a month later, on March 23, the Supreme Court decided to examine three questions: was the document of September 5, 1760, a treaty in the sense of section 88? If yes, did it still have legal force on May 29, 1982? If the answer to both of these questions was yes, were sections 9 and 37 (of the Parks Act) superseded?

It should be noted that the text given for the Murray document of September 5, 1760, was the one that had been submitted to Superior Court by Régent Sioui and not the version published by archivist Arthur Doughty.

On May 24, 1990, Justice Antonio Lamer rendered a ruling some fifty pages long in the presence of Chief Justice Dickson and his colleagues, justices Wilson, La Forest, L'Heureux-Dubé, Sopinka, Gonthier, Cory, and McLachlin. Justice Lamer had taken this case because he felt that it was very important for Quebec. A Supreme Court ruling that confirmed that the Murray document was a treaty in the sense of section 88 of the Indian Act would create a new situation.

Section 88 of the Indian Act was a two-edged sword. On the one hand, it silenced the territorial claims of Indians in most Canadian provinces – mainly in Ontario, where Europeans had dispossessed Indians through a long series of treaties; on the other hand, it put Quebec in a quandary because of the absence there of any treaties. If the Supreme Court ruling meant the creation of new treaties, Quebec would be forced to take account of this. But how? The government of Quebec was not prepared to deal with this unprecedented problem. Furthermore, as we recall, section 88 was reinforced by section 35 of the Charter of Rights and Freedoms (Constitution Act, 1982): "Existing rights – ancestral or issuing from treaties – of Canada's aboriginal peoples are recognized and confirmed." Obviously, this act was bound to be extremely popular in Quebec!□

Justice Lamer had before him the equally split opinions of four judges: Desjardins and Jacques on one side, Bisson and Paré on the other.○ Lamer heard the arguments of Robert Décary and

□ At first glance, the act was a very good thing for Indians, Métis, and Inuit. But the Indian "issue" was increasingly becoming a matter for the courts, and the stunning number of cases involving Indians ended up having a boomerang effect. In medio stat virtus. In Canada, a democratic state, ultimate power is in the hands of Parliament, but this body was largely paralyzed by the Charter of Rights and Freedoms "embedded" in the Constitution Act, 1982, a document that still hasn't been accepted or ratified by Quebec.

○ Judge Bilodeau of the Court of the Sessions of the Peace had not proffered an opinion on the Murray document.

□ *Summary of the five main arguments of the Quebec lawyers as presented in the* Sioui *case (SCR, 1990, pp. 1046–49).*

Quebec's Main Arguments□

First, the document [of September 5, 1760] opens with the words "THESE are to certify that . . . ," which would suggest that the document in question is a certificate or an acknowledgment of the Hurons' surrender, made official by Murray in order to inform the British troops. [Judge] Bisson gave these introductory words an interpretation more favourable to the Hurons: the Hurons did not know how to write and the choice of words only makes clear the fact that the document of September 5, 1760, recorded an oral treaty.

Second, General Murray used expressions which appear to involve him only personally, which do not suggest that he was acting as a representative of the British Crown. Thus, the following expressions are used:

1. "having come to me",
2. "has received under my Protection",
3. "By the Genl's Command".

Although the Hurons had surrendered to His Britannic Majesty, wording of the document in this way could tend to show that Murray intended only to give his personal understanding to protect the Hurons, without thereby binding the British Crown in the long term. Murray, it is argued, had only offered the Hurons military protection and had no intention of entering into a treaty.

Thirdly, the orders given to British soldiers stated in Canada ("no English officer or party is to molest, or interrupt them in returning to their Settlement at LORETTE . . . recommending to the Officers commanding the posts to treat them kindly . . . By the Genl's Command") would more naturally form part of a document such as a safe conduct or pass than of a treaty.

These points bring out the unilateral aspect of the document of September 5: it could be an administrative document issued by General Murray, recognizing that the Hurons had laid down their arms and giving orders to British soldiers accordingly. Finally, the document was signed only by the General's representative with no indication that it had been assented to by the Hurons in one way or another. The main purpose of the document is thus, it is argued, to recognize the surrender, and what was more important to the Hurons, allow them to return to Lorette safely without fear of being mistaken for enemies by the British soldiers they might meet along the way.

Fourth, the reference to a specific event, namely the return journey to Lorette, as opposed to a document recognizing rights in perpetuity or without any apparent time limit, could show that the purpose of this document was not to settle long-term relations between the Hurons and the British. The temporary and specific nature of the document would indicate that the parties did not intend to enter into a treaty.

Fifth, the document does not possess the formality which is usually to be found in the wording of a treaty. First, it is not the General himself who signed the document, but his adjutant on his behalf. Second, the language used in the document does not have the formalism generally accompanying the signature of a treaty with the Indians. Here, for example, are excerpts from the treaty at issue in *Simon* (at pp. 392–93, and 395):

Treaty or Articles of Peace and Friendship Renewed between
His Excellency Peregrine Thomas Hopson Esquire Captain General of the Governor in Chief in and over His Majesty's Province of Nova Scotia or Acadie. Vice Admiral of the same & Colonel of one of His Majesty's Regiment of Foot, and His

Majesty's Council on behalf of His Majesty
and
Major Jean Baptiste Cope, chief Sachem of the Tribe of Mick Mack Indians Inhabiting the East Coast of the said Province, and Andrew Hadley Martin, Gabriel Martin & Francis Jeremiah, Members and Delegates of the said Tribe, for themselves and their said Tribe their Heirs, and the Heirs of their Heirs forever. Begun made and concluded in the manner, form and Tenor following . . .
In Faith and Testimony whereof, the Great Seal of the Province is hereunto Appended, and the party's to these presents have hereunto interchangeably Set their Hands in the Council Chamber at Halifax this 22nd day of Nov. 1752 in the Twenty sixth year of His Majesty's Reign.

The appellant argues that the Hurons did not formalize the document either by their signature (which would not be absolutely necessary to make it a treaty) or by the use of necklaces or belts of shells which were the traditional method used by the Hurons to formalize agreements at the time. Clearly, this argument has weight only if the document accurately indicates all the events surrounding the signature. Otherwise, extrinsic proof of solemnities could help to show that the parties intended to enter into a formal agreement and that they manifested this intent in one way or another.

While the analysis thus far seems to suggest that the document of September 5 is not a treaty, the presence of a clause guaranteeing the free exercise of religion, customs and trade with the English cannot but raise serious doubts about this proposition. It seems extremely strange to me that a document which is supposedly only a temporary, unilateral and informal safe conduct should contain a clause guaranteeing rights of such importance. As [Judge] Bisson noted in the Court of Appeal judgment, there would have been no necessity to mention the free exercise of religion and customs in a document the effects of which were only to last for a few days. Such a guarantee would definitely have been more natural in a treaty where "the word of the white man" is given.

The appellant and the Attorney General of Canada put forward certain explanations for the presence of such guarantees in the document:

1. the free exercise of religion and customs was part of the protection in virtue under which General Murray received the Hurons;

2. the free exercise of religion and customs is mentioned because these benefits had been conferred on Canadians laying down their arms earlier.

As this Court recently noted in *R. v. C. Horse*, [1988] 1 S.C.R. 187, at p. 201, extrinsic evidence is not to be used as an aid to interpreting a treaty in the absence of ambiguity or where the result would be to alter its terms by adding words to or subtracting words from the written agreement. This rule also applies in determining the legal nature of a document relating to the Indians. However, a more flexible approach is necessary as the question of the existence of a treaty within the meaning of s. 88 of the *Indian Act* is generally closely bound up with the circumstances existing when the document was prepared (*White and Bob, supra,* at pp. 648–49, and *Simon supra,* at pp. 409–10). In any case, the wording alone will not suffice to determine the legal nature of the document before the Court. On the one hand, we have before us a document the form of which and some of whose subject-matter suggest that it is not a treaty, and on the other, we find it to contain protection of fundamental rights which supports the opposite conclusion. The ambiguity arising from this document thus means that the Court must look at extrinsic evidence to determine its legal nature.

□ *From Justice Lamer's summary, we can discern the Quebec government's five main arguments (SCR, pp. 1046–47): first, the words "THESE are to certify that" suggest a certificate (but it retains Judge Bisson's explanation to the effect that "the Hurons did not know how to write"). Second, the expressions used seemed to involve Murray personally rather than as a representative of the British Crown: "having come to me," "under my Protection." Third, the orders to the officers and soldiers and the wording "By the Genl's Command" bring to mind a safe-conduct: the document has a unilateral aspect. Fourth, the document had a temporary and specific nature. Finally, there was the absence of formality.*

○ *The National Archives are full of documents that no longer have or never had a range of application. These traces of human activity have a value and an interest that have nothing to do with possible claims. The Hurons themselves keep many documents and objects out of loyalty or respect.*

René Morin, lawyers for the appellant, and those of Jacques Larochelle and Guy Dion, lawyers for the defendants. Representatives from the Attorney General of Canada's office and the National Indian Brotherhood/Assembly of First Nations were also heard.

While the Crown's lawyers used mainly technical and legalistic arguments,□ the main lawyer for the Siouis used all of the ammunition at his disposal.

Justice Lamer Hears Mr. Larochelle . . .

[Why would they have] preserved a pass, made to allow Indians to go from one place to another for 48 hours? No reason, declared Mr. Larochelle:○

Justice Antonio Lamer

Not only did he [Murray?] keep it, but it was kept quite a long time, so that eventually his ancestor – or, rather, his descendant, Mr. Mahon△ – wrote a book from the Murray family papers in which this document was reproduced. You have it in the file; it is called a treaty.

And that is not all. Document D-7, the famous treaty, was printed very long ago. Why, in heaven's name, print a pass the only purpose of which is to allow Indians to get to Lorette

Mahon, Murray's Biographer

△ In a positively glowing biography, Major General R.H. Mahon in effect calls the document a treaty: "Murray's treaty with the Hurons," he writes, "is preserved among the family papers." This comment by Murray's hagiographer is also interesting since it confirms the version given by archivist A. Doughty by using the words "liberty of trading with the *English garrisons*" (author's emphasis).

without being harassed? It makes no sense.□ (Transcript of the Supreme Court, p. 144)

Mr. Larochelle evoked the "facts," putting them in an order that suited his purposes. He raised questions. "Why submit a pass to a notary?" "Why bring it before the Chamber of Canada *[sic]* of the time; why use a 1760 pass to justify their claim to the seigneury of Céleri [Sillery]?"

> They tell us that when this paper was submitted to the Chamber, it was called a certificate of protection by General Murray. This proves that the Indians saw it as a certificate of protection. Error, obvious error. Who named these documents? The clerk of the Chamber.

□ *When and where was D-7 printed? By whom and why? These questions will be examined at the end of part three of this book.*

○ *Brian Dickson was born in Yorkton, Saskatchewan. In that province, people of aboriginal origin comprise 6.2% of the total population, compared to 0.6% in Quebec and 1% in Ontario. The aboriginal population of Saskatchewan comprises 15% of the total aboriginal population in Canada, compared to 10% in Quebec.*

Chief Justice Brian Dickson

... but Listens to Chief Justice Dickson

Mr. Larochelle was eloquent. Eloquent enough to move Justice Lamer? He was very likely preoccupied by the opinions of his chief justice, Justice Dickson, who was well known for his sympathy for the Indians.○ Like many intellectuals of his generation and his region, he was particularly sensitive to the injustices that had befallen the Indians. He was aware of the numbered treaties that had led to the reservation system, and he had read the opinions of senior American jurists and was an admirer of Justice Marshall. He obviously felt guilty, said those who knew him well: as a man of conviction and faith, did he not have a duty to right these considerable wrongs, to the best of his abilities? His opinions had the weight of law, and he took the Supreme Court in a new direction with his rulings on the Indians' claims.

Spurred by the intensification of conflict between the federal government and the provinces, especially Quebec, then encouraged by the White Paper of 1969, the Indians got organized. Some

□ *Lamer became Chief Justice on July 1, 1990.*

○ *SCR, 1990, p. 1035.*

△ *Ibid.*

◇ *Ibid.*

of them remembered that their ancestors had been able to profit from the rivalry between English and French, then from that between British and Americans.

They were also caught in a wave of reaffirmation, a wind of renewal that led them to join forces, in particular, with the ecologists.

Antonio Lamer was on the verge of succeeding Brian Dickson.□ He gave a brilliant demonstration of why he deserved the job of Chief Justice.

The May 24, 1990, ruling is worth reading carefully. The quality of its approach, its volume of information, and its clarity of analysis make it a remarkable text. Justice Lamer spared no effort; he even conducted "personal research." Citing Judge Norris, he noted that "the Court . . . has the right to base itself on its own knowledge of history and on its research."

Thus, he studied the journals of Knox, Montcalm, and Murray; he referred to the work of archivists from Ottawa (Doughty), Albany (O'Callaghan), and Quebec City (Roy); he consulted books by historians – Cadwallader Colden, François-Xavier Garneau, Maurice Ratelle, Jack Stagg; he cited several jurists – Eugène Ortolan, Emer de Vattel, N.A. Mackenzie. Of course, he reviewed the relevant jurisprudence, especially the *Simon* (1985) and *White and Bob* (1964) cases, and he never lost sight of the laws and regulations at issue. To support this extensive documentation – which was, perforce, incomplete – he examined previous rulings and stood them up against the arguments the lawyers had made in his court.

From the very beginning, he admitted that "the task [of determining whether D-7 is a treaty] is not an easy one."○ But he resolutely followed in the footsteps of judges Dickson and Norris in stating "that the courts should show flexibility in determining the legal nature of a document recording a transaction with the Indians."△ As well, "treaties and statutes relating to Indians should be liberally construed and uncertainties resolved in favour of the Indians."◇ This was what Judge Bisson had said.

The Archives Had Opportunities to Purchase the "Murray document"

To my knowledge, neither the Supreme Court nor the Crown's lawyers consulted a contemporary historian on the actual nature of the Murray document. But I discovered that at the time research was ordered by the National Archives of Canada on the respective powers of Sir William Johnson, responsible for Indian affairs in 1760, and James Murray. As well, the Quebec attorney general was interested in Murray's and Amherst's papers, while the bureaucrats of the federal Department of Indian Affairs were gathering information on what the archivists knew about the "laissez-passer issued by James Murray to the Hurons of Lorette, 5 Sept. 1760."

An internal file reveals that this document (D-7) was twice offered to the National Archives of Canada. With regard to the "1760 safe conduct and guarantee of rights by James Murray," Michele Corbett and Patricia Birkett wrote, on November 19, 1976 (see the note on p. 158 where I mention the recent discoveries by Patricia Kennedy), "Although it is well known that at the time of the Conquest many of the Indian tribes received promises of protection, it seems that very few of these written guarantees have survived. Our indexes and logical sources have not provided us with any example, and the specialist in RG 10 has told us that, although he has often seen references to them, he has never seen an actual copy of such an agreement." However, they accorded to D-7 a value of only $75.

In other words, the justice was clearly forewarning that he was going to be flexible in establishing the nature of the document dated September 7, 1760 (D-7) – that is, to affirm that it was a treaty in the sense of section 88 of the Indian Act. In the same breath, he was announcing that any ambiguities would be decided in favour of the Indians.

This desire, previously expressed by Judge Norris and Justice Dickson, among others, seemed to be based essentially upon a deep need to repair past errors. Many judges, however, came to wonder if it was the place of the courts to "correct all the injustices of the past." □

The Indians and Their Treaties

Were the Indians on an equal footing with the Europeans? Were they not in fact disadvantaged in a number of ways?

Judge Norris of the British Columbia Court of Appeal, in one of his rulings,○ recalled a "transaction . . . between, on the one

□ *" It must not be forgotten," wrote Judge Orville Frenette, for example, "that the courts do not have the mandate to correct retroactively all the injustices of the past; this is incumbent, rather, upon the legislators" (RJQ, 1989, p. 1910). Thomas R. Berger, former judge on the British Columbia Supreme Court, expressed his views on the issue in an interesting book called* A Long and Terrible Shadow: White Values and Native Rights in the Americas Since 1492. *(Douglas & McIntyre, 1991). "Among the motives invoked to support his decision (Sparrow, 31 May 1990)," he wrote, "the Court . . . recited the long history of injustice towards Canada's . . . ."*

○ *Excerpt from* White and Bob *cited by Justice Lamer (SCR, 1990, p. 1044). It is a bit of a stretch, however, to link the case that Judge Norris had discussed and the one Justice Lamer had before him. Everything, in fact, was different: the time, the place, the circumstances, the parties, and their intentions.*

□ *SCR 1990, p. 1056.*

◇ *Fredrickson and Gibb, 1980, p. 20. For historian Maurice Ratelle, the Covenant Chain is above all a symbol, a metaphor. "There were frequent misunderstandings and ruptures among the Amerindians," he explains during an interview. "Every year or so, the so-called members [of the Covenant Chain] relit the 'flame of friendship' or fed the roots of the 'tree of peace.' A peace would begin to fall apart the minute it was signed. Often, tribes broke away from the Covenant Chain, but later claimed that they were still part of it." (Translation)*

hand, the strong representative of a proprietary company under the Crown and representing the Crown . . . and, on the other hand, uneducated savages. The nature of the transaction itself was consistent with the informality of frontier days in this Province [British Columbia] and such as the necessities of the occasion and the customs and illiteracy of the Indians demanded."

To make sense of the grab-bag of opinions offered by Judge Norris and Justice Dickson, one must presume the Indians' inferiority – without, of course, denying them the "capacity" to conclude agreements. In effect, Norris and Dickson admitted, as did Justice Lamer, that "the colonial powers recognized that the Indians had the capacity to sign treaties directly with the European nations occupying North American territory."□ In the case of the Hurons of Lorette, Justice Lamer obviously recognized their capacity to conclude a "treaty in the sense of section 88."

Jurists and historians seem to differ, however, on the notion of the Indians' inferiority (or vulnerability).

Thus, "to say that the Indian was the victim of a destructive cultural assault," says a book called *The Covenant Chain,* published by the National Museums of Canada, "is an oversimplification and ignores his role in a two-way encounter."○ Speaking of this

Indian Law versus Indian Ritual

○ Jurists stress that Europeans imposed their legal codes and jargon on the Indians. Yet at the time of the Seven Years' War, according to historian Francis Jennings, the Indians were in fact able to impose their own protocol and style. "At first," he wrote, "the English paid little attention to Indian protocol. . . . As time went on the Europeans adapted themselves to Indian forms of ritual in order to ingratiate themselves with the chiefs or to create a sense of solemn obligation, and the treaty conference became an affair in its own right in which the councils of both sides met each other on formal terms of parity." He then mentions that some Englishmen were exasperated by the Indians' oratory style and long-windedness, while others, who had learned Indian languages, "acquired a taste for Indian rhetoric." Jennings concluded, "Treaty protocol was of Indian manufacture" (*The Invasion of America*, 1976, pp. 120–23).

"Covenant Chain," Francis Jennings, in his latest book, *The Founders of America*, notes with impatience,

> None of our standard histories has noticed the Covenant Chain's existence, preferring instead to blather about a great, imagined savage empire ruled by the Iroquois. The Chain was the reality behind this myth. . . . Among other reasons for the consignment of the Covenant Chain to limbo is the influence of legal conceptions and terminology created for purposes of government rather than history. These conceptions deny the possibility of such political entities as the Chain on the grounds that there could not be independent entities within a sovereignty. . . . In the *form* of Covenant Chain treaty negotiations, the parties were peers.□

A few pages before, Jennings had remarked that "in their Northern Colonies, the English were required to conform to Indian customs in diplomatic negotiations, but in commerce the European way prevailed."○ But, he specified, "business . . . required formal arrangements of a political or diplomatic nature," and he quoted a Seneca to the effect that "Peace and trade we take to be one thing."△

In general, the Indians were able to impose their rituals and language on the Europeans. As Jennings notes, "English colonials, who lacked French finesse in Indian affairs,"◇ agreed to recognize that the Iroquois' Covenant Chain had a special role. They thus ended up relying on a very few individuals who knew how to deal properly with the Indians. And William Johnson was the very best. For their part, the Indians understood their own interests very well and were constantly trying to position themselves advantageously in the situations they were confronted with.□

Perhaps we should stop thinking of the encounter between Europeans and Amerindians as one between civilization and savagery. Frank Talbot, a director of the Smithsonian Institute, prefers to speak of "the encounter of two branches of humankind that had diverged from each other over tens of thousands of years of cultural development."○

□ *Jennings, 1993, p. 216.*

○ *Ibid., p. 182*

△ *Ibid., p. 197.*

◇ *Ibid., p. 217.*

□ *See next page.*
○ *Viola and Margolis, 1990, p. 9*

In fact, Aboriginals and Europeans are simply different. During the period that interests us, around 1760, the Indians – who were on their own territory – were still a force to be reckoned with. To understand this, we must return to the documents of the time. The Indians were omnipresent in reports, memoranda, letters. They were later erased from the "official history," because they lost – a defeat that can be explained in large part by the diseases brought from Europe and consequently by force of numbers. Even the superiority of European weapons, many historians agree, is almost secondary. It wouldn't have tipped the balance. The Europeans needed the Indians. If there's any doubt, one need simply look at the assistance they provided to the Europeans so they could survive, adapt, and travel across the continent.

The Indians: Their Strength and Power

By the nineteenth century, conditions had changed, and the Indians were subjugated in various ways. They no longer held the "balance of power" between the English and the French, or between the British and the Americans; they had been pushed aside. "The War of 1812 marked the end of an epoch in which the Indian nations were a military force. . . . Diplomacy and alliances had served the Iroquois extremely well for almost two hundred years, but they could not resist the inexorable advance of the agricultural frontier. . . . They [the Indians] would not be seen as potential allies; rather they would be sought and destroyed by the now far superior military power of the United States. In Canada, there was no predisposition to eliminate the indigenous population except throught assimilation" (Berger, 1993, p. 64). They were co-opted not because of linguistic problems, illiteracy, or ignorance of laws, but because they were weaker.

After the first half of the eighteenth century, they had gradually ceased to be essential military allies and valuable trading partners.

In recent years, the Indians have received substantial financial assistance from the federal government to make their points of view known, as they did for the James Bay and Northern Quebec Agreement. The Cree nevertheless went to court to attempt to challenge this agreement in the case of the Eastmain dam. The Supreme Court refused to hear the Cree appeal and confirmed the ruling of the Court of Appeal. "They are," the court was saying, "modern partners armed with lawyers whose honoraria for this case amount to $3.5 million. From now on, aboriginals are constrained to respect their contractual agreements, just like everyone else in the country!" (Louis-Gilles Francœur, *Le Devoir*, Oct. 15, 1993; translation).

Erased from "history," the Indians reappeared in force in certain legal rulings. Thus, Justice Lamer surprised quite a few people with his conclusions.

On September 5, 1760, Murray accepted the surrender of the Hurons of Lorette. No historian ever noted this fact, but the evidence is there. In whose name was Murray acting? Could he be considered "the highest ranking officer in the British Army stationed in Canada"□ – especially since, strictly speaking, Canada still belonged to France? That day in Longueuil, wasn't Murray on French territory? Even so, could one not, as did Justice Lamer, "go so far as to say that Murray, as Governor of the Quebec district, might reasonably have been regarded by the Hurons living in that district [Quebec] as the person most competent to sign a treaty with them"?○△

Like some Canadiens and even regular soldiers, the Hurons panicked. The outcome of the war had been devastating, and

□ *SCR, 1990, p. 1040.*

○ *Ibid., p. 1041.*

Murray Established a Passeport System

△ "A very important fact," according to Justice Lamer (SCR, 1990, p. 1040), was that "since 1759 Murray had also acted as military governor of the Quebec district, which included Lorette." According to historian G. Peter Brown, history professor at Carleton University, "Appointed governor of the Quebec garrison, on October 12, 1759, he [Murray] became governor of the Quebec district on October 27, 1760, and governor of the entire province on November 21, 1763" (DCB, 4, p. 616). Murray thus became "Gov of Town & Dependencies of Quebec" on October 27, 1760 (CO 324/40: 150–51). However, on September 23, 1760, Amherst had appointed Murray "governor of the town and Dependencies of Quebec" (NAC, CO 5/59, part 2, ff. 37–9); on October 3, Amherst added "all other parts of dependencies of Quebec."

It is true, as Justice Lamer notes, that during the winter of 1759–60, Murray "used his powers to regulate, inter alia, the currency exchange rate and the prices of grain, bread and meat and to create civil courts and appoint judges" (1040). On January 12, 1760, as we learn from his journal, Murray "[forbade], also, anything to be carried out without a passport." On the previous October 18, he had forced each "French inhabitant" to obtain a passport to transport merchandise outside of the city. On the 30th, he returned to the passport issue.

The misadventure of the Huron Athanase La Plague in the spring of 1762 is very revealing: the safe-conduct given to the Hurons of Lorette in September, 1760, did not keep Murray from requiring passports and respect for certain regulations. (See deposition in Appendix G.)

□ "'The Indians – converted savages –' said Parkman, 'without taking part in the mêlée, excelled in their activity of scalping the dead and wounded after the victory'" (MacPherson Le Moine, 1890, p. 79). This comment is no doubt based on Malartic (1890, p. 319).

○ SCR, 1990, p. 1046.

△ This led Judge Jean-Louis Baudoin, of the Quebec Court of Appeal, on May 17, 1993, in Franck Côté v. Her Majesty (p. 34) to write that "the Supreme Court . . . had decided that a simple safe-conduct permitting the Hurons to cross British lines without worrying well and truly constituted a treaty" (translation).

◇ SCR, 1990, p. 1050.

□ Ibid., p. 1056.

Murray had promised his protection to those who laid down their arms. The Hurons hoped that he would forget their long-standing alliance with the French and, of course, their little prank the previous April 28, during the battle of Sainte-Foy.□ Murray's word alone was not enough; they needed a safe-conduct to return home without being blocked by the British officers who controlled most of the territory between Montreal and Quebec City.

"Several aspects of the wording of the document [Murray's note] are consistent with the appellant's [the Quebec Crown attorney] that it was an act of surrender and a safe conduct rather than a treaty," Justice Lamer recognized.○ Therefore, he sought "extrinsic proof" in order not to reach the same conclusion;△ his "personal research"◇ led him to Knox's and Murray's journals. He examined them closely and discerned two "types of extrinsic proofs." We present the first in the note on pages 122–23, "Justice Lamer's Extrinsic Proof." It consists mainly in his understanding of historical facts. Essentially, it seems quite plausible, except perhaps for the reasons for which the French and French Canadians so feared the "Indians of Sir William Johnson." This overview leads Lamer to conclude:

> Whatever the similarities between a document recording the laying down of arms by French soldiers or Canadians and the document at issue, the analogy does not go so far as to preclude the conclusion that the document was nonetheless a treaty.
>
> . . .
>
> I rely, in particular, on Great Britain's stated wish to form alliances with as many Indians as possible and on the demoralizing effect for the French, the Canadians and their allies which would result from the loss of this long-standing Indian ally whose allegiance to the French cause had until then been very seldom shaken.□

Now that he had laid out the general context, Justice Lamer described the day of September 5 and the events that followed in more detail:

> Let us now turn to the second type of extrinsic evidence proposed by the parties, namely evidence relating to facts which were con-

temporaneous with or which occurred shortly before or after the signing of the document of September 5, 1760.

The respondents first presented evidence that the document of September 5, 1760, was the outcome of negotiations between Murray and certain Indian nations, including the Hurons, who wished to make peace with the British Crown. Knox's Journal reports the following events for September 6 (at p. 384):

> Eight Sachems, of different nations, lately in alliance with the enemy, have surrendered, for themselves and their tribes, to General Murray: these fellows, after conferring with his Excellency, *and that all matters had been adjusted to their satisfaction*, stepped out to the beach opposite to Montreal, flourished their knives and hatchets, and set up the war-shout; intimating to the French, that they are now become our allies and their ennemies. While these Chieftains *were negotiating a peace*, two of our Mohawks entered the apartment where they were with the General and Colonel Burton. [Emphasis added.]

Although it is not entirely clear, Knox appears to be relating here events which took place the preceding day, on September 5. This interpretation is confirmed by the fact that Murray makes no reference in his Journal to any meeting with the Indians on the 6th but mentions one on the 5th, while Knox records no meeting with Indians on the 5th. Both are probably speaking of the same meeting on September 5.□

The foregoing passage shows that the document of September 5 was not simply an expression of General Murray's wishes but the result of negotiations between the parties. This document was thus not simply a unilateral act, a simple acknowledgment or safe conduct, but the embodiment of an agreement reached between the representative of the British Crown and the representatives of the Indian nations present, including the representative of the Lorette Hurons.○

Knox goes on to say that the Mohawks wanted to turn on the various Indian groups allied with the French who had just concluded peace with the British. Murray and Burton intervened and the Mohawks merely made threats against them. What is significant for purposes of this case is that these threats reflected the Mohawks' perception as to the nature of the agreement which had just been concluded between the eight Sachems and Murray. The Mohawks said the following (at p. 385):

□ *Ibid., pp. 1056–57. It is possible that the judge was right; however, I suggest a different hypothesis in part three of this book.*

○ *An attentive reading of documents of the time leads me to believe that the "Eight Nations of Canada" were interdependent and negotiated collectively, at least on certain matters. As for the status of the Hurons of Lorette, we will see other points of view expressed by historians in part three of this book.*

Justice Lamer's Extrinsic Proof

On September 5, 1760, wrote Justice Lamer, France and England were engaged in a war begun four years earlier, which ended with the Treaty of Paris signed on February 10, 1763. About a year earlier, the battle of the Plains of Abraham had allowed the British to take control of Québec City and the surrounding area. During the year following this victory, British troops had worked to consolidate their military position in Canada and to solve the supply and other practical problems engendered by the very harsh winter of 1759.

In his work *An Historical Journal of the Campaigns in North-America for the Years 1757, 1758, 1759, and 1760* (1769), vol. II, at p. 382 (day of September 3, 1760), Captain Knox also relates the efforts of General Murray to win the loyalty of the Canadians. General Murray at that time invited French soldiers to surrender and Canadians to lay down their arms. He had made it widely known that he would pardon those who surrendered and allow them to keep their land. He had also promised them that he would make larger grants of land and protect them. He gave those who responded to his appeal and took the oath of allegiance to the British Crown safe conducts to return to their parishes. Steps were also taken to inform the Indians who were allies of the British of these changes of allegiance so as to ensure that they would not be attacked on the way back.

As the advantageous position and strength of the British troops became more and more apparent, several groups did surrender and it appears that this movement accelerated in the days preceding that on which the document at issue was signed. In his *Historical Journal*, at the entries for September 1, 2 and 3, Knox indicates that:

> The whole parish of Varenne have surrendered, delivered up their arms, and taken the oaths; their fighting-men consisted of five companies of militia: two other parishes, equally numerous, have signified their intentions of submitting to-morrow.

> The Canadians are surrendering every-where: they are terrified at the thoughts of Sir William Johnson's Indians coming among them, by which we conjecture they are near at hand.

> The regulars now desert to us in great numbers, and the Canadian militia are surrendering by hundreds.

In fact, the total defeat of France in Canada was very near: the Act of Capitulation of Montreal, by which the French troops stationed in Canada laid down their arms, was signed on September 8, 1760 and signalled the end of France's *de facto* control in Canada.

Great Britain's *de jure* control of Canada took the form of the Treaty of Paris of February 10, 1763, a treaty which *inter alia* ensured that the "Inhabitants of Canada" would be free to practise the Roman Catholic religion. Some months later, the Royal Proclamation of October 7, 1763 organized the territories recently acquired by Great Britain and reserved two types of land for the Indians: that located outside the colony's territorial limits and the establishments authorized by the Crown inside the colony (SCR, 1990, pp. 1051–52).

Here, Justice Lamer stopped his account to dismiss the point of view of the Crown attorneys. The document of September 5, 1760, was he wrote: "a capitulation comparable to a capitulation of French soldiers or Canadians, which cannot beelevated to the category of a treaty within the meaning of s. 88 of the *Indian Act*" (*ibid.*, p. 1052).

I consider that, instead [he continued] we can conclude from the historical documents that both Great Britain and France felt that the Indian nations had sufficient independence and played a large enough role in North America for it to be good policy to maintain relations with them very close to those maintained between sovereign nations.

The mother countries did everything in their power to secure the alliance of each Indian nation and to encourage nations allied with the enemy to change sides. When these efforts met with success, they were incorporated in treaties of alliance or neutrality. This clearly indicates that the Indian nations were regarded in their relations with the European nations which occupied North America as independent nations. The papers of Sir William Johnson (*The Papers of Sir William Johnson,* 14 vol.), who was in charge of Indian affairs in British North America, demonstrate the recognition by Great Britain that nation-to-nation relations had to be conducted with the North American Indians. . . .

As the Chief Justice of the United States Supreme Court said in 1832 in *Worcester v. State of Georgia,* 31 U.S. (6 Pet.) 515 (1932), at pp. 548–49, about British policy towards the Indians in the mid-eighteenth century:

> Such was the policy of Great Britain towards the Indian nations inhabiting the territory from which she excluded all other Europeans; such her claims, and such her practical exposition of the charters she had granted: *she considered them as nations capable of maintaining the relations of peace and war; of governing themselves, under her protection; and she made treaties with them, the obligation of which she acknowledged.* [Emphasis added.]

Further, both the French and the English recognized the critical importance of alliances with the Indians, or at least their neutrality, in determining the outcome of the war between them and the security of the North American colonies.

Following the crushing defeats of the English by the French in 1755, the English realized that control of North America could not be acquired without the co-operation of the Indians. Accordingly, from then on they made efforts to ally themselves with as many Indian nations as possible. The French, who had long realized the strategic role of the Indians in the success of any war effort, also did everything they could to secure their alliance or maintain alliances already established. . . .

England also wished to secure the friendship of the Indian nations by treating them with generosity and respect for fear that the safety and development of the colonies and their inhabitants would be compromised by Indians with feelings of hostility. One of the extracts from Knox's work which I cited above reports that the Canadians and the French soldiers who surrendered asked to be protected from Indians on the way back to their parishes. Another passage from Knox, also cited above, relates that the Canadians were terrified at the idea of seeing Sir William Johnson's Indians coming among them. This proves that in the minds of the local population the Indians represented a real and disturbing threat. . . .

This "generous" policy which the British chose to adopt also found expression in other areas. The British Crown recognized that the Indians had certain ownership rights over their land, it sought to establish trade with them which would rise above the level of exploitation and give them a fair return. It also allowed them autonomy in their internal affairs, intervening in this area as little as possible (*ibid.*, pp. 1053–55).

□ *SCR, 1990, pp. 1057–58.*
This document is quoted in
its entirety in Appendix G.

Do you remember, when you treacherously killed one of our brothers at such a time? Ye shall one day pay dearly for it, ye cowardly dogs, – *let the treaty be as it will*; I tell you, we will destroy you and your settlement. [Emphasis added.]

The view taken by these Indians was apparently shared by Murray himself. The note written by Murray in his journal on September 5, 1760, indicates that he considered that a peace treaty had been concluded with the Indian nations in question:

> Sepr. 5th. March'd with them myself and on the road, met the Inhabitants who were coming to deliver their arms, and take the oaths, these two nations of Indians, of Hurons and Iroquois, came in & *made their Pace.* [Emphasis added.]

(Knox, Appendix to an *Historical Journal of the Campaigns in North America for the Years 1757, 1758, 1759 and 1760* (1916), vol. III, at p. 831.)

The accounts given by Knox and Murray himself of the events on the days that are critical for this case are quite consistent with British policy, which favoured alliance or at least neutrality for the greatest number of the Indian nations in the newly conquered territories. By holding negotiations to conclude a peace treaty between the Hurons and the British, Murray was only giving effect to this clear policy of Great Britain.

The intervener for the National Indian Brotherhood/Assembly of First Nations provided the Court with some very interesting evidence in this regard. It submitted the minutes of a conference between Sir William Johnson and the representatives of the Eight Nations, including the Lorette Hurons, held in Montréal on September 16, 1760. (*The Papers of Sir William Johnson*, vol. XIII, 1962, at p. 163.)□

. . .

The minutes of this conference refer in several places to the peace recently concluded between the Eight Nations and the English and their allies (at pp. 16–64):

> Bʳ. Wʸ.

> You desired of us to [*see*] deliver up your People who [*may be*] are still among us – [*We*] *As you have now settled all matters wᵗʰ us & we are become firm Friends...*

a Belt

B^r.W.

As we have now made a firm Peace wth the Eng^{sh} & ye 6 Nat^s we shall endeavour all in our Pow^r to keep it inviolably...

a large Belt.

[Emphasis added.]

These words were spoken by spokesmen for the Eight Nations and clearly show that the Indians and Sir William Johnson considered that relations between these Indian nations and the British would now take the form of an alliance ("firm friends"). This new situation was undoubtedly the outcome of the peace concluded between the parties, a peace desired by the Eight Nations as well as the British (". . . we have now made a firm Peace with the English . . .").

Finally, it is worth noting that each of the contributions made by the spokesmen at this conference was followed by the presentation of a belt to solemnize the content of the undertakings that had just been made or the words which had just been spoken. As we saw earlier, the appellant [the Crown] contends that the document of September 5, 1760, is not a treaty, *inter alia*, because the tokens of solemnity that ordinarily accompanied treaties between the Indians and the British are not present. I think it is reasonable to conclude that the circumstances existing on September 5 readily explain the absence of such solemnities. Murray was not given notice of the meeting, and *a fortiori* its purpose, and it was therefore largely improvised. Murray also had very little time to spend on ceremony: his troops were moving towards Montréal and were on a war footing.□ He himself was busy organizing the final preparations for a meeting between Amherst and Haviland in Montréal, for the purpose of bringing down this last significant French bastion of Canada. Although solemnities are not crucial to the existence of a treaty, I think it is in any case reasonable to regard the presentation of belts at the conference of September 16 as a solemn ratification of the peace agreement concluded a few days earlier.○

Lastly . . . the fact that the document has allegedly not been used in the courts or other institutions of our society does not establish that it is not a treaty. Non-use may very well be explained by observance of the rights contained in the document or mere oversight. Moreover, the subsequent conduct which is most indicative of the

□ *Murray, as we know, was in Longueuil, waiting for Haviland and Amherst to arrive. On September 5–6, he was neither moving nor engaged in action. We can, however, agree with Justice Lamer that "Murray had little time to devote to ceremonies," whence the absence of solemnities. It remains to be seen whether Murray thought that he had the authority to do more than receive a "surrender" and issue a safe-conduct.*

○ *What if the peace agreement in question had already been concluded? In fact, Lévis learned on September 2 that his allies were abandoning him.*

□ *See preceding note and my conclusion.*

○ *SCR, 1990, pp. 1056–60.*

△ *Justice Lamer simply mentioned Montreal. The document published in the* Johnson Papers *did not mention a precise location. It was the publisher of the* Johnson Papers *who suggested Montreal.*

parties' intent is undoubtedly that which most closely followed the conclusion of the document. Eleven days after it was concluded, at the conference to which I have just referred, the parties gave a clear indication that they had intended to conclude a treaty.□

I am therefore of the view that the document of September 5, 1760 is a treaty within the meaning of s. 88 of the *Indian Act*.○

Thus, a new and important element was introduced: the meeting at Caughnawaga△ on September 15–16, especially because he alluded to the conclusion of a "lasting peace with the English." For Justice Lamer, this is a "solemn ratification of the peace agreement concluded "a few days earlier" – the one concluded on September 5, 1760, in Longueuil? And was this not, rather, the Oswegatchie meeting? This issue is not within the courts' jurisdiction. Rather, it is the domain of historians, who will have enough problems untangling the web. The subject is new. As I have said, there are few who have studied the outcome of this "French and Indian War" for the Indians, especially those who were allies of the French.

Justice Lamer concluded that the Murray document has the value of a treaty in the sense of section 88 of the Indian Act. As for the range of this "treaty," however, he was very cautious. He stated only that "gathering of some plants . . . pitching a tent using some branches taken from the site and . . . making a fire according to regulations that impose prudence to avoid forest fires" do not constitute a threat. And in this respect, he is correct.

Now, on to the historians.

III

THE MURRAY DOCUMENT
AND THE HISTORIANS

TYPES ATTRIBUÉS A GARAMONT. 1640. (?)		TYPES gravés PAR GRANDJEAN ET ALEXANDRE. 1693. (?)		TYPES gravés PAR LUCE. 1740. (?)		TYPES gravés PAR FIRMIN DIDOT. 1811. (?)		TYPES gravés PAR JACQUEMIN. 1818. (?)		TYPES gravés A LONDRES. 1818. (?)	
ROMAIN.	ITALIQUE.	ROMAIN.	ITALIQUE.	ROMAIN.	ITALIQUE.	ROMAIN.	ITALIQUE.	ROMAIN.	ITALIQUE.	ROMAIN.	ITALIQUE.
A a	A a	A a	A a	A a	A a	A a	A a	A a	A a	A a	A a
B b	B b	B b	B b	B b	B b	B b	B b	B b	B b	B b	B b
C c	C c	C c	C c	C c	C c	C c	C c	C c	C c	C c	C c
D d	D d	D d	D d	D d	D d	D d	D d	D d	D d	D d	D d
E e	E e	E e	E e	E e	E e	E e	E e	E e	E e	E e	E e
F f	F f	F f	F f	F f	F f	F f	F f	F f	F f	F f	F f
G g	G g	G g	G g	G g	G g	G g	G g	G g	G g	G g	G g
H h	H h	H h	H h	H h	H h	H h	H h	H h	H h	H h	H h
I i	I i	I i	I i	I i	I i	I i	I i	I i	I i	I i	I i
" "	" j	J j	J j	J j	J j	J j	J j	J j	J j	J j	J j
K k	K k	K k	K k	K k	K k	K k	K k	K k	K k	K k	K k
L l	L l	L l	L l	L l	L l	L l	L l	L l	L l	L l	L l
M m	M m	M m	M m	M m	M m	M m	M m	M m	M m	M m	M m
N n	N n	N n	N n	N n	N n	N n	N n	N n	N n	N n	N n
O o	O o	O o	O o	O o	O o	O o	O o	O o	O o	O o	O o
P p	P p	P p	P p	P p	P p	P p	P p	P p	P p	P p	P p
Q q	Q q	Q q	Q q	Q q	Q q	Q q	Q q	Q q	Q q	Q q	Q q
R r	R r	R r	R r	R r	R r	R r	R r	R r	R r	R r	R r
S sſ	S sſ	S sſ	S sſ	S sſ	S sſ	S s	S sſ	S s	S s	S s	S s
T t	T t	T t	T t	T t	T t	T t	T t	T t	T t	T t	T t
" "	" u	U u	U u	U u	U u	U u	U u	U u	U u	U u	U u
V v	V v	V v	V v	V v	V v	V v	V vv	V v	V vv	V v	V vv
X x	X x	X x	X x	X x	X x	X x	X x	X x	X x	X x	X x
Y y	Y y	Y y	Y y	Y y	Y y	Y y	Y y	Y y	Y y	Y y	Y y
Z z	Z z	Z z	Z z	Z z	Z z	Z z	Z z	Z z	Z z	Z z	Z z

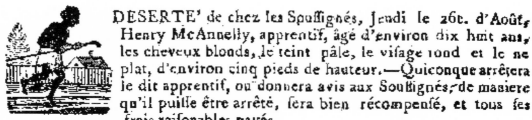

DESERTE' de chez les Souſſignés, Jeudi le 26t. d'Août, Henry McAnnelly, apprentif, âgé d'environ dix huit ans, les cheveux blonds, le teint pâle, le viſage rond et le ne plat, d'environ cinq pieds de hauteur.—Quiconque arrêtera le dit apprentif, ou donnera avis aux Souſſignés, de maniere qu'il puille être arrêté, ſera bien récompenſé, et tous ſes frais raiſonables payés.

Le Public eſt par le préſent averti de ne point le recevoir ou l'employer, parcequ'ils ſerront pourſuivis ſuivant toute la rigueur de la loi.

Québec, 2e. Septembre, 1802.   A. FERGUSON, & Co.

Documents Faribault, Nᵒ 256

THESE are to certify that the CHIEF of the HURON Tribe of Indians, having come to me in the name of His Nation, to submit to His BRITANNICK MAJESTY, and make Peace, has been received under my Protection, with his whole Tribe; and henceforth no English Officer or party is to molest, or interrupt them in returning to their Settlement at LORETTE; and they are received upon the same terms with the Canadians, being allowed the free Exercise of their Religion, their Customs, and Liberty of trading with the English :—recommending it to the Officers commanding die Posts, to treat them kindly.

Given under my hand at Longueil, this 5th day of September, 1760.

By the Genl's. Command,   JA. MURRAY.

JOHN COSNAN,   Archives du Séminaire de Québec

Adjut. Genl.

The table on the facing page shows the evolution of printer's characters since a series of roman characters was developed by Claude Garamond in 1540, followed, 150 years later, by a series created by Philippe Grandjean, then modified by Alexandre and Louis Luce.

Around 1760, the Baskerville, Fournier, and Bodoni typefaces were designed, opening the way for the typefaces of François-Ambroise Didot and his son, Firmin Didot.

Other typeface designers included Jacquemin, who made a new series of boldface roman characters, and Marcellin Legrand. Later came Henri Plon, Eugène Grasset, and Nicolas Cochin, who returned to the earlier fashions.

We can note the evolution of the shape of the "s." In its lower-case form, it had two possible shapes, the short "s" and the long "ʃ," until the early nineteenth century.

In an advertisement from *La Gazette de Québec* of September 2, 1802, we see that within the words the letter "s" always has the long "ʃ" form, except when the letter was in the upper-case form (as in "FERGUSON"). From these observations, we may wonder when the document on this page was written. (See also pp. 155–57.)

The Murray Document
and the Historians

O<small>N THE VERY DAY</small> that the Supreme Court ruled on the appeal by the attorney-general of Quebec, the Bureau du Québec in Ottawa received a copy of the ruling. It is document 20269, and its date of reception is clearly stamped on it: May 24, 1990. The fifty-nine-page document was immediately sent to Quebec City.

Justice Lamer's opinion was clear: "I am therefore of the view that the document of September 5, 1760 is a treaty within the meaning of s. 88 of the *Indian Act*."□ Had this treaty been extinguished in any way? No.○ Did it "render ss. 9 and 37 of the *Regulation respecting the Parc de la Jacques-Cartier* inoperative"?

To answer this question, the justice first had to identify a territory on which "possession of the rights that they [the Hurons] claim to hold" could be exercised. "Further, the Hurons are trying to protect the possibility of carrying on these rites and customs near Lorette on territory which they feel is best suited to such

RÉGENT SIOUI, CONRAD SIOUI, GEORGES SIOUI ET HUGUES SIOUI

et

LE PROCUREUR GÉNÉRAL DU CANADA ET LA FRATERNITÉ DES INDIENS DU CANADA/ L'ASSEMBLÉE DES PREMIÈRES NATIONS

□ *SCR*, 1990, p. 1060.

○ "In view of the liberal and generous approach that must be adopted towards Indians' rights and the evidence in the record," Justice Lamer wrote, "I cannot conclude that the treaty of September 5 no longer had any legal effect on May 29, 1982" (*SCR*, 1990, p. 1066).

□ *SCR, 1990, p. 1069.*

○ *Ibid.*

△ *Ibid., p. 1071.*

◇ *Ibid. And Justice Lamer immediately added, "Murray had been engaged for years in a war the purpose of which was to expand the wealth, resources and influence of Great Britain. It is unlikely he would have granted, without further details, absolute rights that might paralyze the Crown's use of the newly conquered territories" (SCR, 1990, p. 1071). In the judge's mind, Murray is mentioned here in reference to Great Britain. A career soldier, Murray fought where he was told to. He had participated in the siege of Louisbourg in 1758 and in that of Quebec City in 1759. He had been in North America only two years.*

□ *SCR, 1990, p. 1072.*

purposes."□ Justice Lamer stated that Parc de la Jacques-Cartier could be such a place. This "vast area," he emphasized, was not, however, "subject to the rights recognized by the treaty of September 5, 1760."○ He would have to harmonize the "rights that flow from the treaty" with the Crown's policies and objectives.

In effect, he noted, "the British Crown's desire to colonize the conquered land and use that land for its benefit also cannot be doubted."△ Thus, the "Hurons' need to protect the exercise of their customs and the desire of the British conqueror to expand" had to be reconciled. In his opinion, "exercise of the customs" could be protected to the point that "it is not incompatible with its [British] occupancy." In other words, he wrote, "the Hurons, for their part, [through their treaty] were protecting their customs wherever their exercise would not be prejudicial to the use to which the territory concerned would be put." And to make himself perfectly clear, he added,

> The Hurons could not reasonably expect that the use would forever remain what it was in 1760. Before the treaty was signed [*sic*], they had carried on their customs in accordance with restrictions already imposed by an occupancy incompatible with such exercise. The Hurons [of 1760] were only asking to be permitted to continue to carry on their customs on the lands frequented to the extent that those customs did not interfere with enjoyment of the lands by their occupiers.◇

Justice Lamer then commented, "Nonetheless, I cannot believe [there were, evidently, limits to a liberal and generous interpretation] that the Hurons ever believed that the treaty gave them the right to cut down trees in the garden of a house as part of their right to carry on their customs."□ He did not feel it necessary to invoke certain other customs, which were, no doubt, implicitly excluded.

In short, the judgment of May 24, 1990, essentially left open to question the true scope of the new treaty. It was little consolation for the attorney-general of Quebec. "For the exercise of rites and customs to be incompatible with the occupancy of the Park by the Crown," the justice specified, sending the ball back to the Quebec government's court, "it must not only be contrary to the purpose underlying that occupancy, it must prevent the realization of that purpose."□

The Sioui brothers had been well advised to restrain themselves to "the collecting of a few plants," "the setting up of a tent using a few branches taken from the site," and "the making of a fire according to the rules dictated by caution to avoid fires." In his *For an Amerindian Autohistory*, Georges Sioui writes eloquently about the "annual rituals of purification and thanksgiving."○

And who would take a stand against virtue?

As we can see, the Supreme Court opened a door by creating a treaty, but it was careful not to say where this might lead.△ It did not take long, however, for people who were "designated Indians under the *Indian Act*" to take up this issue. There were to be all sorts of opportunities. Among the customs that Murray and the Hurons considered, could they have dreamed of a trade in contraband cigarettes, giant bingo games, and fishing without a permit?

Indians living on reservations do not pay taxes. Not only are the goods they purchase exempt from sales tax, but salaries paid on reservations are not subject to income tax – if they are paid to Indians, of course.◇ In principle, retailers located on a reservation must charge tax if they are selling to non-Indians. Nevertheless, these "special" circumstances have led to the advent of retail activities based on the absence of taxation. And some of these retailers (registered Indians) have stocked their shelves with untaxed products.

The Sioui *Ruling Put to the Test*

There is a curious juridical muddle here – or so it seems to the layperson. It is not my purpose to condemn or cast blame. I simply want to note that some people have tried to profit from a certain lack of legal clarity.

□ *Ibid., p. 1073.*

○ *Sioui, 1992, p. 146.*

△ *"Neither the representative nature of the natural region where the park is located nor the exceptional nature of this natural site are threatened by the collecting of a few plants, the setting up of a tent using a few branches picked up in the area or the making of a fire according to the rules dictated by caution to avoid fires. These activities also present no obstacle to cross-country recreation. I therefore conclude that it has not been established that occupancy of the territory of Jacques-Cartier Park is incompatible with the exercise of Huron rites and customs with which the respondents are charged."*

◇ *Items purchased off the reservation by a status Indian are also exempt from sales tax when they are delivered onto the reservation. At any rate, this is the rule applied by the authorities.*

□ *Ontario Court of Justice (Provincial Division),* Her Majesty v. Marie Elizabeth Vincent. *Grounds for judgment were given orally by His Honour Judge R.G. Masse on Monday, July 29, 1991, in Cornwall, Ont., and in writing on August 16, 1991, in Ottawa, Ont. In the quotations that follow, parenthetical references are for the judgments of 29/7/91 or 16/8/91. I chose this case in particular because of the attention that Judge Masse paid to the testimony of historians Delâge, MacLeod, and Graves (29/7/91: 3). The justices of the Supreme Court seem to have been unaware of this case – which is normal, given the level of the court. But they might themselves have called upon historians to testify and considered their points of view.*

○ *RJQ, 1997, pp. 1722–31.*

This was the case for Elizabeth Vincent, "member of the Band of the Hurons of Lorette," living "on an Indian reservation of the Huron-Wendat village not far from Quebec City."□

"On August 28, 1988," Judge R.G. Masse, of the Ontario Court of Justice, wrote, "Constable Denis Constant of the Royal Canadian Mounted Police received information to the effect that a van, Ford brand, bearing Quebec licence plate JYG 259, was on the Akwesasne Indian Reservation. . . . It must be noted that the Indian reservation at this site straddles two Canadian provinces and one U.S. state. The van was loaded with a quantity of contraband – that is, tobacco liable for customs duties" (16/8/91: 3–4).

A chase, an arrest, a confession. Ms. Vincent admitted everything, including that "there was no duty paid on the tobacco even though it was liable for duty" (16/8/91: 4).

The defence claimed that the "Murray treaty" of September 5, 1760, and the "Jay treaty," concluded between the United States and England on November 19, 1794, "create an exemption in favour of Ms. Vincent that allows her not only to be in possession of commercial goods illegally imported duty free but also to transport commercial goods across the American border without paying duty" (16/8/91: 6).

This trial, which was held in Ontario, provided an opportunity for three historians to give their opinions on the scope of the "Murray treaty."

Denys Delâge, professor of sociology and history at Université Laval, appeared as a "witness for Ms. Vincent." He had prepared a ten-page text called "Contexte historique du traité de 1760 entre les Hurons de Lorette et le général Murray" (Historical context of the 1760 treaty between the Hurons of Lorette and General Murray). The document is dated December 20, 1988, more than one year after the Quebec Court of Appeal ruling.○ At the time of this trial, it was known that the attorney-general of Quebec had appealed to the Supreme Court, but that court had not yet ruled.

The Ontario Crown sought opinions from two expert witnesses: D. Peter MacLeod, an assistant professor of history at the

Denys Delâge

Delâge came to history from sociology and is particularly interested in Indians. In 1985, he published *Le pays renversé. Amérindiens et Européens en Amérique du nord-est, 1600–1664* (Montreal: Boréal Express). He has also published many articles, some of them in the excellent journal *Recherches amériendiennes*, and participated in many radio programmes, including *Les Indiens d'Amérique* (Société Radio-Canada, 1992, HST.10, produced by Jean Desjardins and Louis Martin). As of this writing, he is working on a major history of Indians in Canada in collaboration with Sylvie Vincent. Delâge was co-director, with Jacques Mathieu, of Georges E. Sioui's master's thesis (which became *Pour une autohistoire amériendienne*, Presses de l'Université Laval, 1989) and director of his doctoral dissertation, also published by PUL, in 1994, as *Les Wendats. Une civilisation méconnue.*

□ *Peter MacLeod was in the Ph.D. programme in history at the University of Ottawa. His curriculum vitae includes a number of publications dealing generally with colonial wars in North America. His master's thesis in history (University of Saskatchewan, 1985) was titled* The French Campaign of 1756 in the Lake Ontario Theatre and the Siege and Capture of Chouaguen. *Donald E. Graves is an expert in military history. Before joining the history department of the Department of Defence, he worked at the manuscripts division of the National Archives of Canada and at the Citadel Museum in Halifax. As of 1990, he had several published articles to his credit.*

○ *Graves (1990) mentions "the discrepancy in wording between the text of General Murray's Treaty of 1760 as reported in a decision of the Supreme Court of Canada in* Sioui *and the wording of a transcription of General Murray's copy of the same document as published in the* Report of the Work of the Archives Branch for the Year 1910."

University of Ottawa, and Donald E. Graves, a historian working at the Department of Defence.□

MacLeod prepared a two-part memorandum: a thirty-two-page report called "The Huron of Lorette and the Murray Treaty of 1760," followed by a fourteen-page commentary on Delâge's short study. His document is dated 1990, and he made no allusion in it to the Supreme Court ruling of May 24, 1990. The fact that he used the term "Murray treaty" is explained by the ruling of the Court of Appeal of September 8, 1987, and by the defence allegations.

The same explanation no doubt goes for Graves, who submitted an impressive memorandum, more than fifty pages long, on the "Murray Treaty of 1760," the "Jay Treaty," and the "Treaty of Ghent." The first twenty-two pages dealt with the "Murray treaty." His "historical analysis and opinion" dated from November, 1990, and he had read MacLeod's report, since he referred to it. He also alluded to the Supreme Court ruling to consider the version of the treaty that that court had used.○

□ Delâge, 1988, p. 16.

○ *Ibid., p. 1.*

Denys Delâge's Opinion

In his report, Delâge took the "Murray treaty" for granted without further explanation. "The treaty signed [*sic*] between Murray and the Hurons in 1760," he wrote, "is thus situated within the general context of the English strategy, which was to break the alliance between French and Amerindians and to conclude separate treaties with the latter. I would add that given the leadership exercised by the Hurons (Wyandots or of Lorette) among the other Amerindian nations, the conclusion of a peace between English and Hurons had a scope that greatly surpassed the immediate partners."□

The Hurons before and after 1650

On this subject, Alain Beaulieu writes, "During the Seven Years' War, the French and the English deployed thousands of troops. The some thirty or forty warriors of Lorette, who occasionally formed useful auxiliary troops, were no longer able to make a difference or play a crucial role in the conflicts between France and England in North America. Nor does anything in the available documentation indicate that the Hurons of Lorette continued to play an important diplomatic role after 1650. The French do not seem to have seen them as a group that, beyond its small population, had a decisive political influence" (1994, p. 30). Delâge's text, however, is ambiguous on this account. Although he recognizes that things changed after 1648, he insists on attributing to the Hurons a "prestigious place" and a "decisive role in the councils" that resided mainly in "their traditional mastery of diplomacy" (1988, p. 6).

Delâge set about rehabilitating the role played by the Indians between 1500 and 1760. He attributed to a "chauvinistic and ethnocentric perspective" the importance generally accorded to "the struggle between two colonial powers," "as if the only actors were the French and the English." He stressed that there had been "a third actor whose presence was constant and whose role was decisive: the Amerindians."○

"The Amerindian nations had their own policies, their interests, and the capacity to take all sorts of initiatives," Delâge wrote. Evoking the imbalance between the French and English forces, he explained, "It was the weight and power of the Amerindians'

The drawings engraved on this powder horn (c. 1758) show English soldiers battling the Indians. In the top part, three Indians are hidden behind trees and preparing to fire. Facing them, one Englishman imitates their position and another one is approaching. On the bottom, we can imagine soldiers on exercises. Were they beginning European-style troop movements or conducting target practice Indian-style?

organization that enabled the French to hold on to America." He cited their participation in a number of battles, and mentioned that "they taught the French the rules of guerrilla warfare." □

Skilfully, given the significance of his testimony, he talked a great deal about Amerindians in general, and little of the Hurons. When he mentioned the latter, he tended to talk about them before 1649, when they actually were an important force: "When the Hurons went to see Murray 'to submit,' it meant that they had come to make peace, but it did not mean that they would become simple British subjects. The subsequent events justify this interpretation." ○

For the defence, this was meant to establish for the court that the "Murray treaty" was intended to permit the Hurons of Lorette to trade freely with the English without being taxed – or, at least, without impediments. "The free trade that was accorded to them signified the right to go to the trading posts of the English without being molested."

□ *On this subject, see* Axelrod, Chronicle, *p. 53, and* Côté et al., L'Indien généreux, *p. 139. It should be noted that Delâge was right to stress the importance of Franco-Indian alliances. What remains to be established is the importance of the Hurons of Lorette in these alliances after 1649. A telling remark was once made by a French administrator: "The savages have little to do, being our allies, but they could become a considerable force if they were our enemies" (translation) (NAC, C¹¹B4, pp. 251–56).*

○ *Delâge, 1988, p. 9.*

□ *MacLeod, 1990, p. 6.*

○ *Ibid., p. 10.*

△ *Ibid.*

◇ *Ibid., p. 11.*

□ *Ibid., p. 13 (author's emphasis).*

○ *Ibid., p. 5.*

△ *Ibid., p. 4.*

Peter MacLeod's Opinion

In his "commentary," MacLeod reacted quite strongly to Delâge's text, contesting a number of his statements: "[He] exaggerates the importance of the Amerindians for the defense of New France."□ He reproached Delâge in particular for mixing together "the Wyandots of the Great Lakes and the Hurons of Lorette as if they were all the same. The suggestion that a small band with less than one hundred members [the Hurons of Lorette] wielded the same influence as a powerful confederacy of 20,000 is untenable and unsupported by a single example."○

"Although the treaty of 1760 was negotiated between Murray and the Hurons of Lorette," MacLeod noted, "it was signed only by Murray."△ On the other hand, he agreed with the overall picture that Delâge gave on trade relations between the Indians and the French, although he noted that it "does not establish that this material applies to the very small Huron band living a few kilometres from Quebec [City] in the eighteenth century."◇ As well, he opined, the use of the word "unmolested" in the Murray document "does not necessarily imply the grant of special tax privileges." And he concluded, "Whatever rights they were given by the Murray treaty, those rights were accorded the Hurons of Lorette *upon the same terms as the Canadians.*"□

In his initial statement, MacLeod emphasized the fact that, in his opinion, "the Hurons of Lorette did not engage in economic activities that involved crossing international boundaries, and dealt with the merchants of the town of Quebec":○ "The interpretation placed by the Hurons of Lorette upon the treaty in general, and upon the phrase 'and liberty of trading with the English' in particular, was not preserved, either in the British documents or in the Huron oral tradition."△

Donald Graves's Analysis

Driving the nail in deeper Graves wrote, "MacLeod's conclusion has since been reinforced by the discovery of a second copy of the Treaty of 1760 . . . that contains a different wording." The transcription made by the archivist Arthur Doughty, published in the

The fur trade was based on the encounter between Indian and European. It was, however, much more regulated than is commonly believed.

Report of the Work of the Archives Branch for the Year 1910, specifies "liberty of trading with the English Garrisons recommending it to the Officers commanding the posts to treat them kindly" instead of "liberty of trading with the English:— recommending it to the Officers commanding the Posts, to treat them kindly."□

For Graves, "there is no reason to doubt the reliability and authenticity of the wording [established by Doughty] in Murray's copy and that the word 'garrisons' was intended to be part of [the original] text for three reasons."○ First, the word "garrisons" makes the sentence more comprehensible. Second, when a transcription is made, it is more likely that a word will be omitted than that one will be added. Finally, Murray had begun to settle British merchants in former French trading posts the previous

□ *Graves, 1990, p. 4. It is quite surprising that no one had made this observation before, even though Doughty's transcription had been found by Judge Desjardins in 1985.*

○ *Ibid., p. 5.*

A trade scene taken from a detail of a map of Canada in 1777.
The beaver pelts were used mainly to make hats!

□ *Ibid., p. 20.*

○ *Ruling rendered in writing on August 16, 1991, in Ottawa. Ontario Court of Justice (Provincial Division), D. Akman acting for the Crown and J. Larochelle for the defence. The "grounds for judgment" are 88 pages long. In October, 1993, the Supreme Court rejected Elizabeth Vincent's appeal (Le Soleil, Oct. 15, 1993).*

June, and he had already manifested his intention to maintain the trade system set up by the French, but on behalf of the British Crown.

Like MacLeod, Graves attributed to the Hurons of Lorette "a limited role in the defence of New France in 1759, but, thereafter, [they] do not seem to have had any military significance whatsoever."□

Judge Rommel G. Masse accepted the viewpoints of the two English-speaking historians. Having rejected Ms. Vincent's claims with regard to the "Murray treaty" and the "Jay treaty," he had no choice but to find her guilty, he stated on July 29, 1991.○

Another Expert: W.J. Eccles

At another trial that involved Ms. Vincent,□ this one in Quebec City, the noted historian W.J. Eccles explained "the historical context surrounding the alleged document of September the 5th, 1760, concerning the Hurons of Lorette." His seventeen-page memorandum (with references) is dated February, 1989. It is obvious that he had read Delâge's text, dated December 20, 1988, for he corrected it without ever mentioning Delâge.

A graduate of McGill University (1955), William John Eccles is an expert on New France. From Toronto, where he has made his career, he has always closely watched developments in Quebec historiography. He is observant, hard-working, and argumentative. He is not scared of debate. A historian of the same generation as Guy Frégault, he is a field worker – and archives are his field. His work precedes the era of quantitative, structural history, which obscures people and events behind graphs and trends or themes of the day, such as modernity and identity. When it comes to facts, it is not easy to catch him out. In the introduction to his memorandum, he wrote,

> The document, under date of 5 September 1760, purportedly signed by Brigadier James Murray (the provenance of the document is not given, furthermore Murray was not promoted to Major General until 1762) by no stretch of the imagination can be construed to have been a treaty enacted between the British military command, acting in the name of His Britannic Majesty, and a chief of the Huron band of Lorette, acting for his people. The document is exactly what it is described as being in its body; namely an act of submission of this group of Indians to the British Crown.○

Now, that is clear!△

In broad strokes, Eccles recalled the circumstances surrounding the meeting of September 5, 1760, in Longueuil.

> It was under these circumstances, in this historical context, that the Hurons of Lorette approached Brigadier Murray to offer their submission and make their peace. Certainly, the last thing that Murray would have considered at that juncture of events would have been a treaty of alliance with a handful of pathetic warriors

□ *Quebec Superior Court, no. 200-05-002443-880.*

○ *Eccles, 1989, p. 1.*

△ *It is perhaps surprising that the researchers for the Supreme Court did not bother to look at the historians' memoranda on the subject. Eccles's point of view, in particular, might have helped Justice Lamer to better grasp the historical context.*

□ *Eccles, 1989, p. 4.*

○ *Ibid., p. 13.*

△ *Trudel published* L'Esclavage au Canada français *and* Dictionnaire des esclaves au Canada français *in 1960. He also undertook to paint an accurate portrait of the population of Canada in 1663 and subsequent years.*

totally incapable of offering any resistance whatsoever to the might of British arms. To assert that Murray treated with them as an equal power on this occasion is too ludicrous for words.□

Eccles had entrenched opinions. He also wrote with style:

> To conclude, the Hurons of Lorette were never a force to be reckoned with either by the French, the Indian allies of the French [as Delâge suggests], and most certainly not by the British military forces at Montreal in September 1760. Since 1650 they had existed on the margins of both Canadian and Indian society, a foot in both camps. . . . They submitted to the British and received the reassurance they desired, they would not be put to the sword.○

Eccles's opinion was eminently respectable. But history is woven from innumerable sources that necessitate the work of a number of historians. And it is never finished. Documents are unearthed – such as the Murray document – research tools refined, works written, questions asked. History is very much a living science.

To Eccles's point of view, which was similar to MacLeod's and Graves's, it is interesting to add that of Marcel Trudel. Also a historian of New France, he is a man of his times: open-minded and fiercely independent, he belongs to no historical "school."

Marcel Trudel

Marcel Trudel's Opinion

Like Eccles and Frégault, Trudel is of the generation that does not fear contact with documents. He learned to read and respect them. A patient man, he has enumerated all of the first settlers in New France, as well as the slaves.△ Before jumping to conclusions, Trudel likes to construct a careful chronology of facts, clearly locate the action, and gain an accurate profile of the actors in question.

For the trial of the Mohawks of Kanesatake (Oka), accused of having organized a bingo game "without previously obtaining a permit," Trudel submitted the *Mémoire sur le sauf-conduit accordé aux Hurons par le général Murray le 5 septembre 1760* (Memorandum on the safe-conduct accorded to the Hurons by General Murray on September 5, 1760). This fifteen-page study (undated) was quoted in its entirety by Judge Bruno Cyr of the Court of Quebec in Saint-Jérôme on February 26, 1992.□

Following Justice Lamer's example and citing Judge Norris, who, in *White and Bob*, stated that "the Court has the right to take account ex officio of past or contemporary historical facts . . . and to base itself on its own knowledge of history and on its research," Judge Cyr based himself on Trudel's memorandum to respond to the claim that the Murray document was a "treaty" that was also valid for the "Mohawk community of Kanesatake" and covered a "commercial activity" such as the "organization of bingo games." This memorandum took up more than half of his thirty-page ruling.

Did the "Murray treaty" concern the Mohawks in the Montreal region? This was the first question that Trudel had to answer. According to him, the Indians had made their peace on September 5, 1760, at the meeting in Longueuil. Lévis had learned this abruptly at a meeting in La Prairie on September 2, 1760.○

As for the Murray document, Trudel felt absolutely that it was a safe-conduct.△ And the Hurons were very likely to need one to return to Lorette.

> Of the 14 lines contained in this document, 10 are of the nature of a safe-conduct, and it is only in passing that Murray mentions that the Hurons are submitted to the same conditions as French Canadians, conditions set out in the Act of Capitulation of Quebec City in September, 1759: the ownership "of their houses, goods, effects, and privileges" – that is, the liberty to use them, and, among the privileges, the usual privilege of trading. (Ruling of the Honorable Bruno Cyr, p. 9)

As well, Trudel notes,

□ *Court of Quebec, Criminal and Penal Division, District of Terrebonne, Saint-Jérôme, Feb. 26, 1992, Her Majesty v. Yvan Nicholas.*

○ *Journal des campagnes du chevalier de Lévis en Canada. De 1756 à 1760 (Montreal, 1889), p. 301. See also Casgrain (ed.), Relations et journaux (Quebec City, 1895), Collection des manuscrits, vol. 11, p. 252–53.*

△ *Issuing safe-conducts, passports, and permits was a common practice. Murray issued them constantly after the surrender of Quebec City. The NAC archivist Patricia Kennedy found, in KG1, a large number of "passes" given to Indians in Nova Scotia in 1760, and others authorizing trade with Indians between 1760 and 1765. The Murray document issued to the Hurons of Lorette was not unusual, she writes in a long note dated January 2–8, 1995 (NAC, Manuscripts Division, Ms. Kennedy's personal papers).*

□ Her Majesty v. Yvan Nicholas, *Memorandum by Marcel Trudel, v. 1992, pp. 12–14.*

○ *Ibid., p. 17.*

△ *Court of Appeal, Montreal Court Office, May 17, 1993. Franck Côté, appellant, v. Her Majesty the Queen, defendant. See the ruling by the Honorable Jean-Louis Baudoin and the opinions of his colleagues William S. Tyndale and Jacques Delisle. I am using the version produced by the Court of Appeal. In Superior Court, Franck Côté and some other Algonquins claimed an ancestral right to the territory in dispute. The essay by historian Raynald Parent did not convince Judge Orville Frenette. The ruling rendered in this case is very instructive, especially for its comments on "the origin of Indian title," the Royal Proclamation of October 7, 1763, and the effect of section 35, paragraph 1, of the Constitution Act, 1982, on Indian title (RJQ, 1989, pp. 1893–1913.)*

◇ *Baudoin, 1993, p. 5*

No documentation indicates that the issuing of the document of September 5 to the Hurons was accompanied by the ritual that ordinarily indicates the conclusion of a treaty with the Amerindians. The text is stripped of any juridical wording, and also of any of the symbols that are usually part of treaties with Amerindians. As the conclusion of a treaty between two parties normally requires, this should have had, along with Murray's signature, the mark of the Hurons; this is not at all the case.

"This document is not a treaty," he concludes.

Finally, Trudel regrets that the Supreme Court had been ill-informed on the apparent absence of General Amherst from the Montreal region, on the chronology of events, and on the fidelity of the transcription of the safe-conduct□. Like Graves and Eccles, Trudel endorses Doughty's version, which indicates "freedom to trade with the English garrisons" (according to the translation made by the Public Archives of Canada in 1910–11), giving the document a very different scope. In short, for Trudel, this safe-conduct "takes into consideration the general conditions laid out by the Act of Capitulation of Quebec City."○

Another Trial: The Legal Saga Continues

Before proceeding to my own examination of the Murray document, I will discuss one more case heard recently by the Quebec Court of Appeal.

On or about July 25, 1984, M. Franck Côté, Algonquin Indian, member of the band of Désert River and resident of the Maniwaki reservation, fished with a line without holding the required permit. He and others are accused of refusing to pay the entry fees "provided by the law and the rules" by acceding to the Bras Coupé-Désert ZEC [*zone d'exploitation contrôlée*, wildlife sanctuary].△

"All of these facts are admitted."◇ And others were present, including a group of Native students who were there to be "taught the traditional fishing methods." Franck Côté and the other band members pleaded that the rules invoked could not have a juridical effect on them, due to the protection offered to them by the Constitution Act, 1982.

A ruling was made in Provincial Court in 1988 and in Superior Court, the following year.□ Aside from the terms of the Royal Proclamation of 1763, the defence invoked (in Provincial Court) "treaties," "notably that of Swegatchy, subsequently confirmed by that of Caughnawaga."○ Dissatisfied with the rulings made in these two courts, the "defendants" appealed.

"When the Provincial Court (April 21, 1988) and Superior Court (May 19, 1989) studied the points of law that were the subject of the present appeal," wrote Judge Jean-Louis Baudoin of the Court of Appeal, "neither of them had the benefit of very important rulings by the Supreme Court." He cited various rulings, including *Sparrow* (1990) and *Sioui* (1990), and "reflections and studies," one on a case in British Columbia and another by the Saskatchewan Court of Appeal. "Since 1989," he wrote, "jurisprudence has evolved substantially and we thus should not take the two lower courts to task for not having been able to take account of these changes."△

The wheels of justice turn slowly, and that can be a good thing!

Judge Baudoin took the case before him very seriously and produced a ruling more than sixty pages long. He rejected the appeal "with costs." But he nevertheless recognized that "the source of the right to hunt and fish for subsistence invoked by the appellants is the Treaty of Swegatchy [sic], properly concluded."◇ His two colleagues, judges William S. Tyndale and Jacques Delisle, agreed with him, although the latter differed on one point.□

Her Majesty won the case, but she found herself with a new treaty on her hands!

Of course, Judge Baudoin had read the jurisprudence concerned, and he explained himself by addressing the issue of the "Swegatchy" treaty. (This should have been written "Oswegatchie.") "A treaty with the Aboriginals is an agreement *sui generis*," he noted, "which does not necessarily follow the classic rules of public international law" – to the point that "some of these agreements were not necessarily put in writing." Preparing the ground for his ruling, he added, "Thus, most of the time the colonizer

□ *In Provincial Court* (Her Majesty v. Côté and Attorney General of Quebec), *the case was heard by Judge Jules Barrière, who found "the appellants [the Indians] guilty of the infractions charged." The Honorable Orville Frenette of Superior Court, "for different reasons," essentially agreed with Judge Barrière.*

○ *Baudoin, 1993, p. 8.*

△ *Ibid., p. 12.*

◇ *Ibid., p. 62.*

□*"With respect for the contrary opinion," Judge Delisle wrote, "I cannot accept that exercising a right protected by the Canadian Constitution can be submitted to ministerial discretion, even if judicially reviewable" (Baudoin, Tyndale, and Delisle, 1993, p. 10).*

□ Baudoin, 1993, p. 33.

○ On p. 37 of his ruling, Judge Baudoin added, "One must thus refer to secondary evidence to determine their existence and content." However, on pp. 45 and 46, the judge himself cites the "minutes" of the conference of September 16, 1760.

△ Ibid., p. 37.

◇ See R. Parent, Les institutions. This document contains 32 pages of text and 170 notes, some of which contain at least five or six references. And some references are cited repeatedly with no explanation! It should be noted that Parent works mainly from primary sources – which has its merits – and consults established history very little. This, no doubt, is explained by the colossal amount of pioneering work he has done in the field.

□ Patricia Kennedy, "Des voix dans l'ombre," L'Archiviste, vol. 20, no. 1 (1992): 4 (translation).

○ By "Mémoires," the judge means Sir William Johnson's journal (p. 37). "Certain excerpts of Johnson's Mémoires were produced in the file (M.A. appendix 2, vol. 6, pp. 1870ff). These consist of a series of minutes stating, often in concise form, the agreements between himself [Johnson] and various Aboriginal representatives" (p. 39).

was in a position of superiority, even if only because the juridical concepts used were, in certain cases, unknown to the Aboriginals or difficult to understand or even unintelligible in their cultures."□

These are nice words, but a bit disingenuous. In the case of the "Swegatchy treaty," the judge himself admits that "the written record of the Swegatchy and Caughnawaga treaties have completely disappeared today."○ If this is so, how can one evoke "juridical concepts . . . unknown to the Aboriginals"?

But first of all, let us see how Judge Baudoin came to the conclusion that a treaty was concluded at "Swegatchy." According to his ruling, the testimony of the historian Raynald Parent strongly influenced him.△

The Historian Raynald Parent

A tenacious worker, Raynald Parent began to study Amerindians very early. He has produced a considerable body of work, which has not been widely disseminated and is not well known. His methodology is quite disconcerting: he inundates his readers with references that are difficult to verify.◇ Rarely does he examine his sources or take the time to make links between what he proposes and the documents he cites. Readers who decide to examine them closely are often perplexed. In effect, Parent extrapolates constantly and generalizes easily. Readers cannot help but wish that the historian had let his sources speak more eloquently. In his defence, it must be recognized that "the voice of the Aboriginals is buried under a heap of public documents."□ The sheer volume of collections of Indian records, dispatches, personal journals, and writings of all sorts greatly surpasses the capacities of a single researcher. Thus, one must be careful in interpreting Parent's research.

I do not have access to Parent's testimony or to the "Mémoires" of William Johnson that were presented to Judge Baudoin.○ I do not doubt them, however, since we have seen that there was an important meeting at Oswegatchie in August, 1760. I have in fact seen a number of allusions to "the meeting at

Oswegatchie," a place sometimes identified as La Présentation or Fort William Augustus□ (Amherst's name for Fort Lévis).

According to the judge, Raynald Parent had brought to the Court's attention the minutes of a meeting held on August 21, 1769, at Sault-Saint-Louis in the presence of Indian Affairs agent Daniel Claus and his superior, William Johnson. These minutes are very interesting: they clearly refer to "what you [William Johnson] transacted with the dep. [deputies] of y. [the] Seven confederated Nations of Canada in August 1760, near Swegachy, when . . . you entered into a preliminary Engagement with. . . . " Some words are missing, but the Seven Nations are referred to again. The speaker, "Adighwadooni of Aughquisasne," reminds Johnson of his "preliminary engagement" to ensure the Indians of "the quiet and peaceable Possession of the Lands [they] lived upon and let [them] enjoy free Exercise of the Religion that [they] were instructed in."

Is this reasonably clear?

> After the final Conquest of this Country [continues one of the speakers at the meeting of August 21, 1769), they [the preliminary engagements] were confirmed and ratified by you [Johnson], in behalf of the Great King of England our Father, at a general Congress of all the Ind. nations in Canada, held by you at Caghnawagey,

Controlling the Indians

□ An Indian from Oswegatchie travelling to Montreal was arrested at the Les Cèdres post. Daniel Claus received the complaint and transmitted it to William Johnson on September 8, 1764: "We have submitted to You a vast deal more, than ever we did to the French, who never in Peace, or War, debarred us from going (without their leave) to our Hunting Grounds, – as it is the Case with us now. – Although the Commander in chief of the Army at the settling a Peace with us near Fort Wm Augustus in 1760 had promised, and engaged that if the Country remained in the Possession of the English, we should not only enjoy the same Priviledges [sic] we enjoyed in the time of the French, but still more and greater, – and the usage better – but to our Sorrow, we have not seen the Proofs of it as yet." The three chiefs who addressed Claus were from Oswegatchie. It should not be surprising that they refer to the conference "near Fort Wm Augustus" in 1760 rather than that at Caughnawaga (*Johnson Papers*, vol. 11, pp. 353–54).

□ Baudoin, 1993, p. 40.

○ See Parent, Les institutions. Of its 170 notes, most refer to the Johnson Papers and the RG 10 collection of the National Archives. In his notes, Parent almost never quotes the texts to which he is referring; he does so rarely in the text, simply referring readers to RG 10, to the fourteen volumes (and 13,000 pages!) of the Johnson Papers, or to the ten volumes of the Documents Relating to the Colonial History of the State of New York.

△ "Indian custom ordinarily dictated that no proposition should get a response on the same day it was offered" (Jennings, Invasion, p. 122). The Oswegatchie meeting took place on August 30, 1760; the meeting at Caughnawaga lasted two days, September 15–16, 1760.

◇ Parent, Les institutions, p. 11.

□ Ibid.

○ See the biography of Amherst by Charles P. Stacey (DCB, 4, pp. 22–28). Several historians have suggested cause-and-effect links between Amherst's reluctance to follow the policy of gift giving and Pontiac's uprising. In fact, to be cynical, one would recall that Amherst had often considered offering infected blankets and handkerchiefs to the Indians.

all of which is still fresh in our Memories and we on our side have strictly and inviolably adhered to.□

Johnson had made promises to the Indians in Oswegatchie; there is no doubt of this. But would he not have waited until the surrender of Montreal so that he could verify the behaviour of the Indians "allied with the French," before confirming and ratifying these promises? In fact, they were ratified on September 15 and 16, 1760.

"One month before the surrender of Montreal," Raynald Parent wrote,○ "Johnson signed the treaty of Swegatchy." What did he base this on? The meeting took place on August 30 and the surrender of Montreal on September 8. Why did he mention "one month"? Had he discovered a meeting prior to that of August 30?△

"At this meeting," Parent continued, "the Seven Nations of Canada, including the Algonquins [involved in the Franck Côté case], promised their neutrality in the War of Conquest."◇ In fact, he was taking a risk by listing who was at this meeting. One may wonder, as well, where he found the expression "War of Conquest." In the documents cited in the references?

"In return [for their neutrality]," Parent added, "the British gave the Amerindians a guarantee of possession of the lands on which they lived, respect for and free exercise of their religion, free circulation throughout the North American territory, the establishment of advantageous trade, and continuation of the policy of gift giving."□ The events that followed indicate that Amherst was not up to date on the "policy of gift giving"!○ As for free circulation throughout "North America," this must no doubt be attributed to the historian's enthusiasm. In Caughnawaga, in September, 1760, the only issue was the route between Montreal and Albany!

"Thanks to the negotiations and treaty," Parent concluded, "the English troops were not bothered at all during their march on Montreal." To establish this fact, Parent cites the minutes of August 21, 1760, and ignores Johnson's own reports, J. Amherst's and W. Amherst's journals, and other documents. It was a negotiation, but was it truly a treaty? In the context, could it be more

Conquered or Not?

"As the Indians were never conquered," wrote Parent, "they saw themselves as free beings, not subject to British laws" (*Les Institutions*, p. 12). On this subject, we might note this commentary by William Johnson to the Hurons of Detroit on July 17, 1764. He was reproaching them for several things, and he emphasized "the absurdity of your attempts against us, who have conquered the French, and You" (*Johnson Papers*, vol. 11, p. 281). Again, I quote the note that Amherst sent to Johnson on August 30, 1760: "With . . . the talk you will have from their Sachems, You will be best able to Judge what will be the most likely means to hinder the Indians from joining the Enemy, in which Case, they may be Assured of being permitted to live in Peace and Quiet, and of receiving all the production they can desire."

than a "preliminary engagement"? Johnson himself talked of a treaty, □ but was it not in his interest to aggrandize the event?

An Examination of the Murray Document

In the context of the *Sioui* case, it seems that the exact nature of the document of September, 1760, attributed to Murray is open to question. To borrow from the procedure followed by the judges whose opinions I have examined, we can ask the following questions:

- Where did the photocopy (D-7) presented to the Court come from? Is it possible to establish its authenticity?
- What about printed document D-7a?
- If we accept the validity of these documents, what did their author mean to say?
- What does the historical context tell us?
- Can this document be considered a treaty by historians?
- If no to the above question, could it still have the value of a treaty in the sense of section 88 of the Indian Act?

"History is useless," stated Fustel de Coulanges. This ambiguous statement should be interpreted prudently. The eminent historian meant by this that history must not be subjugated. It is not and must not be used in the service of a cause.○ This is also my opinion.

□ *In a report to Minister William Pitt, dated October 24, 1760* (Johnson Papers, *vol. 3, pp. 272–73).

○ *The goal of history is not to please, to stir the emotions, or to teach lessons; it simply serves knowledge. It proposes to find the truth. Of course, it is not infallible. Knowledge is constantly progressing, thanks to the work of many historians, who are always seeking facts and driven by a critical spirit. Simply, "It is the science of handling and using texts," Joseph Hours said (translation). History is conducted mainly with written documents but, adds Lucien Febvre, also "with everything that the historian's ingeniousness enables him to use" (translation). "Everything in the world," wrote R.G. Collingwood, "is potential evidence for any subject whatever." In a previous work, my co-authors and I tried to show what the world owes to the Amerindians and the Americas* (L'Indien Généreux, *1992). I am not trying here to offer a counterpart to that work. I am simply trying to find the truth.*

□ *See Berger,* A Long and Terrible Shadow: White Values and Native Rights in the Americas since 1492, *in particular, chapter six.*

○ *"England also signed treaties with various groups in the Vancouver region (1850–54) and Ontario (1850–62) that were aimed explicitly at extinguishing the rights of Indians in the Canadian territory. The cession by the Indians of their rights meant the extinction of these rights and impeded them from exercising thereafter any recourse to the government"* (Dupuis, 1991, p. 18).

△ *See Vaugeois,* Québec 1792, *pp. 103, 105.*

Liberality and Ambiguity

It has often been claimed that the Indians distrusted white justice. Perhaps this has always been the case, but some of them nonetheless have not hesitated to seek recourse to it.

From the cases that I have examined, it seems that judges in the "lower courts" have been rather reluctant to accept the innumerable claims that have been presented to them by "treaty Indians." For its part, the Supreme Court went very far with the *Sioui* case. It is certain that its members were aware of this. The jurisprudence that they inherited had come, in large part, from the United States.□ When we consider the powerful American government and its behaviour toward the Indians, it is difficult not to agree that the treaties and laws concerning the Indians should receive a liberal interpretation and that all ambiguity should be settled in their favour. Especially when one admits, with Francis Jennings (1993, p. 312), that "Neither the people nor the government of the United States intended to respect treaty contracts with Indians longer than the Indians could enforce them."

In Canada, history varies from region to region. Thus, the Indians of Ontario were quick to accept the "extinction of their rights to their territory."○ This went so far that John Brant, the youngest of Joseph Brant's sons, elected a representative for Haldimand County (Upper Canada) in 1830, had to give up his seat on the pretext that his fellow-electors were occupying their land without paying the minimum rent required to have the right to vote!△

Finally, we can agree that the opinions of Judge Norris in *White and Bob* or Justice Dickson in the *Simon* case are completely justified. In effect, there is sometimes room for flexibility and liberality. However, in the case underlying the *Simon* case, there in fact exists a document ratified in 1752 by the governor of Nova Scotia, Peregrine Thomas Hopson, and a Micmac chief, Major Jean Baptiste Cope, as well as three other members of "their said Tribe and their Heirs, and the Heirs of their Heirs forever" (SCR, 1985, p. 393). Furthermore, the document is clearly identified as a treaty.

John Brant, 1794-1832

The first question is the following: Can we accept as authentic the document presented in Superior Court by Michel Pouliot on May 18, 1984? As we recall, it was a photocopy – no doubt a photocopy of a copy. It is thus difficult to reach a verdict on the document brought to court by Régent Sioui.

Where did the photocopy come from? Pouliot did not say. Who ordered it made? He was not asked, and he did not say. Since we cannot examine the paper or the ink, we can look at the handwriting. Was it Murray's? It is very unlikely that he wrote out the document produced on September 5, 1760. It may have been the work of Adjutant General John Cosnan, whose name appears on the bottom left. What do we know about this man? Was he Murray's secretary?

Is it possible to establish when the photocopied document was written? With great difficulty, admits an expert, Gilles Durocher of the National Archives. It could be from 1760. There is nothing outstanding about this document, a photocopy of a copy. In fact, its general appearance strongly suggests that it is a retranscribed document.

When he made his ruling, Judge Desjardins noted "the rules of the Canada Evidence Act" and the rules in effect in England. As the original could not be traced, in spite of his insistence, and "in spite of efforts deployed by the appellants to this end," as "the excerpts that were submitted here are not certified by a competent officer," the judge stated that "they do not meet the requirements set out in this matter."□

However . . .

However, the Court declared itself "satisfied with the authenticity of D-7 [a photocopy of a handwritten version of the Murray document] thanks to the testimony of Mr. Armand Therrien, clerk at the Archives du Petit Séminaire de Québec."○ In fact, the judge states, "Mr. Therrien submitted (D-7a), an excerpt of the typed original of D-7. *This original was printed in Halifax in 1760.*"△ On the veracity of the explanations given on this issue, the judge explained, "The printer was set up in Quebec City in 1764 with the publication of the *Gazette de Québec.*"

□ *Desjardins, 1985, p. 15. After noting the rules relating to "evidence for a document," Judge Desjardins (pp. 15–16) wrote, "In addition, the Documentary Evidence Act of 1868, in article 2 (31 and 32 Vict. C. 36, art. 2) states that* prima facie *evidence can be made by a copy of a document certified by the clerk of the Privy Council or by another government officer."*

○ *Ibid., p. 16.*

△ *Author's emphasis. It is obvious that Judge Desjardins was very flexible in his interpretations! D-7 refers to the photocopy submitted by Régent Sioui and D-7a to the printed document kept in the Archives du Séminaire and presented to the Court on May 24, 1984. (This was the entire document, not an excerpt.)*

□ 7c, DCB, vol. 9, pp. 274–76. D-7c seems to have been the photocopy of Georges-Barthélemi Faribault's biography in the *Dictionary of Canadian Biography*. Judge Desjardins felt that D-7 and D-7a were, from all evidence, two versions of a single document; this is correct.

Who had preserved the "printed" copy? From the information obtained, Judge Desjardins understood that "this document (D-7a) comes from the collection of Georges-Barthélemi Faribault, who donated it to the Petit Séminaire de Québec (D-7c). Barthélemi, a merchant and notary, had been appointed clerk of the Parliamentary Archives in 1815. Over the years, he had found and compiled various historical manuscripts, this one among them."□

The judge had another reason for accepting the two "versions" (the photocopy and the printed version): the discovery that he himself had made of a transcription by federal archivist Arthur C. Doughty reproduced in the *Report of the Work of the Archives Branch for the Year 1910* (published in 1912).

Several remarks can be made about the printed version found in the Archives du Petit Séminaire. First of all, we must establish which version, D-7 or D-7a, came first. The judge refers to D-7a as the "typeset original." Strictly, this suggests that the printed version predates the handwritten version; in reality, the judge no doubt used the word "original" as opposed to "photocopy."

Is there any way to establish a chronological order between D-7 (the photocopy) and D-7a (the printed document)? My colleague Gaston Deschênes, a historian and director of Les Éditions du Septentrion, very skilfully found one. Observing the two documents, he was struck by the underlined words in the handwritten version. Some had a single underline, others a double underline, and still others a triple underline. The craft of publishing has some old rules, with codes handed down from generation to generation. A single underline means "italics"; a double underline, "small capitals"; a triple underline, "capitals." And this is exactly what the codes used in the handwritten version correspond to.

The appellant, Régent Sioui, no doubt never learned to mark copy – as this stage in the publisher's work is called – and so he formulated a seductive hypothesis for the Court: if "Chief" and "Huron" were double underlined in the same way as "Brittanick Majesty," it was to indicate a relationship of equals between the two!

Another remark made by Deschênes is that it is very unlikely that someone would have dared to write on an original document. One may reasonably suppose that when the decision was made to print the document of September 5, 1760, a handwritten copy was prepared respecting the original layout or presentation. This is when certain characters were marked for italics, small capitals, or capitals. It is also when changes would have been made – deliberately or not. It is clear that the disappearance of the word "garrisons" and a change to the punctuation originated with this transcription.

What was the purpose of typesetting and printing this document? As Judge Desjardins wrote, the first print shop was established in Quebec City only in 1764.□ Mr. Therrien had suggested that it was printed in 1760. At that time, there were printers in Halifax, Boston, New York, New Jersey, and Philadelphia. Mr. Therrien chose Halifax.○ My research on this was fruitless; I have come to the firm conclusion that in the autumn of 1760 the printer John Bushell did not have the time to print the Murray document.△ And why the rush? Was Murray in a hurry? It is not obvious why he would be. Was it the Hurons? If this were the

□ *Desjardins, 1985, p. 16.*

○ *Why Halifax? Because it is in Canada? New York was no doubt more accessible. We must keep in mind that after September 8, 1760, all of North America was British.*

△ *Or simply had "the heart for the work." Debilitated by alcohol abuse, overwhelmed with debt, Bushell was preparing to form a partnership with his employee, Anthony Henry, in September, 1760. See DCB, vol. 3, pp. 96–97; see also Fauteux,* Introduction of Printing.

◇ *Document D-7 is reproduced on page 92. It can be compared with document D-7a, which is reproduced on pages 79 and 129. It is worth examining the words underlined in D-7 with the characters used in D-7a in the light of the printer's code described by Marius Audin and Gaston Deschênes.*

In *Le Livre* (Robert Morel, 1969), Marius Audin explains (p. 54):
Lower-case roman – that is, noncapital letters . . . is not underlined;
italic, or oblique, lower-case letters are underlined with one line;
roman SMALL CAPITALS, capital letters that are no taller than lower-case roman letters, are underlined with two lines;
CAPITAL LETTERS are underlined with three lines.

In document D-7, "By the Gen^ls command" is underlined with one line to be in italics. In document D-7a, "Chief," "Huron," "Brittanick Majesty," "Lorette," and "John Cosnan" are underlined with two lines. These words are in small capitals in the printed version. "Ja Murray" is underlined with three lines and is in capital letters.◇ It should be mentioned in passing that this is no doubt one of the few treaties in the world that was not signed by one party – the party that gave the order to write it!

MARIUS AUDIN

LE LIVRE

SON ARCHITECTURE
SA TECHNIQUE
PRÉFACE D'HENRI FOCILLON

HAUTE PROVENCE
ROBERT MOREL EDITEUR
LES HAUTES PLAINES DE MANE 04 FORCALQUIER
1969

□ *Desjardins, 1985, p. 17.*

case, they would surely have produced their printed document before 1824.

Print Characters in 1760

My research on Halifax led me to consult documents printed in that city at the time, including a price list published by merchants Nathans & Hart in 1752. To begin with, I wanted to compare the print characters used. For a few days, I read interesting works on the history of typographic characters. Suddenly, something clicked. In 1760, use of the long "s" was still common. But in D-7a, there are no long "s"s. I did not find any studies on the disappearance of the long "s" in typography. But I was able to note for myself the gradual appearance of the short "s" (the one used today), and I asked for observations from colleagues such as Marcelle Cinq-Mars and Jacques Lacoursière, and from archivist Patricia Kennedy of the National Archives. Kennedy contacted an expert at the University of Toronto, Ms. Flemming, who confirmed that the long "s" slowly fell out of use starting in the late eighteenth century.

If document No. 256 of the Faribault collection could not have been printed in 1760, is it possible to clear up the mystery surrounding it? Perhaps. We will return to this.

For the moment, let us return to Judge Desjardins's discovery. "Finally, the undersigned," he wrote, "traced this document [the Murray document] to the National Archives. It is contained in the report that the archivist Arthur G. Doughty submitted to the government in 1912. The document is quoted in its entirety. . . . The court must therefore take judicial cognizance of it and, in virtue of the rules of evidence cited above, the document is *prima facie* evidence."□

The judge then cited an excerpt from Doughty's report in which he mentioned the "certificate granted to the Hurons at Montreal on the 5th of September 1760, three days before the capitulation of Montreal." No doubt pleased that he himself had found a reliable reference for his famous "document," Desjardins did not bother to compare the two texts closely – especially since

Regarding the Letter "s"

In *Le Livre, son architecture, sa technique* (Robert Morel, 1969), Marius Audin relates "how print characters were created, and what they became over time." The evolution of the letter "s" did not draw his attention, but the first typographic examples that he gave show the "s" in the ∫ form *in the beginning or middle of words.* The letter "s" in its current form was found only at the ends of words.

The "Fournier roman" that made a big splash around 1760 was, Audin tells us (pp. 66–67), the subject of two essays: one in the Dutch style and the other rather poetic. In both cases, the ∫ was still present. Among the examples, I noted a text composed in 1797 in characters attributed to the Italian Giambattista Bodoni (ca. 1770): the "s" was in its modern form. He replaced the ∫ within words. But this character did not take hold in France.

Inspired by Bodoni, François-Ambroise Didot designed a new Roman alphabet around 1775 that was greeted with enthusiasm. The use of the "s" spread and replaced the ∫ within words. In 1783, Didot retired, leaving his son, Firmin, to fill his shoes, which he did admirably. From examples that I have found in Audin's book, the long "s" seems to have gradually been abandoned. The French revolution, however, brought an end to this "typographic evolution."

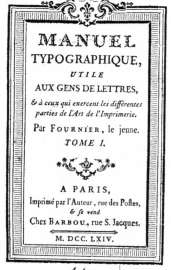

Fournier, for his part, published the *Manuel typographique utile aux gens de lettres.* The excellent library of the government of Quebec has both volumes, which were published in 1764 and 1766. Signed "Fournier, le jeune" (Pierre-Simon Fournier), this work is, of course, impeccably typeset. Out of curiosity, I compared it with the first edition of the *Encyclopaedia Britannica,* which was published from 1768 to 1771. With regard to the use of the long "s", English typography at the time had the same characteristics as French typography: the ∫ was used within words, except for words in capital letters.

I also found two books that discuss specifically the disappearance of the long "s." In *Printing Types: Their History, Forms and Use. A Study in Survivals* (Cambridge: Belknap Press of Harvard University Press, 1966), Daniel Berkeley Updike explained in a footnote (vol. 2, p. 229), "The abolition of the long "s," it is popularly thought, we owe to the London publisher John Bell, who in his British Theatre, issued about 1775, discarded it. Franklin, writing in 1786, says that 'the Round "s" begins to be the Mode and in nice printing the Long "s" is rejected entirely.'" In another note (p. 293), the author states, however, "A statement that John Bell abolished the long 's' in his British Theatre of 1775 is incorrect and should read, 'in his edition of Shakespeare of 1785,' as pointed out in [Stanley] Morison's *John Bell,* pages 105 and 118."

Ronald B. McKerrow was also interested in the evolution of the letter "s." His text was reproduced by Paul A. Bennett in *Books and Printing,* 1991, as "Typographie Debut: Notes on the Long "s" and Other Characters in Early English Printing" (pp. 78–

A meſure que l'expérience a moins de force & que l'on eſt plus ignorant, on voit plus de prodiges mer- veilleux & de belles choſes.

Pierre-Simon Fournier, author of *Manuel typographique*, created this roman typeface around 1762.

82): "From the beginning of printing until towards the end of the eighteenth century 'ſ' was used intitially and medially and 's' finally. . . . In London printing the reform was adopted very rapidly and, save in work of an intentionally antiquarian character, we do not find much use of the 'ſ' in the better kind of printing after 1800. The provincial presses seem, however, to have retained it somewhat longer and it is said to have been used at Oxford until 1824."

Thus, the lower-case "s" evidently was still in the long form within words until the end of the eighteenth century. The short "s" was gradually adopted, in both French and English, starting in the 1780s.

One thing is certain: document D-7a (see p. 79 or 129) could not have been printed in 1760, simply because of the use of the short "s" within words. Thus, in the words in capital letters ("THESE," "MAJESTY," "COSNAN") and at the ends of words ("Indians," "his," "has," "terms," "Canadians," "officers"), the "s" is short, as it should be, but it should have been a long "s" (ſ) in "molest," "customs," "English," and "posts." In my opinion, this typographic use appeared in Lower Canada in the early nineteenth century.

✾✾✾✾✾✾✾✾✾✾✾✾✾✾✾✾✾✾
✾✾✾✾✾✾✾✾✾✾✾✾✾✾✾✾✾✾

EXPLICATION
DES PLANCHES
ET FIGURES
CONTENUES
DANS LE IV. TOME.
PLANCHE XIV.   17

SUPLICES I. Suplice des Eſclaves dans l'Ame-
rique Septentrionale. 2. Suplice des Eſclaves
dans l'Amérique Meridionale. Celui-ci renfer-
me trois differentes actions. D'un côté les femmes
peignent l Eſclave, de l'autre elles peignent le Bou-
ton ou Maſſuë dont il doit être frappé ; dans le milieu eſt repréſentée la manière dont il eſt immolé.
PLANCHE XV.   36
Cette Planche concerne les Ambaſſades & le
Commerce des Sauvages de l'Amérique Septentrionale. Dans le premier ſujet paroît un Sauvage dans
un Conſeil parlant par ſes colliers de porcelaine. Le
collier qu'il tient à la main, eſt repréſenté plus en
grand au bas du ſujet. Le ſecond ſujet eſt une repré-
ſentation de la danſe du Calumet. Au milieu ſur
une natte, ſont le Manitou ou le Génie à l'honneur
duquel ſe fait la danſe, c'eſt un ſerpent, & les armes avec leſquelles on doit combattre. Les ſpec-
tateurs & les Joüeurs d'inſtrumens forment un cer-
cle tout-au-tour dans lequel on voit les deux Com-
battans.   à 2

Excerpt from Lafitau, vol. 4 (1724).

LES hommes corrompent tout, parce qu'ils font eux-mêmes corrompus. Il n'eſt point de crime à qui ils n'aient donné le nom de ver- tu, ni de vertu qu'ils n'aient accuſée de foibleſſe ou de folie ; de ſorte qu'ils ſont capables de louer les plus grands vices, & de con- damner les plus grandes vertus.

Communément c'eſt le préjugé & l'ambition qui dé- terminent le jugement, ra- rement la raiſon.

FIG. 23.

Romain « dans le goût hollandais »
Luce-Fournier, ca. 1750.

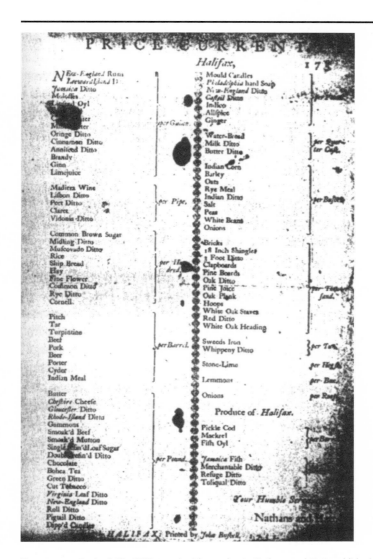

HALIFAX, 1752. On April 13, 1752, two Jewish merchants, Nathans and Hart, published an advertisement in the *Halifax Gazette*. They asked John Bushell, the printer of the newspaper, to prepare a price list. It was one of the first documents to have been printed in Canada.

When placed at the beginning or end of words, the letter "s" is in the short form. Within words, the "s" (or double "s") is in the long form, ſ. Thus, in the second line of the left-hand column, we see "Leeward Iſland"; on the fourth line, "Moloſſes"; farther on, Liſbon, Muſcovado, and so on.

According to Marie Tremaine, the Massachusetts Historical Society has a copy of this document. Here, I used the reproduction presented by R. Arthur Davies in *Printed Jewish Canadiana 1685–1900* (Montreal, 1955).

□ Desjardins, 1985, p. 24.

○ "Printing and transcription produce copies differing in physical details from the original," writes Patricia Kennedy. "The basic principle in tracking treaties should be never to accept texts without question." And, she adds, "Seek the original, but learn to recognize what may be next best." Kennedy, "Treaty Texts: When Can We Trust the Written Word?," in SSHARE - ERASSH, vol. 3, no. 1, 1995.

△ Is this Le Moine's endorsement? Since it is in English, it may have been retranscribed from the document that he had in hand. Otherwise, wouldn't he have made the remark in French, the language in which he was writing? In any case, it indicates that the original was produced before the Court of Sessions of the Peace on January 28, 1804. As we recall, an excerpt of the ruling made on that day was included among the documents submitted to a parliamentary committee on February 18, 1824.

he was preparing to consider D-7 not a treaty (even under the broad interpretation of section 88 of the Indian Act!) but an "act of capitulation"□ that also constituted a "safe-conduct that allowed the Indians to return to Lorette without being molested by English garrisons that they might meet on their way." Under the circumstances, the judge may have felt that he had devoted enough time to the document itself.

Neither Judge Bisson nor Justice Lamer examined the differences between the transcription made by Doughty and the document submitted in Superior Court.○ They took D-7 for a photocopy of an original (that could not be found) and D-7a for a printed version that they did not have to reconsider. It was explained to me that the Court of Appeal did not have to reconsider something that had been ruled on in a court. Does this mean that the fact that Judge Desjardins had recognized that "document D-7 is *prima facie* evidence" settled the question for once and for all? But the question remains: where do documents D-7 and D-7a come from? And are they authentic?

Various Versions of the Murray Document Surface

To my knowledge, the Murray document surfaced at least twice before it was used by Mr. Pouliot on May 18, 1984.

In a systematic search for all documents relating to Murray for the period under consideration, Marcelle Cinq-Mars laid her hands on a historical study on James Murray written by James MacPherson Le Moine and "read in Ottawa on May 23, 1890." "I am indebted," wrote Le Moine, "to General Murray's great-granddaughter, Mrs. Mahon, widow of Colonel Mahon, of engineering, at the Quebec City Garrison in 1864, for the certificate that follows." I have already cited the version given by Le Moine and compared it with Doughty's. I return to it only to indicate that Le Moine, as a dedicated scholar, was good enough to record where his version came from: "The above copied from the original, produced at a special session of the Peace by Vincent of Lorette. Saturday, 28th January 1804."△

On that day, Joseph Vincent had thought to use the Murray document. It perhaps was not very useful before that judge, but it now provides us with valuable information. Even if the document has vanished – recently, it seems – from the pile of papers surrounding Vincent's appearance in court, we still have a transcription that is relatively faithful, since it was made by a meticulous researcher, well respected and with no known interest in the affair.

Aside from the word "garrisons," which is found in Doughty's transcription, we must note the spelling of the name of the adjutant general, John Cosnand. In both Le Moine's and Doughty's versions, this name ends with a "d." But the two versions submitted by Mr. Pouliot bear the name Cosnan, without the final "d." Of course, the handwritten copy, from which the photocopy (D-7) submitted to the court was made, almost certainly could not be the original. I have already explained why. However, since the safe-conduct issued by Murray was for the Hurons, the original was probably given to them. The opposite would be quite surprising – that Murray made an original (for his archives!) and gave a copy to the Hurons.□ I therefore suggest that the original was given to the Hurons and signed by John Cosnand, who had prepared or had someone prepare the "document" to be signed by his superior, James Murray.○

In this perspective, the two main changes that I have noted ("garrisons" and "Cosnand") strongly suggest that D-7 is a transcription made from the original, very probably after 1804.△

Provenance of the Printed Version (D-7a)

The other time that the Murray document surfaced was February 18, 1824, when the Huron chief Stanislas Kotska submitted it to the parliamentary committee headed by Andrew Stuart. Was it the printed document (D-7a) that the parliamentary committee had in hand? Had it been printed at the request of Parliament or by those who decided to present it? Either is possible. In any case, the printed document derives from the marked copy (with the words underlined with single, double, or triple lines), as we have

□ *In this case, one of Cosnand's assistants might have done the work, and so as not to inconvenience his superior (Cosnand) or Murray, he would himself have written "Sign" beside the names John Cosnan [sic] and Ja. Murray. This explanation, however, is unlikely.*

○ *In short, Doughty's version was prepared from the document that Murray had kept with his personal papers, while Le Moine's version was made from the document held by the Hurons, at least until 1804. These two versions correspond on essential points. They have another point in common, Gaston Deschênes observes: both documents used for the transcriptions have disappeared! In effect, in an inventory published in 1985, the National Archives correspondent in Great Britain notes, "The papers have changed hands since the NA's copying. The present owner does not possess the 1759–60 letterbook nor a 1760 Huron Treaty." The National Archives' annual reports are seen as a reliable source by historians, and Murray's journal exists on microfilm. See Appendix B.*

△ *See sidebar on next page.*

seen. Who made the transcription, leaving out the word "garrisons," changing the punctuation, and writing "Cosnan"? Could it have been the priest of Lorette, Abbot Antoine Bédard, or chief Nicolas Vincent's brother Louis, who had a bachelor's degree from Dartmouth College (1781), or Sebastien (or Bastien) Vincent, who studied at Dartmouth at the same time? Perhaps Grand Chief Nicolas Vincent himself? Handwriting comparisons would likely supply an answer.

Various hypotheses could also be formulated as to who printed the document. Around 1820, there were a number of print shops in Quebec City. If the printing had been ordered by the House of Assembly, the work could have been done by John Charlton Fisher, who had become the King's Printer in October, 1823, replacing John Neilson.

Or it might have been printed by Charles Lefrançois, whose presses had been seized on the order of Governor Craig in 1810. Lefrançois had been imprisoned at the same time as the leader of the Parti Canadien, Pierre-Stanislas Bédard. They kept in touch afterward, and Abbot Antoine Bédard, priest of Lorette and Pierre-Stanislas's cousin, was in their circle of friends.□

Document D-7 Dates from after 1804

Other variations in punctuation and the use of capital letters can be discerned. But the presence of the word "garrisons" and the "d" in "Cosnand" enables me to suggest the origins of Doughty's and Le Moine's versions.

"As it is more likely that, when transcribing a document, a word is omitted rather than a word added, it is probable that Murray's copy was written first and then duplicated for the Huron. In doing so, the clerk inadvertently dropped the word 'Garrisons.' It is interesting to note that, in the copy given to the Huron, there is a space between the colon following 'English' and the word 'recommending' although it is not large enough to contain the word 'Garrisons.' In my opinion, the transcribing clerk paused after the word 'English' to refill his pen and then omitted the word 'Garrisons' when he resumed writing. I also note that, in the published version of the treaty, the name of Murray's adjutant, John Cosnan, is misspelled Cosnand." These observations, made by Donald E. Graves (*The Huron of Lorette*, p. 5) are interesting. However, I contend that D-7 was not made in 1760, but dates after 1804.

It is most likely, however, that John Neilson was the printer. As we recall, Andrew Stuart chaired the parliamentary committee formed to hear the Hurons. He was, of course, interested in the presentation of their position and carefully documented it himself. In 1824, Stuart wrote to his friend Neilson to report what had been said in Lorette and requesting "that an hundred Copies of the Lorette Indian Report should be printed." He added, "It is more an introduction to our friend Siouis [*sic*] speech whereof also I send you a copy."□ Many of Neilson's papers are difficult to read, and the parts that are legible, in this case, tell us little more than has already been said. That is, that in 1824, Stuart asked Neilson to print documents relating to the Hurons.

□ *Part of John Neilson's correspondence is preserved at the National Archives in file MG 24, B1. The text quoted here comes from volume 4. The year 1824 is clearly indicated; a stain makes it impossible to identify the month.*

○ *This mission was in part directed against Governor Dalhousie, who then withdrew Neilson's commission as King's Printer! In 1822, the Parti Canadien was fighting against a plan to unite the two Canadas. Petitions by various proponents proliferated, denouncing "the mistaken opinion ... that Canadians of French extraction must remain a distinct people, and that they have a right to be seen as a nation" (DCB, vol. 4, p. 132). The British of Lower Canada (Quebec) no longer wanted to be ruled by a House of Assembly composed of a French-Canadian majority. Governor Dalhousie supported the union plan, which became reality in 1840.*

Not only did Stuart and Neilson have open minds and a sincere interest in the Hurons' claims – of this I am certain – but they had real-estate interests around Lorette. Since about 1816, Neilson had been settling immigrants in the Valcartier region. He obtained lots "from the Jesuits' assets," of which Jeune-Lorette was a part. With Andrew Stuart, he had acquired numerous land concessions.

Neilson accompanied Louis-Joseph Papineau to London in 1823.○ Obviously, this trip was personally satisfying, and he easily convinced his friend, Andrew Stuart, to visit Europe too. In November, 1824, Stuart arrived in Paris, from where he asked Neilson, "knowing your friendly feelings towards the Huron Indians Settled at Lorette," to give them the latest news. Neilson recalled that before his departure, Vallières de Saint-Réal, who had become chairman of the House of Assembly in Papineau's absence, had promised him to prepare a petition from the Hurons for presentation to the king. He had "one copy enclosed to Lieut.-Gov. [in the absence of Dalhousie, who was travelling in England], with a request" that it be sent to the king, he said, keeping another copy for him.

Stuart arranged a trip to London for his Huron friends. They arrived in Liverpool on December 15, 1824, were received by the king on April 7, 1825, and left again for Canada on August 1, 1825.

Andrew Stuart

Huron Chiefs in London

Left to right: Michel Tsioui, Stanislas Kotska, and André Romain. The three Huron chiefs proudly wear earrings, armbands, bracelets, and medals.

In 1823, Louis-Joseph Papineau, leader of the House of Assembly, and John Nielson, representative of Quebec City, were sent to London to protest against the plan to unite the two Canadas, proposed several months before.

More than two years later, four Huron chiefs from Lorette went to England to make their objections known.

During their stay in England, the Huron chiefs posed for the painter Edward Chatfield. A first canvas portrayed Grand Chief Nicolas Vincent (Tsaouenhohoui) holding a wampum belt. The second portrayed Michel Tsioui (Téhatsiendahé), war chief; Stanislas Kotska (Aharathanha); and André Romain (Tsohahissen), council chief.

Both paintings were lithographically reproduced. They were printed in London in 1825 by Charles Hullmandel.

A number of letters, preserved in the Neilson Fund (National Archives, MG 24), give a good idea of the four chiefs' trip to London.

Andrew Stuart had gone first, certainly influenced by Neilson. From London, he went to Paris, arriving in November, 1824.

In a letter dated January 4, 1825, Vincent wrote to people in Lorette, "We landed December 15 at Leverpool *[sic]*." Welcomed by the mayor, they then travelled to London: "Our coach was pulled by four horses that went very fast," the Grand Chief wrote. "On our way, we changed horses so we wouldn't be slowed down. . . . At present, we are in the Capital City of England. His Majesty is absent. He is seven leagues from here. His Majesty will return in one month. The Lords of his council are also absent. One of these ministers [named] Bathurst will be back in 15 days. But our trusted Mr. Stuart is still in France. We have written to him."

Well lodged, well dressed, Vincent assured his people: "We shall advance our business as soon as possible." "We send our compliments to the chiefs," he wrote in ending, "to the Warriors, the Women, and all the people of our village. We hope that you are doing as well as I am."

Weeks passed, and Stuart was still away, "which annoys the Poor Fellows very much." The response of Lord Bathurst,

Nicolas Vincent, ca.1825

secretary of state for the colonies, was sent to him in Paris: no right to the Sillery seigniory was recognized for the Hurons. As well, the under-secretary of state, Wilmot Horton, added, "His Lordship cannot but regret that the Indians should have been encouraged to come to this Country on a Mission which has occasioned much inconvenience and expense and excited hopes which it must have been known could not be realized."

King George IV agreed, anyway, to receive the four chiefs in early April, and he gave each a "superb gold medal." On August 19, they left for Canada on the *Caledonia*.

Had it been a useless mission? John Neilson denied this in a letter of October, 1825, to John Butterworth, a London philanthropist who had hosted the chiefs. While thanking him for this, Neilson regretted Horton's letter in which the right-hand man of Lord Bathurst blamed Papineau and Neilson for having encouraged the Indians to "come to this country."

Neilson, a major property owner in Valcartier with Andrew Stuart, was long faithful to the cause of his neighbours, the Hurons of Lorette.

□ It would be reassuring to be able to verify whether the publisher of the Report of the Work of the Archives Branch for the Year 1910 (published in 1912) made any errors. The handwritten transcription made by Doughty during his trip cannot be found, nor can the one that his staff is supposed to have prepared in the following months, and the staff at the Archives is unable to explain its absence.

○ After threatening "vangéance Sanglante" (bloody vengeance) on French Canadians who took "recourse to arms," Murray added, on July 13, 1760, "Wise Colonists, on the Contrary, who, profiting from past Experience, remain calmly at home, enjoying their Religion, their Property, and, Under the Auspices of a Prince, Father of his country, Sustained and Protected by an Arm so Powerful, will become Rich and prosperous" (RCA, 1918, p. 13). The threat was written in French.

It is difficult to find people as influential as Stuart, Neilson, and Vallières de Saint-Réal who were more committed to the Hurons' cause at the time. Did the Hurons take the Murray document with them to England? There is no allusion to this at all, as we will see.

For the moment, I will return one last time to the various versions of the Murray document, and I will use the transcription prepared by Doughty and published in the *Report of the Work of the Archives Branch for the Year 1910.*□

Murray's Intentions

Now that the most legitimate version of the Murray document has been identified beyond all reasonable doubt, we can investigate what its author meant by it.

"These are to certify" is a formula that does not indicate a treaty, with all due respect to Judge Bisson. In the words "Il est venu à moi" (he came to me) and "il a été reçu sous ma protection" (he was received under my protection), Murray gives his personal commitment. His adjutant specifies that the document was prepared "by the General's Command," although this leaves a slight ambiguity. But the word "command" is unequivocal: it was an order! And the document itself was an order to English officers and soldiers not to molest the Hurons on their way home and to treat them fairly. Finally, only the British party signed the document, while the chief and his tribe are referred to in the third person plural.

As well, the term "under the same conditions as the Canadians" adds an important element. To be precise, and no doubt to reassure the Hurons, Murray told them that they would be able "freely to exercise their religion [obviously, the Catholic religion], their customs," and to enjoy "liberty of trading with the English garrisons." In a manifesto inviting French Canadians to surrender, Murray used essentially the same words.○

The expressions "liberty of trading with the English" and "liberty of trading with the English garrisons" are, of course, not completely synonymous. In any case, it is well established that trade with the Indians was tightly controlled after 1760; traders had to obtain permits for the purpose. The Indians themselves were also controlled. The misadventure of Athanase La Plague, "Christian Huron savage of the mission of Jeune-Lorette," illustrates this well.

□ *SCR, 1990, p. 1071.*

In March, 1762, La Plague asked Murray for permission "to trade." The governor's secretary gave him "a permit or passport . . . for going to trade wherever he wants." La Plague made the mistake of trading with the agent in Chicoutimi, a reserved territory. Indignant, Murray withdrew his permit. The incident is significant. It was the subject of a sworn deposition in Quebec City on December 19, 1765 (reproduced in its entirety in Appendix G).

What can we add? "Liberty of trading" meant access to permits, certainly not the possibility of doing without one.

Finally, there is the word "customs," which has a specific significance. The Canadiens had theirs. After 150 years of common history, French Canadians and their Indian allies shared a few, including, of course, hunting and fishing. In 1760, the Canadiens and Indians resembled each other in quite a few ways.

In talking of "customs," was Murray thinking of permitting the exercise of customs that might contravene the laws and regulations that he and his successors might edict? Justice Lamer seems to have answered this question.□ Over the longer term, Murray, who was involved in a process of conquest, was there to open, not close, the many doors to the future. He knew very well that the Indian question was not under his jurisdiction. For several days, he had been issuing certificates of protection to Canadiens. He wrote one more for the Hurons, his neighbours of the previous winter in Quebec City. He accepted their surrender as he had accepted those of the Canadiens – and under the same conditions, as he took care to note.

From the Meeting of September 5 to the Conference of September 15–16

Could a historian consider the Murray document a treaty? Certainly not. In *The Invasion of America*, Francis Jennings explains

□ Judge Bisson dwells on the words "the free exercise of their religion, their customs, and liberty of trading with the English." The last words are decisive, he writes: "A simple safe-conduct for several days for the trip from Longueuil to Lorette would not require talk of religion and customs" (RJQ, 1987, p. 1727). Justice Lamer says more or less the same thing (SCR, 1990, p. 1048). This remark is absolutely valid. But, as I have noted, Murray repeatedly told the Canadiens that if they surrendered, "they would enjoy their religion, their possessions" and become "wealthy" – thanks, no doubt, to trade.

○ Documents Relating to the Constitutional History of Canada, vol. 1, p. 73.

△ In his ruling (SCR, 1990, p. 1058), Justice Lamer quotes an excerpt from Knox's journal, in which he says to a Mohawk, "Let the treaty be as it will." Since the Mohawks had arrived at Oswegatchie with a letter from Amherst, they could very well have been alluding to the peace negotiations begun on August 30, which resulted in a treaty as circumstances permitted. Justice Lamer (p. 1060) himself suggests that the conference of September 16, 1760, could be a "solemn ratification of the peace agreement concluded a few days earlier." Since he was unaware of the meeting at Oswegatchie, he could refer only to the meeting of September 5, 1760.

the influence that the Indians had on the ritual, or protocol, of treaties concluded between Aboriginals and Europeans, as does Marcel Trudel in the document cited above. On this point, there is no ambiguity.□

Finally, without being truly a treaty, could the Murray document have the *value of a treaty*? The Hurons of Lorette never cited it as such in their innumerable petitions. According to my information, they did not do so in their meeting with the king.

Murray himself would have mentioned it somewhere after 1760. In fact, would he not have done so in his major report concerning the government of Quebec City dated June 5, 1762, in particular when he discussed "the savage tribes residing within the limits of this government"? In order to "make them retain that [language] and as much of their ancient customs as possible, that they might prove of greater use to them in case of war with other nations, at the same time they endeavour'd to attach them to their Interest by every tie. . . . They seem to be well satisfied with the change of Masters," he adds.○ If he had concluded a specific treaty with them, wouldn't he, in all honesty, have reported it?

What is more, could the Murray document be a treaty in the sense of article 88 of the Indian Act? What does this section say? "Subject to the terms of any treaty . . . all laws of general application from time to time in force in any province are applicable to and in respect of Indians in the province." This formulation does not suggest the creation of new treaties.

As well, the Hurons of Lorette, like all Canadian Indians under the "Federation of Seven Fires," also called the Eight Nations, in fact had their treaty.

The meeting of September 15–16, 1760, in Caughnawaga has all of these characteristics.△ No official document has survived, but one of the agents present, Daniel Claus, recorded the essential points. This text was recently found – within the journal of another of William Johnson's agents, Jelles Fonda, who had accompanied Johnson to Montreal in August and September, 1760.

"A Conference lasted at least two days," Jennings wrote. "Indian custom ordinarily dictated that no proposition should get

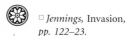

□ *Jennings,* Invasion, *pp. 122–23.*

Jelles Fonda's Journal

Jelles Fonda's journal is preserved in the archives of the New York Historical Society. It is a notebook measuring four by six inches with a marbled cover. Within the journal is an account of a conference that was said, according to various sources, to end on September 16, 1760, in Caughnawaga. The publisher of the *Johnson Papers* attributes the handwriting in the notebook to Daniel Claus, in which case it may have been transcribed by Fonda on the first available page of his journal. Apparently, Fonda was in the region of "Swegatia" in mid-August. He seems to have been in direct contact with the Indians for "discovery" missions. He did not write in his journal from August 24 to September 8. In mid-September, he was in the Oswego region, having recently returned from some business. He was one of William Johnson's agents.

a response on the same day it was offered. By the end of a successful treaty conference, the parties had made a contract that existed in two forms, wampum belts and treaty minutes."□ From what we know of it, the Caughnawaga meeting must have fulfilled these conditions. What has been preserved strongly suggests this.

Thus, the French and Indian War ended for both the Indians and the French. The latter surrendered twice: in Quebec City in 1759 and in Montreal the following year. Their Indian allies had put down their arms in Oswegatchie, Les Cèdres, and Longueuil. They solemnly concluded their treaty in Caughnawaga on September 15–16, 1760, with the interlocutor designated for this purpose by the British authorities, William Johnson, their brother Warraghiyagey.

An Account Written by Fonda

The document above shows two documents of different formats that are attached to each other. This item is identified as the journal of Jelles Fonda. In fact, the journal covers only certain periods in the summer and fall of 1760. It suddenly is interrupted to make room for a long account titled *Speeches of Warriors*, the text of which can be found in Appendix D.

The journal itself has entries from June 29 to August 10, 1760, then from August 10 to September 27, 1760. At the end of the document are several notes recording various transactions.

Comparing the letters attributed to Jelles Fonda (including one of July 9, 1769, reproduced on the facing page) with the journal, it is obvious that it is the same handwriting.

Where was Fonda on September 16, 1760? We do not know, and his journal does not tell us. For the moment, we have only the account transcribed in Fonda's journal to tell us about the conference at Caughna-

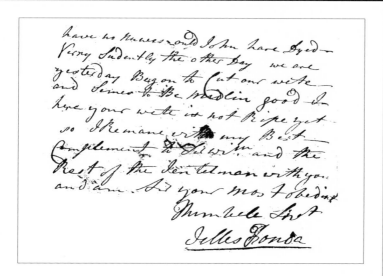

waga. We cannot doubt that this conference took place, even though the dates of September 15 and 16 remain hypothetical, in my opinion.

The staff in the manuscript division of the New York Historical Society has made a transcription of Fonda's journal available to researchers. It is forbidden to photocopy this document or to photograph it using a flash. I used a camera with a special film to obtain the result here.

Epilogue

Oswegatchie, Longueuil, and Caughnawaga

On trial before Judge Bruno Cyr of the Court of Quebec for organizing a bingo game without a permit on or around September 23, 1989, the Mohawks of Kanesatake invoked the *Sioui* ruling of May 24, 1990, in which the Supreme Court gave the value of a treaty to the document of September 5, 1760, given in James Murray's name to the Hurons of Lorette.

How could the Mohawks of Kanesatake claim, in 1992, that this "treaty" also affected them? Given the ruling of the Supreme Court and the opinion of historian Marcel Trudel, for whom the claimed treaty was nothing but a safe-conduct, the Crown, at the time the prosecution, wondered "if there exist two truths with regard to this document [of September 5, 1760]: one juridical, the other historical." □

Justice Lamer had not really declared that the text of the document of September 5, 1760, was a treaty. In one sense, he was no doubt in agreement with Marcel Trudel and most of the historians – that is, with the "historical truth."

But he had to make his ruling in accordance with the Indian Act. Within his reconstruction of the historical context, he accorded the document the value of a treaty in the sense of section 88 of that act.

□ *Cyr, 1992, p. 8. Translation.*

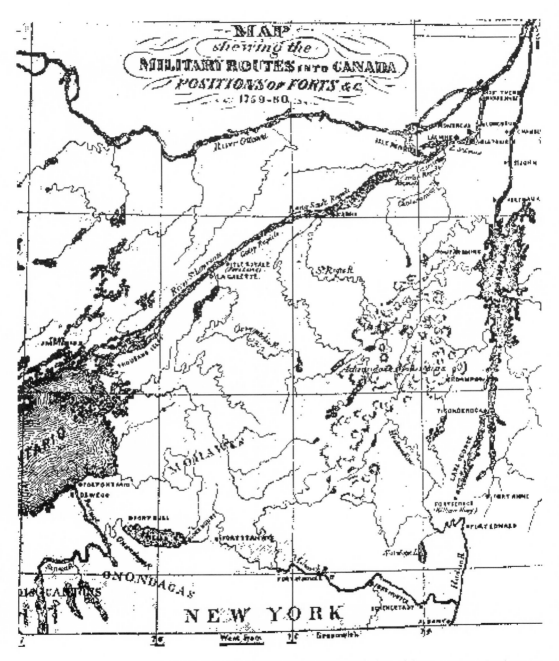

The mouth of the Oswegatchie River is on the south shore of the St. Lawrence River between Lake Ontario and Montreal. The Oswegatchie Indian mission, founded by the Sulpician François Picquet in 1748–49, and Fort La Présentation sat side by side. The place was also called La Galette. A little farther toward Montreal is Isle Royale, on which Fort Lévis was built.

The Sault-Saint-Louis mission at the time of the English victory.

Detail of a painting by Thomas Davies called *A View of Montreal Taken from the Isle St. Helena, 1762*. The artist liked to place Indians in his canvases. Here, they are peacefully paddling canoes.

The small fort known as La Présentation sat on the point of land at the mouth of the Oswegatchie River.

□ Could the Supreme Court re-establish the more reliable version of the "Murray treaty"?

○ Longueuil followed Oswegatchie but preceded Caughnawaga.

△ See pp. 58–60 and the note at p. 60.

What exactly did the Murray document say? In this regard, Justice Lamer was no doubt ready to accept the version of the archivist Arthur G. Doughty. Was there a way for the Supreme Court to make clarifications to the *Sioui* ruling and use them to keep the more faithful version of that document?□ Otherwise, what would courts do when they have to rule on the scope of the "Murray treaty"? Would they use the text accepted by the Supreme Court or the transcription prepared by the archivist of the Dominion, who had convinced Judge Desjardins to accept document D-7?

In fact, other cases should have enabled the Supreme Court to place the meeting of September 5, 1760, in a perspective that encompassed the conference at Oswegatchie on the preceding August 30 and the meeting at Caughnawaga on the following September 15–16.

The Hurons' agreeing to a peace on September 5 was not an isolated incident.○ And they were not the only ones at Longueuil. Who were the Iroquois that Murray mentioned? Might they have been the ancestors of the Mohawks of Kanesatake and Akwesasne?

In fact, we must not discount too quickly the differences between Murray's journal and Knox's.△ If we read the texts of these two men very carefully, we might advance the hypothesis that there were two meetings between the Indians and Murray. In one, Murray was with "two nations of Indians, of Hurons and Iroquois," who "entered and made peace." "At the same moment, three of Sir William Johnson's Indians entered bearing a letter from General Amherst, to which," Murray noted, "I must respond immediately." This was on the 5th.

For his part, Knox reported that between the 5th and the 7th, "Eight Sachems of different nations who had been until recently allied with the enemy came to General Murray in their own names and those of their tribes." What day was this? Knox talks of the taking of Fort Chambly by Haviland, specifying that, the previous evening, his advance guard had arrived at Longueuil. Had the "eight Sachems" met with Murray on the 5th or the 6th? Why not the 6th? On the 5th, "two nations" would have come, and on the 6th, eight nations. This number, eight, makes sense. In Caughnawaga, on September 15–16, the representatives of eight nations met with Johnson.

"While these chiefs were negotiating a peace, two of our Mohawks entered the room, where they found themselves with the general and Colonel Burton." The Indians stared at each other and exchanged insults and threats. It was during this scene that one Mohawk retorted, "Let the treaty be as it will."

On the 5th, Murray made no allusion at all to this set-to or to the fistfight that had threatened to break out.

In short, one might propose the hypothesis that there were two successive "negotiations." Knox's statements leave no doubt about the change of mind of the eight Sachems. "These people, having held discussions with His Excellency, and after all the questions were settled to their satisfaction, went to the shore opposite Montreal, brandished their knives and hatchets, and shouted their war cry, indicating to the French that they were now our allies and their enemies."□

Vaudreuil, who had withdrawn to Montreal, realized that the cause was lost. On the 7th, he attempted to gain some time. Amherst proved to be intractable. He refused certain terms of the proposed surrender. "The English General," Vaudreuil demanded in article 9, "engages to send home the Indian Savages and Moraigans that are part of his army, first, after the signature of the present surrender, and however to prevent all disturbances by those who have not left, the general will give Safe-Guards to those who ask for them, both in the town and in the countryside."

Insulted, Amherst retorted, "The first refused. There have been no cruelties committed by the Savages in our army; and good order will be maintained."

However, he did accept the first part of article 40, which had it that "the Savages or Indians allied with his Very Christian Majesty [the king of France] will be maintained in the lands where they live, if they wish to stay there; they cannot be disturbed under any pretext whatsoever, for having taken up arms and served His Very Christian Majesty." The second part of the article dealt with missionaries.

□ *In my opinion, eight nations were involved in the surrender at Longueuil.*

□ *Johnson assigned his assistant and future son-in-law, Daniel Claus, to see to the "Indians resident" around Montreal, Trois-Rivières, and Quebec City. Claus's responsibility was to make the British respect their agreements with their new Indian allies.*

In article 51, Vaudreuil restated his anxiety about the presence of Indians "after the surrender" of Montreal. "We will take care that the Savages insult none of the subjects of His Very Christian Majesty," Amherst responded.

On September 15 and 16, Johnson brought his Indians together at Caughnawaga. The Six Nations' Covenant Chain met the Eight Nations of the St. Lawrence Valley.

In Oswegatchie, the objective had been to convince the Indians to join the enemy. In exchange for their neutrality, the latter could count on "all the protection that they could wish for," Amherst wrote to Johnson. "We can answer them that they will be allowed to live in peace and tranquillity."

The Indians allied with the French no longer wanted to fight. Had this war been their war alone? The French had tried to convince them that the English wanted them eliminated. As he was leaving Oswego for Montreal via the upper St. Lawrence, Johnson had had a meeting with them. The meeting took place near Fort Lévis. The representatives of the "nine different Indian nations and tribes living in the country around Montreal, bringing together more than 800 warriors," were convinced by his arguments. In exchange for their neutrality, he indicated to minister William Pitt, it had been agreed that "in the future we will treat them as friends and forget all past hostility."

In short, the British had not made specific commitments, as would be evident after the surrender of Montreal.

On September 15, 1760, according to their tradition, the Indians began their negotiations. The next day, they summarized and concluded them. Daniel Claus took notes.□ They were found transcribed into the journal of Jelles Fonda, William Johnson's other assistant.

For a long time, researchers did not know about this document. It even escaped the purview of Francis Jennings, that most thorough historian of the Iroquois. The original is neither in Johnson's papers nor in Daniel Claus's. In 1962, the publishers of the *Johnson Papers* published a thirteenth volume in which the historian Milton W. Hamilton brought together documents that had been left out of previous collections. For the first time, a summary of the meeting of September 16, 1760, was brought to the attention of the experts. It took some time for them to focus on it.□

□ *See Appendix D for the minutes of the meeting on September 16, 1760.*

○ *SCR, 1990, p. 1050.*

Justice Lamer had it in his possession thanks to the National Brotherhood/Assembly of First Nations.○ He had an inkling of its importance, but was not able to accord it all the attention it deserved.

First of all, there are still points to elucidate with regard to the authenticity of this document. The proposed transcription must be verified. Was the document made in Caughnawaga or Montreal? Is the addition of the word "Albany" appropriate? Once these points and others are clarified, the minutes must still be interpreted. In the appendix, I offer some explanatory notes. Here, I shall mention the following points.

Addressing William Johnson, an Indian speaker thanks him for the message that he had sent from Oswego. His appeal for neutrality had been well understood. It was for this reason that this meeting was taking place.

Turning toward the representatives of the Six Nations who had decided at Oswegatchie to follow Johnson to Montreal (in spite of Amherst's attitude at Fort Lévis), he told them that he was happy they were present.

This introduction places the meeting in context very well. The known elements are in place. Everything fits.

Then, returning to the talks held the previous day, the speaker thanks Johnson for having proposed to renew and strengthen the old Covenant Chain, also "for opening the Road from this to your Country." The speaker continued, "We, for our part, assure you to keep it clear of any Obstacle & use it in a friendly Manner."

On whose behalf was this person speaking? "We who are present here as Representatives of 8 Nations," he specified, ". . . will bury the French hatchet we have made use of . . . never to be Seen more by us or our Posterity."

Now that friendship was re-established between the Six Nations and the Eight Nations, it was necessary to verify "ye good-

□ *On September 22,
Amherst ordered "his"
Indians to go home. As
most had already left, only
a few accompanied
Johnson home to the
Mohawk Valley.*

○ *Johnson Papers, vol. 3,
p. 376.*

ness of the Road" and to have "some of every Nation" accompany Johnson on the road back. Here, the style is metaphoric. No doubt, the Eight Nations wanted both to be recognized as allies and, why not, to profit from Johnson's usual generosity.□

The new friends of "Brother Warraghiyagey" had a few special demands. They urgently requested the British to ban the sale and distribution of liquor among their people, asked for blacksmiths to be sent, pleaded for the support of their priests, and "also beg[ged] that you will regulate Trade" so that they would not be exploited.

When the conference reached its close, Ad'yadarouy – one of the chiefs of Caughnawaga – intervened to return to the question of alcohol and the possible discrepancies. He also demanded a new interpreter and, prudently, insisted on "the peaceable Possession of ye Spot of Ground we now live upon, and in case we should remove from it, to reserve to us as our own."

A large necklace of black wampum was given to mark the end of the meeting.

In my opinion, the Caughnawaga meeting summarized the conditions of the peace concluded between the Eight Nations and the British at the end of the Seven Years' War, the last "French and Indian War."

In the following months, Daniel Claus had to intervene so that the Indians of Caughnawaga would not be evicted from the Montreal–Albany route. The new governor of Montreal, Thomas Gage, was reluctant to give the Indians the passes they wanted for the route from Lake Champlain. Although he was concerned with supporting trade between Montreal and Albany, he mistrusted the Indians, who, according to him, were interested only in contraband.○

On February 26, 1761, Claus complained to Johnson about the attitude of Gage, "a perfect stranger to the transactions and engagements that you concluded with the Indians of Canada last autumn." "I think," Claus added, "that if I showed him a copy, he would perhaps not be so strict with them, but would treat them in a friendlier manner; also, I want a copy of said minutes in order

Thomas Gage

to remind the Indians here of what was negotiated, and if strangers were to come, to keep them apprised of the mutual engagements concluded."□

On April 9, 1761, Claus returned to this subject. Gage had refused to give passes to the Indians of Caughnawaga, who complained that the route to Albany, "opened and shown to them last Fall," seemed to be closed once again.

On May 1, Johnson reassured Claus. "I am surprised that General Gage does not allow the Cughnawageys and other Indians living there to come to Albany after having made this one of the articles of the treaty last summer in Caghnawagey. . . . I wrote to General Amherst on this subject."

Claus had made his point. "Whatever promises have been Made," Amherst responded on May 7, "they Shall be Strickly [adhered] to, and So long as they [the Indians] behave well, they Shall have full Liberty for a free and Open trade."

Having received this reassurance for his Indians, Claus was not so reassured when it came to affairs of the heart. Johnson was stunned to learn that his assistant was courting one of his daughters. This man of relatively free morals jealously watched over his children's love lives. Claus ended up winning this point, too. After overcoming the reticence of his boss, he married Nancy Johnson, daughter of William Johnson and Catherine Weissenberg, on April 13, 1762. Although he moved to comfortable quarters near Albany, Claus remained responsible for the Indians of the "Province of Quebec," the new British colony created in 1763.

Claus was thus responsible for the Hurons of Lorette, who had various complaints. On Wednesday, July 28, 1773, he noted in his diary the terms of a long response that he had made to them.○ Recalling that the Hurons had left the Lake Huron region to come and live "among the Whites in Canada," Claus could not say if this change had "proved for the better or the worse." All that he could say on the subject was "whenever a Nation or people quit their Native country in order to settle & abide in any other Nation or Government . . . it is reasonably supposed & expected that

□ *Ibid., p. 348.*
○ *See Appendix H for excerpts.*

Daniel Claus

Nancy Johnson Claus

they are to submit & conform themselves to the Laws Forms & Customs of that Nation or Government."

The meeting of July, 1773, was solemn. The Hurons had presented their demands the previous Monday. Claus accompanied his response with exchanges of belts. He was emphatic. Once, he told the Hurons, this country was governed by the French, but as Providence had ordained the victory of the British army, they could not now have the least objection to conforming to English laws.□

Did Claus know about Murray's safe-conduct? Probably not, and no one thought of taking recourse to it. In any case, Murray had been very clear: "They [the Hurons] are received upon the same terms with the Canadians," he had written. "You must obey the same laws as everyone else," the man in charge of Indian affairs told them. And he was very clear on this subject.

Claus was also charged with territorial claims of the "few surviving Descendants of the Hurons." "As to the White people intermarried with you," he added, "it never was the Intention of the Missionaries to allow them equal Priviledges with the Indians." Later, he insisted, what would be done concerned "only the Indians" of the village, not the "Whites."

In any case, neither the Hurons nor the other Indians of the Eight Nations of Canada had much to say after 1763. With the French defeat, they lost much of their negotiating power. They found themselves, wrote Olive Patricia Dickason, deprived of "their traditional position of negotiation between two rival powers."

Traders rapidly raised their prices – to compensate for losses suffered during the war – and invaded Indian territory. Encouraged by the Canadiens who were still in the Great Lakes region, the Indians revolted, led by Pontiac. The Indians of the "Province of Quebec," for their part, were hesitant to do battle with their brothers.

The American revolution raised the Indians' status temporarily, as both the British and the Americans courted them. Later, they saw another moment of hope with the War of 1812, but after this, nothing.

PRÆVALEBIT ÆQUIOR.

Woodcut from 1758 showing an Indian being solicited by an Englishman and a Frenchman.

The English helped themselves to the land. From 1815 to 1825, the Indians of Canada signed nine treaties, signing away almost all of the peninsula between lakes Ontario, Erie, and Huron. The government paid half or a third of what the land was worth – or less.□

This panoply of treaties leads us to section 88 of the Indian Act:

> Subject to the terms of any treaty and any other Act of Parliament, all laws of general application from time to time in force in any province are applicable to and in respect of Indians in the province,

□ *Olive P. Dickason,* Canada's First Nations, *1992, p. 189.*

This engraving is said to portray the British general John Burgoyne trying to convince his Indian allies to remain loyal to the Crown (1777).

except to the extent that those laws are inconsistent with this Act or any order, rule, regulation or by-law made thereunder, and except to the extent that those laws make provision for any matter for which provision is made by or under this Act.

In other words, provincial laws are applicable to Indians unless they go counter to a provision of the Indian Act, another federal law, or a treaty.

It appears that section 88 protects the Indians against the nasty provinces. But it also confirms the validity of treaties, including those that involve a cession of land. As a consequence, Ontario has no problems, while Quebec has nothing but problems. And the problems get bigger if the Oswegatchie meeting or Murray's safe-conduct have the value of a treaty.□

The Indians of Akwesasne who met in Caughnawaga on August 21, 1769, were quite precise. They recalled the meeting in Oswegatchie in August, 1760, between William Johnson and representatives of the confederated Seven Nations of Canada. Commitments had been made, including for the peaceful and tranquil possession of the land on which the Indians lived, as well as for the freedom to practise the religion they had been taught. Fine. They also recalled that after the surrender of Montreal, these preliminary engagements had been confirmed and ratified at Caughnawaga. Fine. Except, this time, there was a two-day conference, and there is a record of what transpired.

* * *

If the end of the "French and Indian Wars" was quite a catastrophe for the Indians, the recent intensification of federal–provincial disputes has been a windfall, as Aboriginal leaders have well understood. They led Prime Minister Pierre Elliott Trudeau to renounce his traditional positions on the Aboriginal question and accord them an important place in the Constitution Act, 1982, (sections 25, 35, and 37). Later, these leaders strongly influenced the formulation of the proposed Charlottetown accord.

The federal strategists, for their part, decided to play the Aboriginal card. On the international scene, of course, but also domestically. "Political discourse is never innocent."○

From the little wars of yesteryear, the Natives have escalated to judicial guerrilla warfare. Unbelievable sums have been sunk into ridiculous cases. The "Murray treaty" made some people a fortune. Will it do the same for others? And will the treaties of Oswegatchie and Caughnawaga be next? What was the scope of British commitments to the Indians? And in exchange for what were these commitments made? What did Amherst mean by "as [long as] they [the Indians] behave Well"?

□ *Just as they imposed their ritual, the Indians also imposed their emphatic style. If several thousand people are sufficient to constitute a nation, a verbal agreement can very well become a treaty. A piece of paper is no longer necessary – nor, of course, are signatures. Simply the memory of a peace agreement can be evoked as a treaty. Of course, many of these "treaties" became fertilizer. Others were quickly forgotten and had to be revived. Sometimes, they were violated and reformulated, accompanied by new exchanges of gifts. There is thus a wide range of treaties.*

○ *Desbiens,* Comment, *p. 25.*

Conclusion

Quebecers had the impression that relations with the Indians were in fine shape. After all, there had been more than 450 years of common history since the meeting between Chief Donnacona and Jacques Cartier in July, 1534. In ensuing times, innumerable intermarriages had diluted the Indians' blood and Canadianized the French.

Of course, the Indians on the reservations were not very fond of being treated like "damned savages," and for a long time the Canadiens, evolved into Québécois, did not trumpet their Indian blood, or even recognize the cultural contribution of the Aboriginal peoples.

Over time, the history books were amended; the term "savage," in its first, somehow attractive sense, was abandoned. Quebecers even came to identify proudly the Indian ancestors that they found within or just outside of their family trees.

Many found the arrangements linked to the James Bay and Northern Quebec Agreement, involving the Cree and Inuit of Quebec (1975), a bit expensive, but they resigned themselves to the agreement without protest. They accepted the supplementary agreement of 1978, this one involving the Naskapis. Premier René Lévesque had extended his hand to the Aboriginals of Quebec, he was open and attentive, and no one took offence.

The some sixty thousand "registered Indians" in Quebec had their share of problems, but when they compared themselves to their brethren in other provinces, they found nothing to envy. In every way, on every level, their situation was better: inferior to that of other Quebecers, but still preferable to those of "registered Indians" living in the rest of Canada. Protection of Native languages, average income, housing, social problems – all indicators led then, and still lead now, to similar conclusions.

In the early 1980s, observers with a finger to the wind sensed a gathering storm. Mr. Lévesque and his faithful collaborator, Éric Gourdeau, were to serve as lightning rods. In London, the delegate general for Quebec put himself at the disposal of the Aboriginals at the very time when major manoeuvres were afoot to repatriate the Canadian constitution. Like most Quebecers from outlying regions – Abitibi, Mauricie, Saguenay-Lac-Saint-Jean, the North Shore, the Gaspé – Gilles Loiselle was at ease with the Indians, who reminded him of his hunting companions, his partners in adventure, his schoolmates.

Slowly but surely after 1985 the conditions were created for great misfortune to befall Quebec.

The clouds burst during the summer of 1990. In May, the Supreme Court issued a series of rulings in favour of the Indians. On June 22, 1990, the Meech Lake Accord died, thanks mainly to an Indian, Elijah Harper. The Quebec *indépendantistes* were almost grateful to him for having helped to illustrate the impasse in which the 1982 Constitution placed Quebec. But many also wondered where the rumbling revolt among the Indians, who, ironically, were pointing an accusing finger at Quebec's "distinct society," would lead us.

It didn't take long to find out. The Oka crisis erupted. On July 11, 1990, two shots killed a member of the Canadian armed forces. Canada was in the headlines around the world. The federal authorities consoled themselves with the fact that, temporarily at least, Quebec was taking the rap. The crisis hit rock bottom when we saw masked "warriors" signing agreements with Judge Alan B. Gold.

The authorities had lost control of the situation. For many Quebecers, it was a hellish situation.

□ La Presse, *Feb. 22 and Mar. 12, 1994. Translation.*

○ L'Actualité, *Dec. 1, 1993, May 1, 1994. Translation.*

The Aboriginal spokespeople took turns knocking Quebec. Harper had simply said "No." George Erasmus, chief of the Assembly of First Nations of Canada, and Ovide Mercredi, at the time the vice-chief of Manitoba, were short of neither prejudices nor insults, which were expressed in English. The French-language media grew tired of translating it all. The journalists kept to themselves the shouts of "French SS" and "Go back to France!" that they heard in their travels.

From a war of words, it was easy to move to a multifaceted guerrilla war. The Indians returned to their "little war." Added to their jibes were contraband activities, contempt for the law, and provocative gestures.

Tolerance has its limits, as the residents of Châteauguay and Oka reminded the authorities, with the media echoing their protests. Lysiane Gagnon, of *La Presse*, tried to set the record straight. In a series of very-well-documented articles, she summarized the Jay Treaty of 1794 and a certain form of trade. To answer the attacks directed against Quebec, she turned to studies by Robin Philpot, Jean-Philippe Chartrand, and Bradford Morse. "At a time when the English-Canadian (and part of the American) intelligentsia claims to see the pinnacle of anti-Indian racism in Quebec," she wrote in January, 1994, "it is surely worthwhile to make some comparisons and to see clearly where Quebec is situated when it comes to treatment of the Aboriginal minority."□

For his part, Jean Paré, the editor of the magazine *L'Actualité*, devoted several pages to the Aboriginal issue. In a 1994 editorial, Paré did not mince his words: "Civil disobedience has a noble history," he noted. He denounced tax fraud and delinquency, then recalled "the complacency toward gangs, which, in the absence of democracy, make law among the Aboriginals." He was not shy about accusing federal politicians of having "tolerated banditry" on the Akwesasne, Kahnawake, and Oka reservations: "This was arranged by the enemies of the sovereignist movement and their secret services, and today they are doing battle with their own mercenaries!"○

☐ L'Actualité, Dec. 1, 1993.
Translation.

Paré was not at all certain that the "warriors" of Oka were in the majority among the Indians, or that most of the Indians were in agreement with the means used. Although some were no doubt privately jubilant, it was more politic to applaud Elijah Harper's "historic gesture." "For the first time," said Montagnais chief Réal McKenzie, "we realized that it is impossible to govern Canada without the participation of the Indians. It was at that moment that we acquired true political power."☐

* * *

Less spectacular, but equally significant, was the long march of the Siouis. Georges Sioui, the oldest of the four brothers charged, was a man deeply immersed in Aboriginal culture. Obviously, he is very proud of their judicial victory. He has good reason to be.

The road to the *Sioui* ruling of May 24, 1990, was dotted with pitfalls. All indications are that in 1982, the Siouis had no precise plan. They had had themselves arrested by the forest-conservation agents apparently without trying to. But they no doubt knew that they were infringing on some regulation or other.

In a weak position at their trial in Superior Court, they tried the "treaty coup." Georges Sioui, with a doctorate in history, was well versed not only in the distant past of the Wendats (Hurons), but also in the Indian Act and the Constitution Act, 1982. Is it pure coincidence that the Siouis were arrested six weeks after promulgation of the latter law? One thing is certain: Georges Sioui knew about section 35, which confirmed the recognition of rights arising from treaties.

The Siouis' lawyer, Michel Pouliot, went to court with a photocopy of a handwritten document, which was impossible to date simply by visual examination. The judge was quite skeptical. He asked for the original or an acceptable reference, but none was forthcoming. Instead, Mr. Pouliot brought a printed version that he said was from 1760. Not only did the courts not question the authenticity of either version, but they used the less reliable version, even though it was known that a transcription had been made by the federal archivist Arthur G. Doughty.

As a result of rules or tradition, the Appeal Court tends to be much more attentive to jurisprudence than to facts and documents. "Two elements are no longer open to debate before us," Judge Bisson noted, "the authenticity of document D-7 [and] the authority that Governor Murray had on September 5, 1760."□ As we recall, document D-7 is a photocopy of a document that is impossible to authenticate, and its text is different from the text that Judge Desjardins accepted. We should also recall that this judge had refused to see the terms of a treaty in the document, which had no doubt led to his not examining it more closely.

It was clear that James Murray had neither the authority nor the capacity to sign a treaty with the Indians. This right was reserved for William Johnson, who exercised it according to the orders he received.

In any case, the document attributed to Murray was not a treaty. "As the Hurons did not know how to write, they could not have signed it," explained Judge Bisson. This is quite a surprising statement when we look at all the known treaties, from the Great Peace of Montreal to the treaty of July 18, 1764, with the Hurons of Detroit, which bear totemic signatures alongside the signature and seal of Sir William Johnson.

For Judge Bisson, the references to freedom of religion, customs, and trade were "decisive words."○ However, these words were constantly used by Murray, and most of them are found in the surrender of Quebec City. In fact, had Murray not specified that "they are received upon the same terms with the Canadians"? Why are these words not decisive? Do they not have a greater scope than those chosen by the Court of Appeal?

This was the viewpoint of Judge Robet Legris of Superior Court△ in another trial concerning Elizabeth Vincent, who was "charged with not collecting sales tax on tobacco when she sold it to Whites." Her lawyer, Jacques Larochelle, evoked the "Murray treaty," among others, and referred to the recent ruling by the Court of Appeal.

After carefully studying the context of the time, after reading the paper by historian Denys Delâge and John Knox's journal,

□ *RJQ, 1987, p. 1726.*

○ *Ibid., p. 1727.*

△ *RJQ, 1990, pp. 821–22.*

□ *Ibid., p. 821.*

○ *Ibid., p. 822.*

△ *Sioui, 1989, p. 146.*

Judge Legris did not hesitate. "The English," as he understood it, "were seeking to break the last lines of support for the French army: the Canadien regulars, the Canadien militia, and the Indians allied with the French. To each of these, Murray offered peace, amnesty, and the protection of His British Majesty."□

"The Hurons of Lorette," Judge Legris concluded, "were offered the same treatment as all other Canadiens. The expression 'freedom of trade with the English' ... guaranteed the Hurons access to trading posts up to then controlled by the English without risk of being turned away or molested. . . . I conclude that the treaty of 1760 gives no more nor less rights to the Indians of Lorette than to all other inhabitants of New France."○

As we know, for the Supreme Court, there was still enough ambiguity to make the Murray document a treaty in the sense of the Indian Act, and thus in the sense of the Constitution Act, 1982. In 1760, the military power represented by Murray had amnestied the Hurons. In 1990, the judiciary transformed this gesture into a treaty.

Following the example of the 1982 law, does this judgment not lead to a dead end?

∗ ∗ ∗

Treaty or not, does the Murray document give the Hurons of Lorette particular rights? The Supreme Court had recognized a treaty, but it did not pronounce on the existence of particular rights for the Hurons of Lorette or for the descendants of members of the Confederacy of Seven Fires (or Eight Nations).

On February 26, 1992, Judge Bruno Cyr, of the Court of Quebec, District of Terrebonne, concluded that he did not believe that the "Murray treaty" allowed the Mohawk community of Kanesatake to organize a bingo game without an appropriate permit.

In May, 1982, "the Siouis finished their annual rituals of purification and thanksgiving."△ Logically, their victory in the Supreme Court should have enabled them, if necessary, to revive certain traditions and reinvigorate their spiritual life. Justice Lamer seemed ready to recognize this. But to the great distress of the Siouis, the "treaty" has since been hijacked. Will it ever end?

It took fifteen years of judicial battles to come to the ruling of May 26, 1995, rendered by Judge France Thibault of Superior Court. Judge Thibault concluded that "the permission accorded to the Hurons of Lorette to freely exercise their customs did not relieve them of the obligation to collect taxes," which the accused, Gabriel Sioui, retailer of the Huron Village, had failed to do.

During this trial, Jacques Larochelle preferred to base his argument on the free exercise of customs, rather than on the "freedom to trade" also evoked in the "Murray treaty." After having heard "Mr. Sioui's expert," Denys Delâge, and the attorney general, Alain Beaulieu, "the court has privileged the report of the latter, who painted a detailed picture of the Huron Nation of Loretteville."□

Adhering to the point of view of the Crown prosecutor, René Morin,○ Judge Thibault believed it "unlikely that he [Murray] would have accorded to the Hurons of Lorette, without more specification and under the term 'customs,' absolute sovereignty on the territory of their reservation."△ "Although they [the Hurons of Lorette] enjoy special treatment, in certain regards," the judge wrote, "the historical context does not lead to the conclusion that the English and the Hurons could have understood, at the signature of the Murray treaty, that they would not be subject to application of English laws."◇

* * *

As these cases were moving through the courts, the people responsible for Aboriginal and Quebec organizations created a group to encourage a rapprochement through reflection on relations between Aboriginals and Quebecers.

In the autumn of 1993, this group, the Aboriginal and Quebec Peoples' Equality Forum, published a manifesto [see Appendix J] clearly demonstrating their feeling that the future is still full of promise:

□ *RJQ, 1995, p. 33.*

○ *Ibid., p. 22.*

△ *Ibid., p. 33.*

◇ *Ibid., p. 38.*

At the present time, the legal instruments at our disposal are not adapted to the reality of the collective and national rights of the Quebec people and the Aboriginal peoples. The Forum considers it necessary to create a common charter, founded on the Universal Declaration of Human Rights, that will allow us to protect the fundamental individual rights of persons, equality of sexes, collective rights, and national rights.

This resolution fit within the perspective of one of the first political moves made by René Lévesque: a vote in the National Assembly (March, 1985) recognizing the Aboriginal nations of Quebec and certain fundamental rights accorded to them.

Finally, to conclude, I cannot resist the temptation to emphasize that according to the Forum's manifesto, the political autonomy desired both by the eleven Aboriginal peoples in Quebec and by the Québécois people supposes "the setting up of governments founded not on the racial or ethnic character of persons under it, but on a territorial basis."

Appendices

INDIAN ALLIANCES
IN WILLIAM JOHNSON'S HANDS

William Johnson was victorious both on the battlefield and in his diplomatic efforts. The Iroquois, who had recommended Johnson for the position of superintendent of Indian affairs, considered him one of theirs and named him Warraghiyagey. His marriage to Molly Brant in 1759 – she was around twenty-one years old, and he was forty-two – reinforced his integration into the Native world without diminishing his loyalty to the Crown.

The couple were perfectly at ease in both societies, the foundations of a new world. He learned Mohawk; she, English. He could dress in Indian style, and she could receive guests in European fashion. They were equally skilful, generous, and knowledgeable.

William Johnson's seal

American archivists, slowly becoming aware of Johnson's enormous role, began to collect his papers. Edmund Bailey O'Callaghan, a good friend of Louis-Joseph Papineau's, fled to the United States after the Battle of Saint-Denis in 1837. As archivist of New York State, he helped to collect Johnson's papers and began to publish them. He put out some thirteen thousand pages, an eloquent sign of the enormity of Johnson's work and activity. This thirteen-volume collection (with an index as a fourteenth volume) is today the main monument to Johnson's memory.

Johnson's first major residence, Fort Johnson, on the banks of the Mohawk River, has been restored. The second residence, Johnson Hall, located some ten miles north, in Johnstown, is now within a park and has become an interesting interpretation centre under the direction of Wanda Burch.

William Johnson is doubtless one of the most important characters in the history of the United States. He now generally has a place of honour in American history books.

Canadian historians were long unaware of Johnson. They found his name in documents, but forgot him immediately.

Fort Johnson

JOHNSON HALL

Johnson was the prototypical American entrepreneur. As he was among the first of his type, the British did not like him much. They took him for a man of the forest, more like a savage than a civilized man. All known portraits of Johnson show him dressed in European style, with all the outside signs of wealth and his baron's title. At the time, men did not pose in their everyday clothes.

Johnson headed an enormous organization. His fortune and the scope of his business affairs made him a powerful man: his title of colonel of the Six Nations and his appointment as superintendent of Indians are a good indication of his rise; his intelligence, energy, and ambition did the rest.

He was the nightmare of the Frenchman Dieskau in the Battle of Lake George in September, 1755. His successes and immense popularity restored confidence to the British and pride to the Americans.

He was the artisan of the breaking up of the Franco-Indian alliances.

Wanda Burch, current director of Johnson Hall

Appendix A

Chronology
The Covenant Chain from 1677 to 1760

1677

Agreements are signed in Albany between the Iroquois and some of their allies, on the one hand, and the Colony of New York and other English colonies, on the other. It was the beginning of a new "Covenant Chain" that was to be frequently renewed in various ways over the years to come. According to the vocabulary of the time, if the chain was forgotten it would rust and break; when it was repaired, it was consolidated, and it would shine and triumph.

1744

A particularly active year on the diplomatic front. A number of meetings solidify the "Covenant Chain" or "Chain of Friendship." The Iroquois refuse to march against the French, even though one of their chiefs, Canassatego, states that he can influence the "Praying Indians" and says he is certain that they will not take up arms against the English. He says that he has planted a certain antipathy against the French in their minds.

This engraving is taken from the book by the Jesuit missionary Joseph-François Lafitau, titled *Mœurs des sauvages amériquains, comparés au mœurs des premiers temps* (1724). Although this portrayal is rather imaginative – which was not the case for Lafitau's text – we note the importance of the wampum belt in the speaker's hand and in the foreground. "Brothers, with the help of this belt, I open your ears so that you can hear. . . . "

1745

The Irishman William Johnson becomes the colonel of the Indians of the Six Nations.

1753

The term "Chain of Friendship" is used instead of "Covenant Chain." The Indians of the Ohio River want to resist the French, but, at the same time, they want the Virginians to give up their settlements on the Ohio. Meanwhile, the French, under the orders of Governor La Galissonière, treat the Ohio River Valley as the key to the continent.

1754

An important congress is held in Albany in June and July involving representatives of the English colonies and the Six Nations. The terms "Covenant Chain" and "Chain of Friendship" are used. The Mohawks take the initiative and ask for William Johnson to be appointed superintendent of Indian affairs.

Border incidents on the Ohio River. George Washington is responsible for the death of Jumonville. One month later, he must surrender Fort Necessity. Feelings run high in Albany.

1755

Edward Braddock, commander-in-chief of the British armed forces in North America, gives a commission to William Johnson, in the name of the king, for the "sole Management & direction of the Affairs of the Six Nations of Indians & their Allies . . . giving [him] full Power & Authority to treat & confer with them as often and upon such matters as [he may] judge necessary for His Majestys Service."

Johnson must report on his negotiations and all other matters of import.

All persons who had occupied the position of leader of said nations were by this order enjoined to stop intervening. Johnson also had the right to appoint a secretary and one or several interpreters and to pay them an appropriate salary.

1755

French victory at Monongahela. Braddock is killed, but not before accomplishing his most important act: the appointment of Johnson. George Washington, for his part, is strongly affected by this experience: his career is not starting well. Neither the Canadiens nor the Indians, however, are able to defeat him. And he is no fool! For proof, one can peruse General Washington's expense account during the War of Independence, published by Marvin Kitman in *George Washington's Expense Account* (New York: Harper & Row, 1988).

1756

A royal commission is awarded to Johnson. He also becomes a baronet.
Montcalm captures Fort Oswego (Chouaguen) on Lake Ontario.

1757

Montcalm captures Fort William Henry but cannot keep Indians from massacring part of the English garrison.

1758

The famous treaty at Easton, through which the Indians hope to regain some territorial rights, is signed.

Montcalm's victory at Carillon (Ticonderoga). The previous year, his exploits had excited the Indians. "Given his reputation and his exploits," the Indians of Michillimakinac explained, "we had believed that his head was lost in the clouds. But in fact, you are small, my father, and it is in your eyes that we find the grandeur of the tallest pines and the alertness of eagles" (Bougainville, 1993, p. 207).

The ends of Lake Ontario were guarded by Niagara to the west and Kingston to the east. To the south, Oswego sat at the mouth of the Oswego River. It was a convenient spot, as it also commanded the route to Albany via the Mohawk River. In a sense, Oswego was almost as strategically valuable as Niagara. In fact made up of three forts (Ontario, Chouaguen erected by the French, and George), Oswego fell to Montcalm in the summer of 1756. Montcalm's early campaigns in North America were promising. A medal was struck in honour of the victory at Oswego in which the place was portrayed with obvious exaggeration. Today, we can visit Fort Ontario, on the right bank, which has been restored. (John Henry Walker, MSQ.)

1759, March 22

Johnson says that he has met deputies of the chiefs of the Nations (of the region of Canajoharie). These chiefs want action to be taken against Niagara very soon. Johnson is so convinced that they are sincere that he is sure he will have no difficulty gathering eight hundred Indians to achieve this goal.

He writes to Jeffery Amherst, the new commander-in-chief of the British armed forces in North America, "that the Fort would be no very difficult Conquest, as I could Invest it with Indians to favour the Attack, and with them Cut off all Succours from coming to it." In Johnson's view, the capture of Fort Niagara would reverse the fortunes in the region and bring the Indians allied with the French over to the English: "I am of Opinion the Reduction of Niagara will Overset the whole French Indian Interest, and Trade, and throw it into Our hands."

1759, May 23

Amherst informs Johnson that he has decided to undertake the campaign against Fort Niagara, but that the command has devolved to Brigadier General John Prideaux. Amherst therefore asks Johnson to assist Prideaux as best as he can, especially by gathering Indians to help.

Amherst sends two hundred of the best and lightest rifles to arm the Indians.

1759, May 24

Johnson informs Amherst that he has sent a message to the nations living near the Susquehanna River asking them to meet him at Fort Stanwix. The Upper Nations will meet him at Oswego, while the Mohawks and other Indians will leave from the fort with him.

Johnson states that he is confident that the rifles sent by Amherst will be useful, but he specifies that the Indians who bring their own guns will want to be compensated.

In July, 1759, Johnson captured Fort Niagara and took Pierre Pouchot prisoner. Pouchot nevertheless managed to rally the French forces. He commanded Fort Lévis, facing La Galette (La Présentation), in the summer of 1760. "For Canada (that is, at the time, the St. Lawrence Valley)," Guy Frégault wrote, "losing Niagara meant being cut off from all the *pays d'en haut* (the region of the Great Lakes and the Ohio), and also seeing one of the boulevards of Montreal fall" (Frégault, 1955, pp. 156–57).

1759, July 25

Johnson writes to Frederick Haldimand, commander of Fort Oswego, "Niagara July 25th, 1759. I have the pleasure to inform you that we had the good fortune yesterday to beat the French army which came to the Enemys assistance, and this morning the effort surrendered by Capitulation, for further particulars I refer you to Mr Moncrief. You'll please to forward the French Garrison, who are on their way to New York, with a proper Escort, from thence, if convenient, if not this Escort is to proceed with them." Prideaux is killed during the siege of Fort Niagara, so Johnson takes command of the troops.

1760, February 13

The Six Nations end the discussions held at Onondaga between them and the representatives of the Oswegatchies, Caughnawagas, Conesedagas, and others delegated by twenty-two nations allied with the French.

The deputies of the twenty-two nations make it understood that they want to remain neutral: "Let us abide by Our Old Engagement of Friendship, and not meddle with their Quarrel, otherwise We shall be ruined, to Join One or the Other, while both bear hard upon Us, who are the Native Owners of the Land they fight about."

The twenty-two deputies say that their peoples have adopted the French religion.

The Indians allied with the French invite the Onondagas to Caughnawaga, "where a Council Fire is Lighted and wait Your Arrival; Your Friends there look for you very soon over the Ice, have Stop'd all the Young Warriors, till You Come."

Johnson tells the Onondagas that he has sent a number of messages to the Oswegatchies asking them to leave the French and return to their homeland, and that the Indians allied with the French have often betrayed the Onondagas. As a consequence of this, Johnson recommends that they refuse the invitation and to ask the deputies of the twenty-two nations to come to Onondaga or to him.

1760, March 7

Johnson informs Amherst that there has been a meeting between the deputies of the Six Nations and the Caughnawagas, Shawendadys (?), Oswegatchies, and other "French Indians." The deputies of the Six Nations have given him a report, which he includes in his letter to Amherst.

Johnson also receives two Indians from Oswegatchie who assure him that the majority of the Oswegatchies want to settle among the Six Nations in the spring, as he has requested. Johnson does not believe that they are sincere with regard to the English, but thinks, rather, that these statements by the Oswegatchies result from the weakness of the French and the distress of the Oswegatchies: "There have also been two Swegatchy Indians here to Assure me, that the greatest part of their people, where Determined to leave that Settlement, & come among the Six Nations in the Spring. I am far from thinking, that this Seeming good Disposition of their proceeds from any real regard for us, but the low Circumstances of the Enemy and their own Distresse."

Johnson uses this occasion to ask Amherst for his pay as "colonel of the Indians of the Six Nations."

1760, March 16

Amherst writes to Johnson commenting on the attitude of the Indian Nations of Canada, who have invited the Indians allied with the English to come and make peace at Caughnawaga.

According to Amherst, the Indians of Canada believe that they are superior in spite of their political error in their choice of allies and must bear the consequences: "I See, that the French Indians assume a

Superiority, which, from the present low Circumstances of their pretended Friends the French, little becomes them, and could not have been Expected; but however, since they persist in so obstinate & Impolitick an Attachment, they must take the consequences that will Ensue from a Continuance of the War."

1760, April 27

Johnson informs Brigadier General Gage that the Six Nations have met with the French commander at La Galette. According to their report, it seems that the French are continuing their policy of pressure on and intimidation of the Indians, and Johnson believes that this practice will soon be a problem for the French.

Johnson has given orders to all of his officers in trading posts to send groups of Indians to Canada and La Galette to obtain information and prisoners.

1760, May 12

Johnson announces to Colonel Haldimand that merchandise — presents for the Indians — is en route to Oswego. Johnson reminds Haldimand of the policy of presents and recommends that he be on good terms with the Indians, both friends and enemies; an opportune gift to an Indian who is influential in his tribe will always have good results in terms of keeping this tribe loyal to English interests.

In the shipment of merchandise, there is some for Niagara; Haldimand will send this merchandise to Colonel Eyre (at Niagara).

1760, May 30

Johnson writes to Haldimand to tell him how he should treat the "French Indians." He includes an excerpt from a letter from General Amherst to him dated May 28, 1760, in which Amherst explains his policy toward the Indians who are living near the English. After recalling that the Indian policy is Johnson's jurisdiction in the northern region, Amherst writes "that such of the French Indians as chuse to come and live among Us, may be received, altho' they might decline joining His Majestys Arms; All I require of these, is to remain quiet, and not to go to and fro with intelligence, as from the Moment they can do this, they can be no longer looked upon as friends, & consequently must be treated as Enemies." (The complete letter is in *Johnson Papers,* vol. 10, pp. 156–57.)

Johnson announces that his representative, Lotteridge, has received orders to assist Haldimand.

Johnson also informs Haldimand that he has offered twenty pounds sterling to any Indian who brings him back a well-informed prisoner: "that I would over, and above that [clothing the Indians] give them Twenty pound for an intelligent Prisoner, which I hope they will be able to bring in soon, and thereby clear up all doubts concerning the fate of Quebec."

1760, June 26

Johnson answers Amherst's letter containing a message to Daniel Claus and adds an excerpt of a letter from Colonel Haldimand concerning the request for peace made by the Oswegatchies. As he has done with other Indian allies of the French, Johnson sends an invitation to the Oswegatchies to return to the Six Nations. As they have not committed a hostile act since their request for peace the previous year, while he was in Oswego, Johnson believes that they could be accepted and included in the Confederation friendly to the English.

Johnson is sure that he will be able to unite them with the Six Nations; as well, these Oswegatchies will be very useful in helping to navigate the rapids, since they are expert river pilots: "I make no Doubt, I shall then be able not only to make them join, but with the six Nations conduct the Army into Canada thro that difficult Navigation as they are the best Pilots that way."

1760, July 4

Johnson answers Haldimand's letter announcing the arrival of the Indians from Oswegatchie and the reason for their arrival. He advises Haldimand to have a meeting with these Indians. The Onondagas will assist Haldimand in this meeting: they have played a large role with the Indians of Oswegatchie.

Johnson is not worried that the Indians of Oswegatchie may obtain information on English projects: "I trust we are now so sufficient, that there is little to be feared from any Intelligence they could now pick up, if so inclined." Johnson specifies that he has orders from General Amherst to win over enemy Indians and that a number have already defected from the French, including the Indians of Oswegatchie: "Several of them having for some time past abandoned the French and are now settled among the five Nations, as well from other Quarters as from Swegatchy."

Johnson thus asks that these Indians be warmly received: "From thence I am of Opinion that when such Indians come (of whatever Nations), and offer to be friends, they should not be refused."

Amherst, who is on his way to Oswego, will see under what terms and conditions these enemy Indians will be received.

1760, July 9
Amherst arrives at Oswego.

1760, August 10
Amherst leaves Oswego, heading for Fort Lévis.

1760, August 17
Amherst is at Oswegatchie.

1760, August 22
Cannon fire is directed at Fort Lévis.

1760, August 25
Bombardment of Fort Lévis by Amherst intensifies. Pouchot, the French commander of the fort, complains about the treatment he is receiving from Amherst:

> Sir, I have noted at the moment that the fort I have the honour of commanding for my master the King is being bombarded with cannon fire. I did not believe that I deserve such hard treatment from Your Excellency.
> I dare, Sir, to appeal to your generosity in this matter of war, and I do not believe that I have put myself in a position in this case to have proved myself unworthy. If necessity puts me in the position to surrender the fort, I hope to merit favourable treatment, if you wish that I request conditions.
>
> With profound respect, Sir
> Your very humble and obedient servant,
> Pouchot

1760, August 28
Johnson warns Amherst that three "French Indians" have arrived and announced that thirty more will follow. They have told Johnson that Murray's army has arrived at Montreal.

1760, August 29
In the evening, Captain Jacobs arrives with enemy Indians. Jacobs has also brought a letter from a French priest (probably Roubaud), who asks for peace in the name of the Indians.

1760, August 30

Johnson confers with the Indians.

1760, September 6

"The army passed by the Cochnawaga Indians, who promised the General, that they would observe a strict neutrality: upon which he gave orders that they should not be molested" (Mante, 1772, p. 310).

1760, September 8

Capitulation of Montreal.

1750, September 15–16

Treaty of Caughnawaga. The "Covenant Chain" triumphs. The old treaty of alliance between the Six Nations and the Seven (or Eight) Nations of Canada is permanently re-established! Had it existed previously? It was certainly a coveted alliance. See Appendix D.

This chronology was enhanced by correspondence from William Johnson and by Jeffery Amherst's journal.

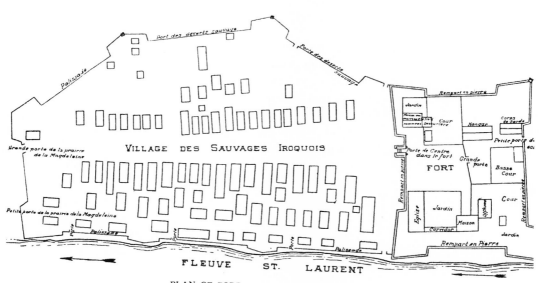

PLAN OF FORT AT CAUGHNAWAGA, 1754

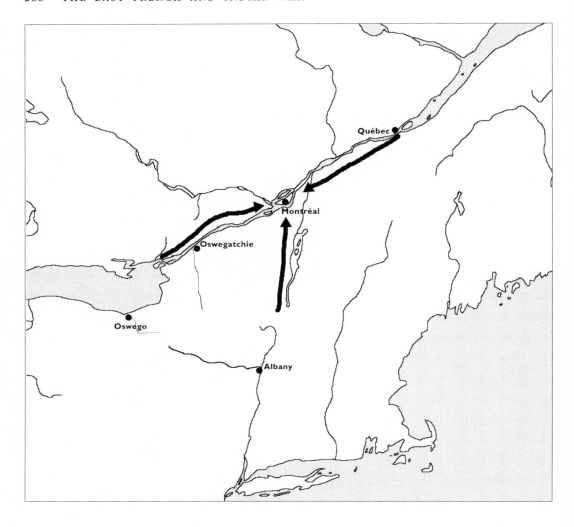

Appendix B
Safe-conduct of September 5, 1760

Arthur Doughty's version
and the Supreme Court's version

*The safe-conduct issued to the Hurons by Murray
on September 5, 1760*

The original of the document issued by Murray to the Hurons of Lorette on September 5, 1760, was found in the Murray papers kept by a Mrs. Murray in Bath, England. The text was published in English in the *Report of the Work of the Archives Branch for the Year 1910* (pp. 50–51), and in French in *Rapport sur les archives du Canada pour 1910* (pp. 50–51).

In 1985, an envoy of the National Archives of Canada traced part of the collection to a James P. Murray: "The papers have changed hands since the NA's copying," he noted in his report. "The present owner does not possess the 1759–1760 letter book nor a 1760 Huron Treaty."

(Translation done by the Archives.)

These are to certify that the chief of the Huron Tribe of Indians, having come to me in the name of his Nation to submit to His Britannick Majesty and make Peace, has been received under my protection with his whole Tribe, and henceforth no English Officer or party is to molest or interrupt them in returning to their settlement at Lorette and they are received upon the same terms with the Canadians, being allowed the free Exercise of their Religion, their Customs and liberty of trading with the English Garrisons recommending it to the Officers commanding the posts to treat them kindly.

Il est par les présentes certifié que le chef de la tribu des Hurons s'étant présenté à moi, au nom de sa nation, pour se soumettre à Sa Majesté Britannique et faire la paix, a été pris sous ma protection ainsi que sa tribu entière ; et dorénavant nul officier ou corps anglais ne devra les molester ou les arrêter à leur retour à leur colonie de Lorette ; ils seront traités de la même façon que les Canadiens et jouiront du libre exercice de leur religion, de leurs coutumes et de la liberté de trafiquer avec les garnisons anglaises, recommandation étant faite aux commandants des postes d'user de bons procédés envers eux.

Given under my hand at Longuil this 5th day of September, 1760.

Sigd   Ja. Murray

By the Generals Command

Sigd   John Cosnand

Adjt   Genl.

Endorsed

Copy of a certificate granted by Genl Murray to the Huron Indians.
5th Sept: 1760

Donné sous ma signature à Longuil ce 5me jour de septembre 1760.

(Signé)   Ja. Murray

Par ordre du général

(Signé)   John Cosnand

Aide-major général.

Endossé :

Copie d'un certificat délivré par le général Murray aux sauvages hurons.

In the *Sioui* ruling of May 24, 1990, the Supreme Court used the following version.

(Traduction)

THESE are to certify that the CHIEF of the HURON tribe of Indians, having come to me in the name of His Nation, to submit to His BRITANNICK MAJESTY, and make Peace, has been received under my Protection, with his whole Tribe ; and henceforth no English Officer or party is to molest, or interrupt them in returning to their Settlement at LORETTE ; and they are received upon the same terms with the Canadians, being allowed the free Exercise of their Religion, their Customs, and Liberty of trading with the English : — recommending it to the Officers commanding the Posts, to treat them kindly.

PAR LES PRÉSENTES, nous certifions que le CHEF de la tribu des HURONS, étant venu à moi pour se soumettre au nom de sa nation à la COURONNE BRITANNIQUE et faire la paix, est reçu sous ma protection lui et toute sa tribu ; et dorénavant ils ne devront pas être molestés ni arrêtés par un officier ou des soldats anglais lors de leur retour à leur campement de LORETTE ; ils sont reçus aux mêmes conditions que les Canadiens, il leur sera permis d'exercer librement leur religion, leurs coutumes et la liberté de commerce avec les Anglais : nous recommandons aux officiers commandant les postes de les traiter gentiment.

Given under my hand at Longueil, this 5th day of September, 1760.

By the Genl's Command,

JOHN COSNAN   Ja. MURRAY

Adjut. Genl.

Signé par moi à Longueil, ce 5ᵉ jour de septembre 1760.

Sur l'ordre du général,

JOHN COSNAN   Ja. MURRAY

Adjudant général

Appendix C

Excerpts from the Act of Capitulation of Montreal, September 8, 1760

This translation comes from Short and Doughty's *Documents Relating to the Constitutional History of Canada, 1759-1791*, pp. 25–36. The articles that could affect Natives living in villages (including the Hurons), because they referred to Canadiens and/or to Natives, are the following:

Art. 4

"The Militia after evacuating the above towns, forts and posts, shall return to their habitations, without being molested on any pretence whatsoever, on account of their having carried arms."

Amherst's answer: Granted.

Art. 8
"The Officers, Soldiers, Militia, Seamen and even the Indians, detained on account of their wounds or sickness, as well as in the hospital, as in private houses, shall enjoy the privileges of the cartel, and be treated accordingly."

Amherst's answer: "The sick and wounded shall be treated the same as our own people."

Art. 27
To this article, which claimed freedom of religion for the inhabitants, as well as the obligation for them to pay tithes and usual

taxes to the clergy, Amherst answered: "Granted; as to the free exercise of their religion, the obligation of paying the tithes to the Priests will depend on the King's pleasure."

Art. 37

This article generally claimed "peaceable property and possession of the goods" for all Canadiens, including merchandise and fur pelts, with the freedom to sell them to the French and English.

Amherst's answer: "Granted."

Amherst answered by referring to article 26, which recognized the right of the Compagnie des Indes and private citizens to ownership of their pelts.

Art. 39

"None of the Canadians, Acadians or French, who are now in Canada, and on the frontiers of the colony, on the side of Acadia, Detroit, Michillimaquinac, and other places and posts of the countries above, the married and unmarried soldiers, remaining in Canada, shall be carried or transported into the British colonies, or to Great-Britain, and they shall not be troubled for having carried arms."

Amherst's answer: "Granted, except with regard to the Acadians."

Art. 40

Another demand from Governor Vaudreuil: "The Savages or Indian allies of his Christian Majesty, shall be maintained in the Lands they inhabit; if they chose to remain there; they shall not be molested on any pretence whatsoever, for having carried arms, and served his most Christian Majesty; they shall have, as well as the French, liberty of religion, and shall keep their missionaries.

Amherst's answer: "Granted," except for the end of the article relating to the powers of the vicars-general and the bishop to send new missionaries to the allied Indians.

Art. 41

This article demanded that "The French, Canadians, and Acadians" not be forced to take up arms against the French.

Amherst answered, simply: "They become Subjects of the King."

Art. 42

"The French and Canadians shall continue to be governed according to the custom of Paris, and the Laws and usages established for this country, and they shall not be subject to any other imposts than those which were established under the French Dominions."

Amherst's answer: "Answered by the preceding articles, and particularly by the last."

Art. 46

"The inhabitants and Merchants shall enjoy all the privileges of trade, under the same favours and conditions granted to the subjects of his Britannic Majesty, as well as in the countries above, as the interior of the colony."

Amherst's answer: "Granted."

Art. 55

"As to the officers of the Militia, the Militia, and the Acadians, who are prisoners in New-England, they shall be sent back to their Countries."

Amherst's answer: "Granted except what regards the Acadians."

Appendix D
The Conference of September 15–16, 1760, at Caughnawaga

On September 16, 1760, eleven days after General Murray issued the safe-conduct to the Hurons of Lorette and eight days after the capitulation of Montreal, an assembly of Indians chaired by William Jonson, superintendent of Indian affairs, ended. This assembly was formed of representatives of eight nations,[1] who renewed the alliance of peace and friendship among themselves first, and following this, with the Six Iroquois Nations.

The notes for this meeting, which aimed to reproduce the words of the Indian speakers, are drawn from *Johnson Papers*, vol. 13, pp. 163–66 [Conference at Caughnawaga, September 16, 1760]. Here, we do not transcribe the crossed-out words, and we spell out abbreviated words where necessary.

At the moment, it is impossible to specify the origin of these notes, found in the archives of the New York Historical Society. They come from a copy attributed to Daniel Claus. But the text was integrated into the journal of Jelles Fonda, who accompanied William Johnson in August, 1760.

---

1. *See Maurice Ratelle, 1991, pp. 15–16. The author mentions that the reference to "eight nations," when there were seven missions or villages, is explained by the presence of two nations at Oka (Iroquois and Algonquins). Jean-Pierre Sawaya (1993, pp. 12–13) notes that depending on the case, there were seven, eight, or nine villages, and he specifies that "village and nation were equivalent." Around 1760, there were the following villages: Kahnawake, Oswegatchie, Akwesasne, Kanesatake, Odanak, Wôlinak, Lorette, and Pointe-du-Lac. As "fire is the symbolic representation of the council of a nation" or village, the term was a federation of fires. A fire might include up to three nations. This was the case for Kanesatake (Oka), where Iroquois, Algonquins, and Nipissings cohabited.*

[*Montreal, September 16, 1760*]

1. Brother Warraghiyagey[2]

We are glad to meet you and thank you for your friendly Advice sent us from Oswego, that we should keep out of the Way[3]; We have paid a due Regard thereto and thank the Great Spirit above who allows us to meet together this Day in so Friendly a Manner.

a String[4]

2. Brethren of the Nations[5]

It gave us great Pleasure of your having resolved at Swegachy to accompany our Brother Warraghiyagey as far as here, Your coming along was very necessary and of mutual Service. We therefore most sincerely return you our hearty Thanks for it.

a Belt[6]

Montréal, 16 septembre 1760

1. Frère Warraghiyagey[2],

Nous sommes heureux d'être avec vous et nous vous remercions de cet avis amical que vous nous aviez envoyé d'Oswego, de nous tenir à l'écart[3]. Nous en avons tenu bon compte et nous remercions le Grand Esprit qui nous permet de nous réunir aujourd'hui dans une atmosphère si amicale.

une branche de porcelaine[4]

2. Frères des Nations[5],

Nous avons été très heureux que vous ayez décidé à Oswegatchie de suivre jusqu'ici notre frère Warraghiyagey. Votre venue était d'une grande nécessité et à notre avantage réciproque. C'est pour cela que nous vous présentons nos chaleureux remerciements.

un collier de porcelaine[6]

---

2. Sir William Johnson's Indian nickname. Note that in their relations with the English, the Indians of the English colonies used the term "Brother" when they addressed representatives of the British authorities, in order to mark their equality. Under the French régime, the allied Indians called themselves "children" when addressing their governors.
3. The English authorities had warned the Indians allied with the French to remain neutral. Not all Indians did so; some, like the Hurons, withdrew only at the very end of the conflict.
4. Presentation of a string of wampum to confirm the words.
5. The Indian speaker is here no doubt addressing the representatives of the Six Nations who had followed Johnson to Caughnawaga.
6. Presentation of a wampum belt.

3. Brother Warraghiyagey

We heard and took to heart the good Words you spoke to us yesterday ; We thank you most heartily for renewing and strengthning the old Covenant Chain[7] which before this War subsisted between us, and we in the Name of every Nation here present assure you that we will hold fast the Same, for ever hereafter.

4. Brother Warraghiyagey

We are greatly obliged to you for opening the Road from this to your Country;[8] we on our parts assure you to keep it clear of any Obstacles & use it in a freindly Manner —

5. Brother Warraghiyagey

You desired of us to deliver up your People who are still among us[9] — As you have now settled all matters with us & we are become firm Friends. We who are present here as Representatives of 8 Nations do assure you that what you desired shall be fully agreed to as soon as possible.

a Belt

3. Frère Warraghiyagey,

Nous avons entendu et pris à cœur les bonnes paroles que vous nous avez dites hier. Nous vous remercions chaleureusement de renouveler et de renforcer l'ancienne Chaîne d'alliance[7] qui subsistait entre nous avant cette guerre : au nom de chacune des nations ici présentes, nous vous assurons que nous nous y tiendrons fermement à tout jamais.

4. Frère Warraghiyagey,

Nous vous sommes grandement reconnaissants de nous ouvrir le chemin qui va d'ici à votre pays[8] ; de notre côté, nous vous assurons de le garder libre de tout obstacle et de nous en servir en amis.

5. Frère Warraghiyagey,

Vous avez désiré que nous vous remettions ceux de vos gens qui sont encore parmi nous[9]. Puisque vous avez réglé avec nous tous les problèmes et que nous sommes devenus de solides amis, nous, ici présents en qualité de représentants de huit nations, vous assurons que ce que vous avez demandé sera entièrement accordé aussitôt que possible.

un collier de porcelaine

---

7. *The "Covenant" or "Accord" concluded periodically (sometimes each year) between the Iroquois nation and the Dutch, then between the Iroquois nation and the English of New York, was called, depending on the case, a rope or an iron chain, which evoked a more solid link. Because an iron chain might rust, this became a silver chain around 1677. (See Appendix A.)*
8. *The Indians of Canada had been authorized to begin trade between Canada and the state of New York, which, in principle had been forbidden under the French régime. This authorization, however, was soon placed in doubt by the English governor of Montreal.*
9. *That is, the English taken prisoner during the war.*

6. Brother Warraghiyagey

We also agreable to your Desire yesterday will burry the french hatchet we have made Use of, in the bottomless Pit, never to be Seen more by us or our Posterity. —

a Belt

7. Brethren of the 5 Nations[10] —

In Return to your Belt of Yesterday Whereby you told us that as you Brother Warraghiyagey had finished every thing with us you on your part had something to say which was that as there had been during this War a Division & Disunion between us ; and desired us to re-unite & be firm Friends as heretofore, We hereby assure all here present that we with pleasure agree to your friendly Proposal and reunite as formerly

8. Brother Warraghiyagey

With Regard to the String you spoke by yesterday of your Returning as soon as pos-sible to your homes and of your leaving two Persons behind to transact Business in your Absence[11] and at the same time told us to send some of every Nation with you to Albany[12] in order to try the goodness of the Road, we are ready whenever You go to accompany You.

6. Frère Warraghiyagey,

Conformément à votre désir exprimé hier, nous enterrerons la hache de guerre française, dont nous nous sommes servi, dans un puits sans fond, pour que ni nous ni nos descen-dants ne la revoyions plus.

un collier de porcelaine

7. Frères des Cinq-Nations[10],

En réponse à votre collier de porcelaine d'hier, par lequel vous marquiez que votre Frère Warraghiyagey en ayant fini avec nous, vous aviez quelque chose à ajouter, à savoir que, vu la division et la mésentente survenues entre nous durant cette guerre, vous désiriez rétablir cette union et être comme auparavant de soli-des amis, nous assurons tous ceux qui sont ici présents que nous acceptons avec plaisir votre offre d'amitié et que nous reformons l'union comme par le passé.

8. Frère Warraghiyagey,

Votre déclaration d'hier, accompagnée d'une branche de porcelaine, annonçait que vous retourniez chez vous aussi tôt que pos-sible et que vous laissiez ici deux personnes pour traiter des affaires en votre absence[11] et, en même temps, vous demandiez d'envoyer avec vous à Albany[12] quelqu'un de chacune des nations pour éprouver la qualité du chemin :

---

10. *We understand here that the speaker, a Mohawk from Sault-Saint-Louis, is addressing the other Indians of the Five Nations: during the last war, they had finally taken the side of the English, while the Indians of the Eight Nations had turned neutral after fighting on the French side.*

11. *We know, in particular, that Daniel Claus was to act as Johnson's representative in Montreal. Had he written these notes? We know that he asked for a copy in February, 1761 (Johnson Papers 3, p. 348).*

12. *Johnson lived a few miles northwest of Albany, on the Mohawk River (today Fort Johnson, New York). In 1762, he moved ten miles away, to a magnificent residence called Johnson Hall (today Johnstown, New York), where he died in July, 1774.*

nous sommes prêts en tout temps à vous accompagner.

a String —

une branche de porcelaine

9. Brother Warraghiyagey

9. Frère Warraghiyagey,

As we have now made a firm Peace with the English & the 6 Nations[13] we shall endeavour all in our Power to keep it inviolably. There is one thing Brother Warraghiyagey we understand you have great Plenty of, which is Liquor, as that is the only thing which can turn our heads and prove fatal to us, we who now represent 8 Nations here present entreat you in the most earnest Manner not to suffer any of your People to sell or give any to us.

Maintenant que nous avons conclu une paix durable avec les Anglais et les Six-Nations[13], nous allons nous appliquer de toutes nos forces à la maintenir inviolable. Il y a une chose, Frère Warraghiyagey, que, comprenons-nous, vous avez en grande quantité : les spiritueux. Comme c'est la seule chose qui puisse nous faire tourner la tête et se révéler fatale pour nous, nous qui représentons ici huit nations vous demandons de la manière la plus pressante de ne pas tolérer qu'un seul de vos gens nous en vende ou nous en donne.

a large Belt[14]

un large collier de porcelaine[14]

10. With another large Belt they made the same Request to the 6 Nations not to bring any Liquor to their Country

10. En présentant un autre large collier de porcelaine, ils demandèrent aussi aux Six-Nations de ne pas apporter de spiritueux dans leur pays.

a Belt

un collier de porcelaine

11. Brother Warraghiyagey

11. Frère Warraghiyagey,

Every thing being now settled between us in the most friendly Manner which we rejoice at ; We have only to acquaint you that our Young Men are soon going upon the hunt and perhaps may happen to come to some of your Posts, that you will give Strict charge to the Officers of every Post along not to suffer any Person to dispose of any Liquor to any of our

Tout étant maintenant réglé entre nous de la façon la plus chaleureuse, ce dont nous nous réjouissons, nous voulons seulement vous faire savoir que nos jeunes gens partent bientôt à la chasse et se présenteront peut-être à l'un ou l'autre de vos postes ; nous vous demandons d'enjoindre rigoureusement aux officiers de chacun des postes de ne permettre à personne

13. That is, the Six Iroquois Nations.
14. A belt with several strings of wampum.

People that may come there as it might be productive of Disputes & ill Consequences between them & your People which might shake the Friendship now so happily strengthned and which by all Means I will endeavour to avoid.

de vendre des spiritueux à quiconque de nos gens qui pourrait y aller : cela pourrait amener entre eux et vos gens des disputes aux conséquences désastreuses, et affecter l'amitié que nous venons avec tant de bonheur de renforcer ; ce que de tous mes moyens je vais m'efforcer d'éviter.

a black Belt

un collier de porcelaine noire

12. Brother Warraghiyagey

12. Frère Warraghiyagey,

It is proper for you to know the Way our Affairs were managed while under the Care of the french which is that Smiths &ca were allowed to work for Us upon that Governments Expence.[15]

Il convient que vous sachiez comment nos affaires étaient menées du temps qu'elles étaient sous la conduite des Français et ceci en particulier : des forgerons et d'autres étaient autorisés à travailler à notre service aux frais du gouvernement[15].

13. Brother Warraghiyagey

13. Frère Warraghiyagey,

We are heartily thankfull to the General[16] for his Goodness in allowing our Priests to remain & instruct us as usual, and we shall endeavour to make a good Use of it, as He is now the head of all here, & had subdued our former Superiors, who maintained our Priests, they must suffer & cannot subsist without your Assistance ; Therefore we beg you will not be worse than our former Friends the french. And also beg that you will regulate Trade so that we may not be imposed upon by the People our new Brothers

Un chaleureux merci au général[16], qui a eu la bonté de permettre à nos prêtres de rester et de continuer à nous instruire ; comme il est à la tête de nous tous maintenant et qu'il a soumis nos anciens maîtres, qui entretenaient nos prêtres, ceux-ci seront malheureux et ne pourront subsister sans votre secours. C'est pourquoi nous vous demandons de ne pas leur être moins favorable que nos alliés d'auparavant, les Français ; comme aussi de réglementer dans le commerce de façon que vos gens, nos nouveaux frères, n'abusent pas de nous.

15. In effect, under the French régime, the government supplied blacksmiths, gunsmiths, and surgeons to the Indians as needed.
16. General Amherst, commander-in-chief of the British troops.

a Belt

un collier de porcelaine fin

here ended —

Then arose Ad'yadarony chief of the Warriors of Caghnawagy and addressed himself to Sir William in the Following Manner

[le procès-verbal se poursuit quand même] À ce moment se leva Ad'yadarony, chef des guerriers de Kahnawake, qui s'adressa à Sir William en ces termes

14. Brother Warraghiyagey

The Sachems having finished the Good Work of Peace which is agreable to all our young Men, I shall offer something in behalf of them, which I beg you will take Notice of. Should any of the young People thro' Imprudence or Liquor drop or make Use of any foolish or rash Expression to You or those you leave behind, we beg you will not take Notice of them, but of us now present who are their chiefs.

14. Frère Warraghiyagey,

Les chefs ayant terminé la bonne œuvre de paix si agréable à tous nos jeunes gens, je veux vous offrir de leur part quelque chose que je vous demande de prendre en considération. Si l'un ou l'autre de nos jeunes gens, manquant de prudence ou sous l'effet de spiritueux, laisse échapper ou utilise des propos insensés ou irréfléchis à votre endroit ou à l'adresse de ceux que vous avez laissés à votre place, nous vous demandons de ne pas prendre garde à eux, mais de vous en reporter à nous ici présents qui sommes leurs chefs.

a Warriors Belt

de la part de guerriers, un collier de porcelaine

15. Brother Warraghiyagey

As we are now linked together in the Chain of Friendship; we the Warriors have one Request more to make which is that if Mr Purthuit[17] alias Ohowa late Interpreter to Onontio[18] should apply to you to be further employed that Way, you will not hear to it, but let him go with his former Master over the great Lake and let us have one of your own People to act as Interpreter

15. Frère Warraghiyagey,

Maintenant que nous sommes liés ensemble dans la chaîne de l'Amitié, nous, les guerriers, nous avons une autre requête à vous présenter : si monsieur Perthuis[17], autrement dit Ohowa, jusqu'ici interprète auprès d'Onontio[18], vous demande de servir encore en cette qualité, ne l'écoutez pas, laissez-le s'en aller avec son ancien maître au-delà du grand lac, et désignez un de vos gens pour nous tenir lieu d'interprète.

---

17. *Louis Perthuis [Purthuit], interpreter for the Iroquois, probably served at Fort Duquesne in 1755 and was highly praised by Commander Contrecœur (Papiers Contrecœur, Presses de l'Université Laval (1952), pp. 253, 365).*
18. *That is, the French governor-general.*

gave a string of Wampum

here ended the Meeting

September 16th. 1760
Brother Warraghiyagey

    As every Matter is now settled to our mutual Satisfaction we have one Request to make to You who have now the Possession of this Country, That as we have according to your Desire kept out the Way of your Army, You will allow us the peaceable Possession of the Spot of Ground we live now upon, and in case we should remove from it, to reserve to us as our own.

a large black Belt

on présenta une branche de porcelaine

ici prend fin l'assemblée
[le procès-verbal reprend]
16 septembre 1760
Frère Warraghiyagey,

    Toutes les affaires étant terminées à notre satisfaction réciproque, nous avons une demande à vous présenter, à vous qui êtes entré en possession de ce pays : comme nous sommes demeurés, selon votre désir, à l'écart de votre armée, accordez-nous la tranquille possession du coin de terre où nous vivons et si nous devions nous en retirer, réservez-le-nous comme notre bien propre.

un large collier de porcelaine noire

The notes for Appendix D were written in collaboration with the historian Marcel Trudel.

Appendix E

The Royal Proclamation of 1763 and Indian Territory

By the proclamation of October 7, 1763, the king of Great Britain determined the boundaries of the four governments to be established in North America: the Province of Quebec (new name for the old French colony on the St. Lawrence), East Florida (today's Florida to the Apalachicola River), West Florida (from the Apalachicola River to Lake Pontchartrain and the Mississippi River), and Grenada (to which responsability for several other islands was added). This proclamation also specified how the king intended to reserve lands for the exclusive use of the Indians.

The text that refers to the new Province of Quebec and the reservation of lands for the Indians is the following:

Purpose

First – The Government of Quebec bounded on the Labrador Coast by the River St. John, and from thence by a Line drawn from the Head of that River through the Lake St. John, to the South end of the Lake Nipissing; from whence the said Line, crossing the River St. Lawrence, and the Lake Champlain, in 45. Degrees of North Latitude, passes along the High Lands which divide the Rivers that empty themselves into the said River St. Lawrence from those which fall into the Sea; and also along the North Coast of the Baye des Châleurs, and the Coast of the Gulph of St. Lawrence to Cape Rosières, and from thence crossing the Mouth of the River St. Lawrence by the West End of the Island of Anticosti, terminates at the aforesaid River of St. John.

. . .

The Indian Provisions

And whereas it is just and reasonable, and essential to our Interest, and the Security of our Colonies, that the several Nations or Tribes of Indians with whom We are connected, and who live under our Protection, should not be molested or disturbed in the Possession of such Parts of Our Dominions and Territories as, not having been ceded to or purchased by Us, are reserved to them, or any of them, as their Hunting Grounds – We do therefore, with the Advice of our Privy Council, declare it to be our Royal Will and Pleasure, that no Governor or Commander in Chief in any of our Colonies of Quebec, East Florida. or West Florida, do presume, upon any Pretence whatever, to grant Warrants of Survey, or pass any Patents for Lands beyond the Bounds of their respective Governments, as described in their Commissions. . . .

And We do further declare it to be Our Royal Will and Pleasure, for the present as aforesaid, to reserve under our Sovereignty, Protection, and Dominion, for the use of the said Indians, all the Lands and Territories not included within the Limits of Our said Three new Governments, or within the Limits of the Territory granted to the Hudson's Bay Company, as also all the Lands and Territories lying to the Westward of the Sources of the Rivers which fall into the Sea from the West and North West as aforesaid.

And We do hereby strictly forbid, on Pain of our Displeasure, all our loving Subjects from making any Purchases or Settlements whatever, or taking Possession of any of the Lands above reserved, without our especial leave and Licence for that Purpose first obtained.

. . .

We do, with the Advice of our Privy Council strictly enjoin and require, that no private Person do presume to make any purchase from the said Indians of any Lands reserved to the said Indians, within those parts of our Colonies where We have thought proper to allow Settlement: but that, if at any Time any of the Said Indians should be inclined to dispose of the said Lands, the same shall be Purchased only for Us, in our Name, at some public Meeting or Assembly of the said Indians, to be held for that Purpose by the Governor or Commander in Chief of our Colony respectively within which they shall lie.

Appendix F

Were the Indians the King's Subjects?

Letter from Sir William Johnson
to Commander-in-Chief Thomas Gage, October 31, 1764

In this letter, Johnson, superintendent of Indian affairs, wrote that one must not too easily "insinuate that the Indians call themselves Subjects." Letter reproduced from *Johnson Papers*, vol. 11, pp. 394–96.

Dear Sir —

Altho the Words of the late Treaty[1] may at first appear extraordinary, yet, I am not at a loss to Account for them, as I know it has been verry customary for many People to Insinuate that the Indians call themselves Subjects, altho I am thoroughly convincend they were never so called, nor would they approve of it — tis true that when a Nation find themselves pushed, their Alliances broken, and themselves tired of

Même si les termes du dernier traité[1] peuvent à première vue sembler hors de l'ordinaire, je ne suis pas embarrassé de les justifier ; je sais qu'il est très habituel chez bien des gens de laisser entendre que les Amérindiens se déclarent sujets, bien que, selon ma profonde conviction, on ne les ait jamais ainsi qualifiés et que, d'ailleurs, ils ne l'accepteraient pas. Certes, lorsqu'une nation se trouve à bout,

---

1. *The treaty of 1764, concluded in Detroit between Sir William Johnson and the Hurons of that region. This treaty of peace, friendship, and alliance made no mention of Indians being subjects of Great Britain, something that Johnson wanted to explain to Gage (text in* Documents Relating to the Colonial History of New York, *vol. 7, p. 650s). It should be noted that in a letter written the previous day to the Lords of Commerce on this same treaty, Johnson gave the same explanation (ibid., p. 674).*

a War, they are verry apt to say many civil things, and make any Submissions which are not agreeable to their intentions, but are said meerly to please those with whom they transact Affairs as they know we cannot enforce the observance of them. But you may be assured that none of the Six Nations,[2] Western Indians &ca. ever declared themselves to be Subjects, or will ever consider themselves in that light whilst they have any Men, or an open Country to retire to, the very Idea of Subjection would fill them with horror. — Indeed I have been Just looking into the Indian Records, where I find in the Minutes of 1751 that those who made the Entry Say, that Nine different Nations acknowledged themselves to be his Majestys[3] Subjects, altho I sat at that Conference, made entrys of all the Transactions, in which there was not a Word mentioned, which could imply a Subjection, however, these matters (notwithstanding all I have from time to time said on that Subject) seem not to be well known at home, and therefore, it may prove of dangerous consequence to persuade them that the Indians have agreed to things which (had they even assented to) is so repugnant to their Principles that the attempting to enforce it, must lay the foundation of greater Calamities than has yet been experienced in that Country, — it is necessary to observe that no Nation of Indians have any word which can express, or convey the Idea of Subjection, they often say, "we acknowledge the great King to be our Father, we hold him fast by the hand, and we shall do which he desires" many such like words of course, for

que ses alliances sont détruites et qu'elle est elle-même lasse de se battre, elle est tout à fait portée à se montrer aimable et à poser des gestes de soumission qui ne correspondent pas à ses intentions, mais c'est là seulement pour contenter ceux avec qui elle a affaire: elle sait bien que nous ne sommes pas en mesure d'y faire donner suite. Vous pouvez être assuré qu'aucune des Six-Nations[2], que les Amérindiens de l'Ouest et autres ne se sont jamais dits sujets ou ne s'estimeront tels aussi longtemps qu'il en restera un seul homme ou qu'ils trouveront une terre où se retirer : la seule idée de sujétion les comblerait d'horreur. Je viens tout juste d'examinier les archives concernant les Amérindiens et j'ai trouvé dans les procès-verbaux de 1751 que ceux qui y ont tenu la plume écrivent que neuf diverses nations se sont reconnues sujettes de Sa Majesté[3] : or, j'étais présent à cette assemblée, j'en ai noté toutes les délibérations : on n'y a pas prononcé un seul mot qui impliquât une sujétion. Pourtant, malgré tout ce que de temps à autre j'ai répété là-dessus, on ne semble pas suffisamment éclairé sur cette question en Angleterre. Par conséquent, il peut se révéler dangereux de faire croire que les Amérindiens ont été d'accord sur des points qui, même s'ils les ont acceptés, sont tellement contraires à leurs principes que tenter d'y donner suite pourra faire naître des désastres plus importants que ceux que ce pays a jamais subis. Il faut le remarquer, chez aucune nation amérindienne on n'a de mot qui puisse exprimer ni évoquer l'idée de sujétion ; ils disent souvent « nous reconnaissons le grand roi pour notre père,

---

2. *The Six Iroquois Nations.*
3. *This was the assembly held in Albany in July, 1751, before Governor Clinton of New York. It brought together a number of Indian nations, including the Six Iroquois Nations: the minutes mention Indians who declared themselves subjects of Great Britain (text in* Documents Relating, *vol. 6, pp. 717–26).*

which our People too readily adopt & insert a Word verry different in signification, and never intended by the Indians without explaining to them what is meant by Subjection. — Imagine to yourself Sir, how impossible it is to reduce a People to Subjection, who consider themselves independant thereof both by nature & Scituation, who can be governed by no Laws, and have no other Tyes amongst themselves but inclination, and suppose that it's explained to them that they shall be governed by the Laws Liable to the punishments for high Treason, Murder, Robbery and the pains and penaltys on Actions for property of Debt, then see how it will be relished and whether they will agree to it, for without the Explanation, the Indians must be Strangers to the Word, & ignorant of the breach of it.
[...]

For my part I have agreable to your letter only given You my private Sentiments on the Subjection mentioned in the Treaty,[4] as to a Freind in whom I can thoroughly confide, for I would not take upon me to censure the insertion of these Words done by any Officer Commanding an Army, as probably his Motive might be well intended.
[...] Cher Monsieur,

nous le tenons ferme par la main et nous ferons ce qu'il désire », et bien de ces paroles que nos gens retiennent trop volontiers en leur prêtant un sens tout différent, en aucun cas voulu par les Amérindiens, à qui on n'a pas expliqué ce qu'on entend par sujétion. Représentez-vous, Monsieur, combien il est impossible d'amener un peuple à se soumettre quand il fonde son indépendance à la fois sur la nature et sur l'habitat, des gens que ne régisse aucune loi et qui n'ont point d'autres liens entre eux que des dispositions communes. Supposez qu'on leur explique qu'ils seront régis par des lois, qu'ils seront passibles de châtiments pour haute trahison, meurtre, brigandage et soumis à des peines s'ils sont poursuivis en justice pour dettes: voyez alors si cela sera de leur goût et s'ils pourront l'accepter, car à défaut de le leur expliquer, ce mot *sujétion* leur demeurera forcément inconnu et ils n'auront pas conscience d'y manquer.
[...]

Quant à moi, conformément à votre lettre, je ne vous ai exprimé, sur la sujétion dont fait mention le traité[4], que mes sentiments personnels, comme à un ami sur qui je puis tout à fait compter, car je ne prendrais pas sur moi de reprocher à celui qui a le commandement de l'armée, d'avoir inséré ce mot, sans doute avec des intentions valables.

(Traduction de Marcel Trudel)

---

4. *That of 1751.*

Appendix G

Deposition of Athanase La Plague, Huron de Lorette, December 19, 1765

What is the scope of the "Murray treaty"? What did Murray himself mean by freedom of customs and of trade? The deposition below provides an interesting view on these questions. (Text drawn from collection MG, 23, I, 13, vol. 1, Docments from the late eighteenth century, *Sharpe Papers*, "Charges against James Murray, 1765-1767".)

Departement de la ville de Quebec dans la Province de Quebec (Savoir)

La Deposition d'Athanase La Plague Sauvage Huron Chrétien de la Mifsion de la Jeune Lorette prise par devant moi L'honorable Guillaume Gregory Ecuier Juge en Chef de sa Majesté pour la dite Province qui ayant fait Serment Sur la Sainte Evangile dit

Que dans le Mois de Mars de l'An Mille Sept Cents Soixante & deux le Deposant demanda à son Excellence Jacques Murray Escuier Gouverneur de Quebec, la permifsion d'aller en traite de Quelques effets chés les Nations Sauvages du petit Nord Vulgairement nommés les Montagnais ou Tête de Boules, qui habitent sur le Lac S^L Jean, la Rivière Saguenay & aux environs.

Qu'en consequence Monsr Cramahé le Secretaire de son Excellence donna au Deposant un permis ou pafseport bien & duement Signé & Scellé pour faire la traitte ou bon lui sembleroit. Et que quand ledit Secretaire lui remît ledit permis, il lui commanda de faire ses efforts pour encourager les Sauvages des Terres de decendre afin de Trafiquer dans les Postes.

Que le Deposant fit lire led^t permis par Monsr le Lieutenant Jean Montresor, Ingenieur (que le deposant avoit conduit par les bois dans l'hyver 1759, de Quebec a la Nouvelle Angleterre pour porter des Nouvelles à Monsr le General Amherst) et par plusieurs autres Officiers Anglois qui lui dirent que ledit permis etoit bon, qu'il n'avoit rien a craindre, qu'il pouvoit trafiquer par tout ou il voudroit & que quand même il reviendroit par les autres Gouvernemens de Montreal ou des trois Rivieres, personne ne lui toucheroit une Epingle.

Que le deposant ayant été fourni de Marchandises par Monsr Foye & Monsr Werden (deux Bourgeois Anglois) il partit en Raquettes avec quatre autres Sauvages de sa Nation, & dans les Bois eu le malheur de perdre son fils Ainé.

Qu'en Chemin ils firent la Chafse & la traite avec les Montagnais mais la Saison etant trop avancée pour revenir par les Bois ils pafserent par la Riviere de Saguenay & etant arrivés a Chigoutimi le Commis de Monsr Jean Gray Agent des Postes, lui dit que puisqu'il etoit la il lui seroit plus avantageux de lui Vendre ses Pelleteries & autres effets que de les porter a Quebec, & qu'il lui en donneroit le prix courant de Quebec.

Que le deposant ayant accepté cette proposition le Commandant Monsr Thomas Fortye Lieutenant des troupes & le Sieur Robert Forbe commis des Postes au quinze de Juin 1762. ou environ donnerent au Deposant bien & duement Signé un etat des Pelleteries & autres effets, que le deposant & ses Camarades laifsoient audit poste de Chigoutimi pour la valleur d'environ cinq Mille francs.

Que le deposant etant arrivé a Quebec vers la fin dud^t mois de Juin, une Garde de Soldats, avec la Bayonnette au bout du Fusil, le Vinrent chercher a bord du Batiment dans lequel il etoit monté & l'ayant mené chés ledit Sieur Cramahé le Secretaire, il lui demanda son permis, & le deposant n'ayant point de Soupçon le lui remît. Sur cela le dit Sieur Cramahé prît led^t permis en presence de Monsr Thomas Mills Major de la place, Et le deposant ne Sait pas ce qu'il est devenu depuis

Qu'ensuitte ledit Sieur Mills mena le deposant chés son Excellence Monsr Le Gouveneur Murray, qui lui dit « *te voilà donc Athanase! Pourquoi as tu été a mon Poste?* » le Deposant repondit que c'etoit en consequence d'un permis de son Excellence, alors son Excellence lui dit qu'il confisqueroit son Butin. Le Deposant ne pouvant d'abord S'im-maginer que le Gouveneur lui parloit Serieusement & le voyant cepen-dant entrer en Colere, sortit dans le defsein d'y retourner une autre fois.

Qu'après ce tems la le Deposant fut plusieurs fois chés le Gouver-neur mais que ses Domestiques avoient eu beau l'Annoncer, la porte lui avoit toûjours été refusée sous pretexte que son Excellence avoit à faire.

Qu'on prit au Deposant jusquà Son Canot & son Fusil sans qu'on lui ait rendu ni l'un ni l'autre depuis ce tems la, qu'il n'a Jamais receu aucune Satisfaction pour les Pelleteries & autres effets qui lui avoient été Saisis, mais qu'on lui dit que le tout avoit été confisqué, & que quand même une partie de leur produit auroit été employée a payer ses Dettes, ce nétoit ni de sa connoifsance ni de son Consentement.

       his

Signed Athanase + Laplague   Sworn before me at Quebec the
           mark   19th day of December 1765
                                  Signed Wm Gregory Ch. Justice

Truly read by me
    Geo. ... Allsopp.   A True Copy
                                     D.A.N.B.

I have here used the transcript prepared by Richard Lortie and edited by Maurice Ratelle.

Appendix H

Excerpts from the Journal of Daniel Claus, from July 26, 1773, to August 10, 1779

Sent to Canada to represent Sir William Johnson, superintendent of Indian affairs, the officer Daniel Claus went to see the Hurons in Lorette on July 26, 1773, to listen to their requests. The next day, he went to Lieutenant-Governor Cramahé to see the Jesuits' titles to Lorette (more precisely, their titles to the Saint-Gabriel seigniory). The following day, he answered the Hurons. Another meeting with the Hurons took place on July 30. When Claus returned to Montreal, he received the Mohawks of Kahnawake and Akwesasne.

These excerpts here are from Claus's journal, reproduced in *Johnson Papers*, vol. 13, pp. 624–33. We have spelled out the abbreviated words.

26. July at a Meeting with the Lorette Indians, at their Village, the Speaker B [...] proceded as follows :

Brother
When our Ancestors lived at [...]¹, la Grand Isle in Lake Huron² our father the Priest³ acquainted us he saw it inconvenient

Le 26 juillet, lors d'une assemblée avec les Amérindiens de Lorette, à leur village, l'orateur B [...] s'exprima comme suit :

Frère,
Du temps que nos ancêtres vivaient à [...]¹, la Grande Île dans le lac Huron², notre Père, le prêtre³, nous fit savoir qu'il trouvait

---

1. *Blank in the text.*
2. *Huronia and Wendake are not islands. However, the Jesuits probably translated "Wendat" as "inhabitants of an island." George Sioui (1994, p. 15) explains, "On the cosmology level, the Wendats considered the world an island carried on the back of a turtle."*
3. *The evacuation of Huronia in 1650 was conducted under the supervision of the Jesuit Ragueneau, but here "the Priest" should be interpreted as the Jesuits, collectively.*

for him as well as us to remain there any longer and there fore proposed our moving to (*to where our lines were and That*) towards Quebec where we should want for neither Land or anything else, Accordingly we agreed to his request & followed him & at our arrival at [Quebec] Three Rivers he settled us there where we remained some Years with the Arundax the Original Indians of that Country[4] then the Priest who we then looked upon as our spiritual as well [as] temporal [guide] removed us to Sillery formerly called St. Mishel when the priest[5] saw they had improved the Environs of that place he removed them to Quebec, afterwards to the Island of Orleans, after which to St. Foy, then old Lorette and lastly to this place called New Lorette where we now have lived 75 Years[6] and have been looked after by all Indian Nations from Tadoussack to Niagara as their Superiors and obeyed as such, we have invited the Mohawks to this Country & procured their Settlements[7] being considered by all the Nations in the above Light & original Proprietors of this Country we are at present come to that disagreable period of not being Masters of one Foot of ground [*without*] being [*told*] shuffed back & forward like a foot Ball, altho

désavantageux pour lui comme pour nous d'y demeurer plus longtemps ; c'est pourquoi il nous proposa de nous transporter du côté de Québec où nous ne manquerions ni de terres ni de quoi que ce soit. Par conséquent, nous avons consenti à sa demande, nous l'avons suivi. À notre arrivée aux Trois-Rivières, il nous y a établis et nous y sommes restés quelques années avec les Arundax, les premiers Amérindiens de ce pays[4]. Après quoi, le prêtre que nous regardions alors comme notre guide spirituel et temporel nous fit déménager à Sillery, que l'on appela d'abord *Saint-Michel* ; quand ce prêtre[5] vit que ces Hurons avaient développé les alentours de ce lieu, il les fit se transporter à Québec, puis à l'île d'Orléans, ensuite à Sainte-Foy, à l'Ancienne-Lorette et, enfin, à cet endroit dit *Jeune-Lorette*, où nous vivons maintenant depuis 75 ans[6]. Et nous avons été considérés par toutes les nations amérindiennes, de Tadoussac à Niagara, comme étant leurs supérieurs et nous avons été respectés comme tels. Nous avons invité les Mohawks dans ce pays et leur avons assuré des établissements[7]. Considérés par toutes les nations, à cause de notre supériorité, premiers propriétaires de ce pays, nous en sommes arrivés à présent à cette situation fâcheuse de

---

4. According to Marcel Trudel, the speaker made a mistake: there was no Huron settlement at Trois-Rivières after the destruction of Huronia. As for the word "Arundax," it designates the Algonquins. See Sawaya, 1993, p. 13.
5. Here again, "the Priest" can be taken in the collective sense to designate the Jesuits in charge of the Huron group. The word may also designate specifically the Jesuit Pierre Millet, who directed the transfer from Ancienne-Lorette to Nouvelle-Lorette.
6. The account that the speaker gave of the Huron migrations does not always correspond to historical fact. In fact, when they arrived from the Great Lakes in 1650, under the supervision of the Jesuits, the Hurons stayed first in Quebec City, near the Hôtel-Dieu. In 1651, they were taken to Île d'Orléans, from where they began to return in 1656 to take refuge again in the town of Quebec. In April, 1668, they were in the Jesuit Notre-Dame-des-Anges seigniory. The following year, they moved to the Jesuit seigniory in Sillery, on the Saint-Michel hill (to a place called Sainte-Foy), and then went to a neighbouring Jesuit seigniory, Saint-Gabriel, where they founded Lorette (today Ancienne-Lorette). They left there in 1697 for another part of the same seigniory, which became Jeune-Lorette, where they were when Claus went to meet with them. (Commentary by Marcel Trudel.)
7. According to Marcel Trudel, there is no historical proof that the Hurons held this superiority over the Indian nations from Tadoussac to Niagara, and the Hurons were not at all behind the Mohawk settlements of Sault-Saint-Louis and Lake of Two Mountains. Georges Sioui (1994, pp. 15–18) defends this thesis based on Sagard and Charlevoix.

the Priest assured us when he removed us hither That we should have what Land we pleased [and] for our Village and marked out The Spot himself[8] which we now claim 2 years before he built this church, which we have showed you at your Arrival here this day as to writing Brother We See you cant imagine we should have secured our Claim by being entire Strangers to it [at present] and consequently were more so 40 years ago, all we have to rely on is our Memory & the Justice of our Superiors for we can with Truth assure you to be so as we tell you and the then living priest had the two Statues you see on. each side of him over the Church Door put up in token [of] and Confirmation of said Limits and some of our old People now living were present when the Spot was marked out to them by that Priest who 5 years after died. And Now Brother the present Priest[9] [leases] Sells & leases away the Land his [former] Predecessor granted us for our Village and for ought we know may if in his Power entirely dispossess us of said Grant & let us shift for ourselves in the Wilderness.

ne plus être maîtres d'un seul pied de terre, poussés d'un côté et repoussés de l'autre comme un ballon. Pourtant, le prêtre nous avait assuré, en nous faisant venir en ces lieux, que nous aurions ce qu'il nous plairait de terre. Quant à notre village, il[8] en marqua lui-même l'endroit que nous réclamons deux ans avant de bâtir cette église que nous vous avons montrée à votre arrivée ici aujourd'hui...

Frère,

Nous le voyons bien, vous ne pouvez pas vous imaginer que nous aurions pu prouver notre droit parce que nous sommes à présent tout à fait des étrangers, et que nous en étions par conséquent davantage 40 ans auparavant ; le seul appui que nous ayons, c'est notre mémoire et la justice de nos supérieurs, car nous pouvons, en toute vérité, vous assurer qu'il en est comme nous vous le disons, et le prêtre qui vivait alors avait, en garantie et confirmation des limites, placé les deux statues que vous voyez de chaque côté au-dessus de la porte de l'église ; quelques-uns de nos anciens qui vivent encore étaient présents quand le lieu leur en a été marqué par ce prêtre, décédé cinq ans plus tard. Et aujourd'hui, Frère, le prêtre actuel[9] vend et loue la terre que son prédécesseur nous a concédée pour notre village et, pour autant que nous le sachions, il peut, si c'est en son pouvoir, nous déposséder entièrement de cette concession et nous laisser à l'abandon dans le désert.

---

8. *This does not refer to the Jesuit Millet, but to the Jesuit Pierre-Daniel Richer, in charge of the mission from 1716 to 1761. He constructed a first chapel in 1722, then a second in 1730; the latter still stood in 1773. See L.-S.-G. Lindsay,* Notre-Dame de la Jeune-Lorette de la Nouvelle-France, *pp. 38s, 112ss.*
9. *This was the Jesuit Étienne-Thomas-de-Villeneuve Girault, who succeeded Richer in 1761 and who was still in charge of Lorette in 1773. He remained there until 1790.*

Wherefore Brother we beg you will consider our Distress and do us that Justice which you think we in Reason & Equity deserve. Recommending ourselves our Women & children to your Protection and Paternal Care, hoping[9] that you will not expose your Children, to that Dilemma of being driven out of house & home.

Gave a Belt —

The Speaker likewise spoke in behalf of their Warriors that they were hemmed in by the white people with Regard to their hunting Grounds at Tadoussack &ca which was never the Case before so that in every respect their Situation was to be pitied, and they beg we may be supported in the Right & Priviledges granted us by our present Royal Sovereign & Father by his proclamation of 7th October 1763.[10]

Brother

We beg of you likewise to take into Consideration the house we were shewing you & that the Road may be turned by the side of it which amount to a very trifling spot of a few feet which when we begun to build the house we did not imagine would occasion the least Difficulty of having the Road turned the small space it requires. And therefore flatter ourselves that we the Hurons descendants of the most respectable Tribe of Indians in This Country may be gratified in this here trifleing & in our Opinion Just Request, and were we to die this Instant we we could not vary from

C'est pourquoi, Frère, nous vous supplions de considérer notre détresse et de nous accorder cette justice que, selon vous, nous méritons en toute raison et équité. Nous nous recommandons, nous, nos femmes et nos enfants à votre protection et à votre sollicitude de père et nous espérons que vous ne soumettrez pas vos enfants à cette double nécessité d'être chassés de leur maison et de leur pays.

Ils ont présenté un collier de porcelaine.

En outre, l'orateur déclara au nom des guerriers qu'ils étaient entravés par les Blancs sur leurs territoires de chasse à Tadoussac et ailleurs, ce qui ne s'était jamais produit dans le passé, et il s'ensuit qu'à tout point de vue, leur état devrait faire pitié : ils demandent d'être soutenus dans les droits et privilèges qui, dit-il, nous ont été accordés par notre actuel Souverain et Père, en vertu de sa proclamation du 7 octobre 1763[10].

Frère,

Nous vous demandons aussi de prendre en considération la maison que nous vous avons montrée : le chemin qui la longe pourrait être déplacé, ce qui met en cause une petite parcelle de quelques pieds : quand nous avons entrepris la construction de cette maison, nous ne pouvions pas imaginer qu'il y aurait la moindre difficulté à déplacer le chemin sur le court espace qu'il fallait. C'est pourquoi nous nous flattons, nous les Hurons descendants de la plus respectable tribu amérindienne de ce pays, qu'on nous accordera cette demande de peu d'importance, mais que

---

10. *This proclamation, among other things, ensured the Indians of lands that had been reserved for them within the province of Quebec.*

what we related above relative to our Limits granted us as by our spiritual fathers.

Then the old Speaker N... addressed himself to me saying that as their head Man [Outahtidarrio] was dead he beg'd to recommend an other in his Place naming Simonet alias Onhegtidarrio who by the unanimous Opinion & Consent of the whole Village was looked upon equal to the Task being a sensible Man & well acquainted with their Affairs.

Gave a Belt

and said they had finished what they had to say.

Then another cheif [...] spoke in behalf of thier Women & Chidren that their Condition was deplorable on Account of the Loss they sustained by The Frost which destroyed every Necessary of Life the Ground usually produced for them & were quite in Despair how to keep themselves from perishing for want of food, and likewise beg'd for some Cloths for them & their Children.

Recommending themselves to the Comisseration of the Gentlemen present likewise —

The Warriors beg'd for Amunition & Axes, towards their going on the hunt.

[...]

27th [July]. Went to Governor Cramahes[11] to examine into the Jesuits Title to Lorette, found they were given to them by one of the first Settler, in Canada Mr. Chissart[12] afterwards confirmed by his Descendant

nous croyons équitable ; et dussions-nous mourir sur le champ, nous ne pourrions pas modifier ce que nous venons de vous dire au sujet des limites que nous ont accordées nos pères spirituels.

Puis, le vieil orateur N... s'adressa à moi-même en déclarant que leur chef [Outaghtidarrio] étant décédé, il désirait en recommander un autre à sa place, soit Simonet, autrement dit Onhaghtidarrio, qui, de l'avis et du consentement unanime de tout le village, était jugé digne de cette tâche, homme sensé et bien au fait des affaires.

Ils ont présenté un collier de porcelaine et déclaré qu'ils avaient terminé ce qu'ils avaient à dire.

Ensuite, un autre chef [...] vint dire, au nom de leurs femmes et enfants, que leur condition était lamentable, à la suite de la perte subie par une gelée qui a détruit tout ce qui, produit par leur terre, était nécessaire à leur subsistance ; ils avaient perdu tout espoir de s'empêcher de périr par manque de nourriture, et ils demandaient aussi un peu de vêtements pour eux et leurs enfants. Ils se recommandaient, en outre, à la commisération des personnes présentes.

Les guerriers demandaient des munitions et des haches, en vue de leur départ pour la chasse.

[...]

Le 27 [juillet], je me rendis chez le gouverneur Cramahé[11] examiner les titres des Jésuites sur Lorette. Je constatai que ce lieu leur avait été donné par l'un des premiers habitants du Canada, monsieur Giffard[12], puis

---

11. Hector-Theophilus Cramahé [Camahes] was only lieutenant-governor, but he administered the country when the governor, Guy Carleton, was absent.

11. *Hector-Theophilus Cramahé [Camahes] was only lieutenant-governor, but he administered the country when the governor, Guy Carleton, was absent.*

12. *Clause wrote "Chissart." Robert Giffard had received the concession of a seigniory called Saint-Gabriel, measuring two leagues by ten leagues, on April 16, 1647. On November 2, 1667, he donated it to the Jesuits. An area of 2.5 leagues had been detached on March 15, 1651 for the Hurons. See Trudel,* Le terrier du Saint-Laurent en 1663, *p. 115.*

Mr. du Chêne[13] and they the Jesuits gave the Indians what land they thought sufficient to build their Village upon and 40 Acres[14] of Land for planting of Corn &ca with the proviso if they remained under the Guidance & Direction of the Jesuits otherwise to revert to the Society again And now their spiritual fathers indiferent [to] what becomes of the poor Indians, under the English Government pretend that the Indians have forfeited their Claim to that Land by shaking off the Missionaries Awe and Inspection over them & by that means want re enter into the possession of the Lands granted to them & throw them upon our hands or perhaps want us to pay a Consideration from us for the same, which therefore ought to be thought of & remedied.

[...]

Quebec 28th. July 1773.
Answer to the Hurons of Lorette upon their Speech of Monday last.
Brethren

I have considered upon your speech you made me last Monday at your Town, and with Regard to your being prevailed upon by your Fathers the Jesuits to leave your original place of Abode in Lake Huron and follow him to live among the Whites in Canada. I cant say anything about whether your change of habitation proved for the better or the worse you must look for that to Yourselves & the Priest. All I have to observe upon the Subject is that whenever a Nation or people quit their Native Country in order to settle & abide in

confirmé par son descendant, monsieur Duchesnay[13] ; les Jésuites avaient donné aux Amérindiens ce qu'on jugeait suffisant pour y bâtir leur village et 40 arpents[14] de terre pour y cultiver le maïs, etc., à la condition qu'ils demeurent sous la conduite et direction des Jésuites ; sinon, cela devait retourner à la Compagnie [de Jésus]. Et aujourd'hui, sous le gouvernement anglais, leurs pères spirituels, indifférents au sort des pauvres Amérindiens, prétendent que ces Amérindiens ont perdu leur droit sur cette terre en s'affranchissant du respect et du contrôle de leurs missionnaires et ces Jésuites désirent reprendre possession des terres qu'ils leur ont accordées et les reprendre de nos mains et s'en remettre à nous, ou peut-être veulent-ils que nous leur en fassions compensation, ce qui est à voir et résoudre.

[...]

Québec, le 28 juillet 1773.
Réponse aux Hurons de Lorette et leur discours de lundi dernier.

Frères,

J'ai réfléchi sur le discours que vous m'avez adressé lundi dernier dans votre village. Quant à ce que vous ayez été persuadés par vos Pères, les Jésuites, de quitter le lieu de votre habitation originelle dans le lac Huron pour les suivre et venir vivre parmi les Blancs au Canada, je ne saurais dire si ce changement de demeure a été pour le meilleur ou pour le pire : c'est à vous et au prêtre d'en débattre. Tout ce que je puis faire remarquer là-dessus, est que lorsqu'une nation ou un peuple abandonne son pays natal pour s'établir et

---

13. *Du Chêne in Claus's journal. This was Juchereau-Duchesnay, a descendant of Nicolas Juchereau of Saint-Denys, who probably married one of Giffard's daughters.*
14. *The text says 40 acres, but it is 40 arpents, a French measurement in force at the time (an arpent is 0.85 acre). According to a 1793 document, this "reserve called the Forty Arpents" would have been made on March 7, 1742 (Lindsay,* Notre-Dame, *p. 314s).*

any other Nation or Government they [...] it is reasonably supposed & expected that they are to submit & conform themselves to the Laws Forms & Customs of that Nation or Government, which I dare say you have experienced while this Country was Governd by the French. Now as Providence would have it that by the Success of the Brittish Army this Country became Subject to the Crown of England you have seen that the English Laws have taken place with the French Inhabitants of the Country and they are ruled & Governed by them its therefore supposed you cannot have the least Objection of conforming to these Laws as you have done to the french and submit to the Opinion & Decision of those that are the Rulers & Lawgivers & have a better Insight & Knowledge in Matters of property &ca. than you can have.

And therefore with Regard to your Complaint of your Village being hemmed in by Tenants of the Jesuit your Father, I have been with the Governor this Morning, who had summoned the Jesuit of your Village[15] before him in order to examine him about this Matter of your Dispute and who entirely [denies] and flatly denies that ever any Agreement was Made by his Predecessor[16] with regard to any certain Boundry of your Village as he never could find the least Note or Memorandum among his Papers concerning it, and that your Village was full large at present for the few surviving Descendants of the Hurons and as to the White people intermarried with you it never was the Intention of the Missionaries to allow tham equal

habiter chez une autre nation ou sous un autre gouvernement, on peut raisonnablement espérer que ces gens-là vont se soumettre et se conformer aux lois, systèmes et coutumes de cette nouvelle nation ou de ce nouveau gouvernement : je crois pouvoir dire que vous l'avez fait du temps que ce pays était dirigé par les Français. Or, maintenant que la Providence a voulu que, grâce au succès de l'armée britannique, ce pays se trouve soumis à la Couronne d'Angleterre, vous avez constaté que les lois anglaises ont été mises en place chez les habitants français de ce pays et qu'ils sont régis et gouvernés par elles ; on peut donc supposer que vous ne pouvez avoir la moindre objection à vous conformer à ces lois, comme vous l'avez fait à l'égard des lois françaises, ni à vous soumettre à l'opinion et à la sentence de ceux qui gouvernent, légifèrent, voient et connaissent mieux que vous ce qui concerne la propriété, etc.

C'est pourquoi, au sujet de votre grief que votre village serait entravé par les tenanciers du Jésuite votre Père, je suis allé chez le gouverneur ce matin, il a convoqué devant lui le jésuite de votre village[15] pour l'interroger sur l'objet de votre dispute : ce dernier nie entièrement et carrément qu'il ait jamais été passé aucun accord par son prédécesseur[16] au sujet des limites de votre village, et qu'il ne saurait là-dessus en trouver la moindre note dans ses archives ; à présent, affirme-t-il, votre village suffit amplement aux quelques descendants qui survivent des Hurons ; quant aux Blancs qui se sont mêlés parmi vous par mariage, il n'a jamais été dans l'intention des missionnaires de leur accorder des privilèges égaux à ceux des Amérindiens.

---

15. *The Jesuit Girault.*
16. *The Jesuit Richer.*

Priviledges with the Indians. The Secretary of the Province was likewise sent for with the Records to examine into the Title of your Mission whereby it appears that the Land you live on was to all intents & purposes a Deed of Gift from a french Genleman Mr. Chiffary afterwards du Chéne[17] to the Jesuits at this Place for spiritual Services, so that they are the sole and lawfull proprietors of said Seigneurie, without the least hint or Clause of Your having the least Right or Claim to a Foot of Ground in it, and therefore what you are in Possession of now is entirely at the Will & Disposal of the Jesuits and no One can with Justice or Equity take their Right from them. However the Governor ready & willing to serve you as far as in him Lies will prevail upon the Jesuits to release you the Spot your Village is built upon as well as your Plantation Ground of 40. Acres and have it surveyed by the Surveyor General and the Lease and Plan thereof deposited in the Secretaries Office & a Copy thereof furnished you with for your Use & Behoof of the Indians of your Town only exclusive in every Respect of the Whites intermarried with you they being not able to shake of the Duties of Subjects by Intermarrying with Indians. And now having finished my Answer to your Land Complaint I confirm it with this

Belt.

Brethren

Your choice of the chief you proposed to me to assist Onhaghtidarrio I have no Objection against being sensible of his being capable to supply that place well & I do by this Belt confirm him as such

On a fait venir aussi le secrétaire de la Province avec ses registres, pour étudier le titre de votre mission. Il appert que la terre sur laquelle vous vivez a fait l'objet, à toutes fins pratiques, d'un contrat de donation entre un gentilhomme français, M. Giffard, puis Duchesnay[17], et les Jésuites de ce lieu en vue du ministère spirituel ; ils sont donc les seuls et légitimes propriétaires de cette seigneurie, sans qu'il soit fait la moindre allusion ni mention du moindre droit que vous auriez à un pied de terrain ; par conséquent, ce que vous occupez est à l'entière disposition des Jésuites et personne, en toute justice et équité, ne peut leur enlever leur droit.

Cependant, le gouverneur, toujours disposé à vous rendre service dans la mesure de son pouvoir, entend donc persuader les Jésuites de vous reconcéder les lieux sur lesquels est bâti votre village ainsi que votre terre à cultiver de 40 arpents : le tout sera arpenté par l'Arpenteur général de la Province, le contrat et le cadastre en seront déposés au bureau du Secrétaire, on vous en donnera copie pour l'usage et les besoins des seuls Amérindiens de votre village, les Blancs qui se sont mêlés à votre population par mariage ne pouvant se libérer de leurs devoirs de sujets en épousant des Amérindiens. Ayant terminé ma réponse à votre grief concernant la terre, je la confirme par

ce collier de porcelaine.

Frères,

Quant au choix du chef que vous me proposez pour assister d'Onhaghtidarrio, je n'ai aucune objection, étant convaincu de sa capacité à bien remplir ce poste et, par ce collier de porcelaine, je le confirme comme chef.

---

17. *On these people, see notes above.*

A Belt

Un collier de porcelaine

As to your other Requests & Cravings I shall comply with as far as in my Power. Procured them 2 Barrels of Pork & 3 of Flower 50 lb of Powder & 100 lb Shot, half a Johs. to the Women and ditto ditto for fresh Meat ans some Bread Pipes Tobacco & a Dram.

They thanked me for my Answer & what I gave them and departed

[...]

30th [July]

Two Chiefs Limanet & Athanas with their Interpreter a french Metiss came to me & told me the Governor had sent for them & they had a Letter from the Jesuit & desired me to go with them. I told them if the Governor wanted me he could send when they came to the Governor he kicked the Interpreter out adours & then sent for me & told me that he could not bear these half breed Indians & never would let them come near them. he said [he] had sent for these Chiefs about the removal of the house[18] that if the owner would have removed quietly he'd pay for the Expence of doing it otherwise he'd order it to be done at the Indians Expense which he Desired I would tell these Chiefs and they departed he then showed me the Condition upon which the Jesuits granted the 40 Acres which were as above related. The chiefs told me would wait at my Lodging when I met them. They in a pitifull manner repeated to me their Situation concerning their Lands & said they intended if I approved to petition the King in person about it. I told them that the King left these Matters to Sir William to whom I should

En ce qui concerne vos autres demandes et vos besoins, je veux y accéder autant qu'il est en mon pouvoir. (Je leur ai fourni 2 barils de lard et 3 de farine, 50 livres de poudre et 100 de plombs, un demi [?] aux femmes, autant de viande fraîche, du pain, des pipes, du tabac et un « misérable ».)

Ils me remercièrent de ma réponse et de ce que je leur avais donné, puis se retirèrent.

[...]

Le 30 [juillet]

Deux chefs, Limanet et Athanase, et leur interprète, un métis français, vinrent me trouver pour me dire que le gouverneur les avait demandés ; ils avaient une lettre du jésuite et désiraient que je les accompagne. Je leur dis que si le gouverneur avait besoin de moi, il me le ferait savoir quand ils seront devant lui. Le gouverneur jeta l'interprète à la porte et me fit demander. Il me déclara qu'il ne pouvait pas supporter ces sang-mêlés et qu'il ne les laisserait jamais fréquenter les Hurons. Il avait, me dit-il, fait venir ces chefs au sujet du déplacement de la maison[18] : si le propriétaire veut bien qu'on la déplace sans dispute, j'en ferai les frais, sinon je donnerai ordre qu'on le fasse aux frais des Hurons. C'est ce qu'il désirait que je réponde aux chefs, qui se retirèrent. Il me fit voir alors les termes de la concession faite des 40 arpents par les Jésuites, termes que j'ai décrits plus haut.

Les chefs m'avaient dit qu'ils m'attendraient chez moi pour me rencontrer. Ils me décrivirent de nouveau, d'une triste façon, leur situation concernant les terres et me dirent qu'ils projetaient, si j'étais d'accord, de pré-

---

18. *The house that blocked the road, as mentioned above.*

report the whole & they should have an decisive Answer either this Winter or on my Return next Spring which satisfied them. Athanas delivered me his petition to Sir William.

[...]

10th [Montreal]

Called the Caghnawageys & Aughquisasnes who waited for me about what I gave the Priest in french Writing. I told them they must either send the Priest about his Business or allow Him to manage their Village with regard to private party disputes among themselves as well as their spiritual Matters as both were in a manner so connected that the one could not prosper without the other being conformable to it. Then delivered them the Belt the Mohawks spoke to Sir William about touching their hunting Grounds being encroached upon by the Canada Indians since the Conquest & that they desire them most earnestly to desist for the future.

Aquirandonquas then replied that the Belt was of too much Import to give an Answer upon without the concurrence of the whole Confederacy which by the first Opportunity they would assemble & consider upon. In the mean time they must entreat the Mohawks to leave off selling any more of their hunting Grounds[19] or at least acquaint them how far they had sold that [they] might know their Bounds. As they believed the real Reason of the Scarcity of Game proceeded from that illegal practice of theirs & that perhaps they

senter une pétition au roi lui-même à ce sujet. Je leur dis que le roi avait laissé ces problèmes à Sir William [Johnson], à qui je ferais rapport la-dessus : ils devraient recevoir une réponse décisive cet hiver ou lors de mon retour le printemps prochain ; ce qui les contenta. Athanase me remit sa pétition à l'intention de Sir William.

[...]

Le 10 [août, à Montréal]

Ai convoqué les gens de Kahnawake et d'Akwesasne qui m'attendaient à propos de ce que j'avais communiqué à leur missionnaire, dans une note en français. Je leur dis : vous devez soit renvoyer le prêtre à ses affaires, soit lui permettre d'assumer la direction de votre village quand surviennent parmi vous des disputes à caractère privé ou quand il s'agit du domaine spirituel ; ces deux cas sont si étroitement liés que dans le premier il ne peut y avoir aucune chance de réussite s'il n'est pas conforme au second. Ils me remirent alors le collier de porcelaine qui avait accompagné le discours de Sir William [Johnson] au sujet de leurs territoires de chasse sur lesquels empiétaient les Amérindiens du Canada depuis la conquête ; ils souhaitaient d'une façon fort pressante que ces Amérindiens y renoncent à l'avenir.

Aquirandonquas répondit là-dessus que le collier de porcelaine avait trop d'importance pour donner réponse sans l'accord de toute la confédération, que l'on comptait réunir à la première occasion, pour étudier cette question. Entre temps, ils doivent prier les Mohawks de cesser de vendre leurs territoires de chasse[19] ou, à tout le moins, de faire

---

19. *The Mohawks (those of the Hudson Valley) had started to cede some parts of the hunting territories in the upper reaches of the Hudson River; this is what is alluded to here. It may also refer to the hunting territories gained in old Huronia, between Lake Ontario and Georgian Bay.*

might soon sell their planting Grounds & Village, meaning the Canada Indians.

They observed among one another that they believed the Mohawks wanted to pick a Quarrel by their Belt.

savoir aux autres Amérindiens jusqu'où ils en ont vendu pour que ceux-ci en connaissent les limites. Ils croient, en effet, que la véritable cause de la rareté du gibier vient de cette pratique illégale et que peut-être les Amérindiens (on pensait à ceux du Canada) en viendront bientôt à vendre leurs terres à culture et leur village.

Ils firent remarquer entre eux qu'ils pensaient que les Mohawks cherchaient une mauvaise querelle autour de ce collier de porcelaine.

(Traduction et commentaires préparés par M. Marcel Trudel)

The notes for Appendix H were prepared by Marcel Trudel.

Appendix I

Excerpts of the Constitution Act, 1982

The Constitution Act, 1982

amended by

Constitution Amendment Proclamation, 1983

(SI/84-102)

CONSTITUTION ACT, 1982

PART I

CANADIAN CHARTER OF RIGHTS AND FREEDOMS

Whereas Canada is founded upon principles that recognize the supremacy of God and the rule of law :

Guarantee of Rights and Freedoms

1. The *Canadian Charter of Rights and Freedoms* guarantees the rights and freedoms set out in it subject only to such reasonable limits prescribed by law as can be demonstrably justified in a free and democratic society.

La Loi constitutionnelle de 1982

modifiée par la

Proclamation de 1983
modifiant la Constitution

(TR/84-102)

LOI CONSTITUTIONNELLE DE 1982

PARTIE I

CHARTE CANADIENNE DES DROITS ET LIBERTÉS

Attendu que le Canada est fondé sur des principes qui reconnaissent la suprématie de Dieu et la primauté du droit :

Garantie des droits et libertés

1. La *Charte canadienne des droits et libertés* garantit les droits et libertés qui y sont énoncés. Ils ne peuvent être restreints que par une règle de droit, dans des limites qui soient raisonnables et dont la justification puisse se démontrer dans le cadre d'une société libre et démocratique.

Fundamental Freedoms

2. Everyone has the following fundamental freedoms :
(a) freedom of conscience and religion ;
(b) freedom of thought, belief, opinion and expression, including freedom of the press and other media of communication ;
(c) freedom of peaceful assembly ; and
(d) freedom of association.

General

25. The guarantee in this Charter of certain rights and freedoms shall not be construed so as to abrogate or derogate from any aboriginal, treaty or other rights or freedoms that pertain to the aboriginal peoples of Canada including
(a) any rights or freedoms that have been recognized by the Royal Proclamation of October 7, 1763;
and
(b) any rights or freedoms that now exist by way of land claims agreements or may be so acquired. (SI/84-102)

26. The guarantee in this Charter of certain rights and freedoms shall not be construed as denying the existence of any other rights or freedoms that exist in Canada.

27. This Charter shall be interpreted in a manner consistent with the preservation and enhancement of the multicultural heritage of Canadians.

Libertés fondamentales

2. Chacun a les libertés fondamentales suivantes :
a) liberté de conscience et de religion ;
b) liberté de pensée, de croyance, d'opinion et d'expression, y compris la liberté de la presse et des autres moyens de communication ;
c) liberté de réunion pacifique ;
d) liberté d'association.

Dispositions générales

25. Le fait que la présente charte garantit certains droits et libertés ne porte pas atteinte aux droits ou libertés — ancestraux, issus de traités ou autres — des peuples autochtones du Canada, notamment :
a) aux droits ou libertés reconnus par la proclamation royale du 7 octobre 1763 ;
b) aux droits ou libertés existants issus d'accords sur des revendications territoriales ou ceux susceptibles d'être ainsi acquis. (TR/84-102)

26. Le fait que la présente charte garantit certains droits et libertés ne consitue pas une négation des autres droits ou libertés qui existent au Canada.

27. Toute interprétation de la présente charte doit concorder avec l'objectif de promouvoir le maintien et la valorisation du patrimoine multiculturel des Canadiens.

PART II

RIGHTS OF THE ABORIGINAL
PEOPLES OF CANADA

35. (1) The existing aboriginal and treaty rights of the aboriginal peoples of Canada are hereby recognized and affirmed.

(2) In this Act, "aboriginal peoples of Canada" includes the Indian, Inuit and Métis peoples of Canada.

(3) For greater certainty, in subsection (1) "treaty rights" includes rights that now exist by way of land claims agreements or may be so acquired.

(4) Notwithstanding any other provision of this Act, the aboriginal and treaty rights referred to in subsection (1) are guaranteed equally to male and female persons. (SI/84-102)

35.1 The government of Canada and the provincial governments are committed to the principle that, before any amendment is made to Class 24 of section 91 of the "*Constitution Act, 1867*", to section 25 of this Act or to this Part,
(a) a constitutional conference that includes in its agenda an item relating to the proposed amendment, composed of the Prime Minister of Canada and the first ministers of the provinces, will be convened by the Prime Minister of Canada ; and
(b) the Prime Minister of Canada will invite representatives of the aboriginal peoples of Canada to participate in the discussions on that item. (SI/84-102)

PARTIE II

DROITS DES PEUPLES
AUTOCHTONES DU CANADA

35. (1) Les droit existants — ancestraux ou issus de traités — des peuples autochtones du Canada sont reconnus et confirmés.

(2) Dans la présente loi, « peuples autochtones du Canada » s'entend notamment des Indiens, des Inuit et des Métis du Canada.

(3) Il est entendu que sont compris parmi les droits issus de traités, dont il est fait mention au paragraphe (1), les droits existants issus d'accords sur des revendications territoriales ou ceux susceptibles dêtre ainsi acquis.

(4) Indépendamment de toute autre disposition de la présente loi, les droits — ancestraux ou issus de traités — visés au paragraphe (1) sont garantis également aux personnes des deux sexes. (TR/84-102)

35.1 Les gouvernements fédéral et provinciaux sont liés par l'engagement de principe selon lequel le premier ministre du Canada, avant toute modification de la catégorie 24 de l'article 91 de la « *Loi constitutionnelle de 1867* », de l'article 25 de la présente loi ou de la présente partie :
a) convoquera une conférence constitutionnelle réunissant les premiers ministres provinciaux et lui-même et comportant à son ordre du jour la question du projet de modification ;
b) invitera les représentants des peuples autochtones du Canada à participer aux travaux relatifs à cette question. (TR/84-102)

PART IV

CONSTITUTIONAL CONFERENCE

37. *[Section 54 provided for the repeal of Part IV one year after Part VII came into force. Part VII came into force on April 17, 1982 thereby repealing Part IV on April 17, 1983.]*

Section 37 read as follows :

37. (1) A constitutional conference composed of the Prime Minister of Canada and the first ministers of the provinces shall be convened by the Prime Minister of Canada within one year after this Part comes into force.

(2) The conference convened under subsection (1) shall have included in its agenda an item respecting constitutional matters that directly affect the aboriginal peoples of Canada, including the identification and definition of the rights of those peoples to be included in the Constitution of Canada, and the Prime Minister of Canada shall invite representatives of those peoples to participate in the discussions on that item.

(3) The Prime Minister of Canada shall invite elected representatives of the governments of the Yukon Territory and the Northwest Territories to participate in the discussions on any item on the agenda of the conference convened under subsection (1) that, in the opinion of the Prime Minister, directly affects the Yukon Territory and the Northwest Territories.

PARTIE IV

CONFÉRENCE CONSTITUTIONNELLE

37. *[L'article 54 prévoyait l'abrogation de la partie IV un an après l'entrée en vigueur de la partie VII. La partie VII est entrée en vigueur le 17 avril 1982 abrogeant ainsi la partie IV le 17 avril 1983.]*

L'article 37 se lisait comme suit :

37. (1) Dans l'année suivant l'entrée en vigueur de la présente partie, le premier ministre du Canada convoque une conférence constitutionnelle réunissant les premiers ministres provinciaux et lui-même.

(2) Sont placées à l'ordre du jour de la conférence visée au paragraphe (1) les questions constitutionnelles qui intéressent directement les peuples autochtones du Canada, notamment la détermination des droits de ces peuples à inscrire dans la Constitution du Canada. Le premier ministre du Canada invite leurs représentants à participer aux travaux relatifs à ces questions.

(3) Le premier ministre du Canada invite des représentants élus des gouvernements du territoire du Yukon et des territoires du Nord-Ouest à participer aux travaux relatifs à toute question placée à l'ordre du jour de la conférence visée au paragraphe (1) et qui, selon lui, intéresse directement le territoire du Yukon et les territoires du Nord-Ouest.

PART IV.1

CONSTITUTIONAL CONFERENCES

37.1 *[Section 54.1 provided for the repeal of Part IV.1 and section 54.1 on April 18, 1987.]*
Part IV.1 (section 37.1), which was added by the Constitution Amendment Proclamation, 1983 (SI/84-102), read as follows :

37.1 (1) In addition to the conference convened in March 1983, at least two constitutional conferences composed of the Prime Minister of Canada and the first ministers of the provinces shall be convened by the Prime Minister of Canada, the first within three years after April 17, 1982 and the second within five years after that date.

(2) Each conference convened under subsection (1) shall have included in its agenda constitutional matters that directly affect the aboriginal peoples of Canada, and the Prime Minister of Canada shall invite representatives of those peoples to participate in the discussions on those matters.

(3) The Prime Minister of Canada shall invite elected representatives of the governments of the Yukon Territory and the Northwest Territories to participate in the discussions on any item on the agenda of a conference convened under subsection (1) that, in the opinion of the Prime Minister, directly affects the Yukon Territory and the Northwest Territories.

(4) Nothing in this section shall be construed so as to derogate from subsection 35 (1).

PARTIE IV.1

CONFÉRENCES CONSTITUTIONNELLES

37.1 *[L'article 54.1 prévoyait l'abrogation de la partie IV.1 et de l'article 54.1 le 18 avril 1987.]*
La partie IV.1 (article 37.1), qui avait été ajoutée par la Proclamation de 1983 modifiant la Constitution (TR/84-102), se lisait comme suit :

37.1 (1) En sus de la conférence convoquée en mars 1983, le premier ministre du Canada convoque au moins deux conférences constitutionnelles réunissant les premiers ministres provinciaux et lui-même, la première dans les trois ans et la seconde dans les cinq ans suivant le 17 avril 1982.

(2) Sont placées à l'ordre du jour de chacune des conférences visées au paragraphe (1) les questions constitutionnelles qui intéressent directement les peuples autochtones du Canada. Le premier ministre du Canada invite leurs représentants à participer aux travaux relatifs à ces questions.

(3) Le premier ministre du Canada invite des représentants élus des gouvernements du territoire du Yukon et des territoires du Nord-Ouest à participer aux travaux relatifs à toute question placée à l'ordre du jour des conférences visées au paragraphe (1) et qui, selon lui, intéresse directement le territoire du Yukon et les territoires du Nord-Ouest.

(4) Le présent article n'a pas pour effet de déroger au paragraphe 35 (1).

PART V

PROCEDURE FOR AMENDING THE CONSTITUTION OF CANADA

38. (1) An amendment to the Constitution of Canada may be made by proclamation issued by the Governor General under the Great Seal of Canada where so authorized by
(a) resolutions of the Senate and House of Commons ; and
(b) resolutions of the legislative assemblies of at least two-thirds of the provinces that have, in the aggregate, according to the then latest general census, at least fifty per cent of the population of all the provinces.

(2) An amendment made under subsection (1) that derogates from the legislative powers, the proprietary rights or any other rights or privileges of the legislature or government of a province shall require a resolution supported by a majority of the members of each of the Senate, the House of Commons and the legislative assemblies required under subsection (1).

(3) An amendment referred to in subsection (2) shall not have effect in a province the legislative assembly of which has expressed its dissent thereto by resolution supported by a majority of its members prior to the issue of the proclamation to which the amendment relates unless that legislative assembly, subsequently, by resolution supported by a majority of its members, revokes its dissent and authorizes the amendment.

(4) A resolution of dissent make for the purposes of subsection (3) may be revoked at any time before or after the issue of the proclamation to which it relates.

PARTIE V

PROCÉDURE DE MODIFICATION DE LA CONSTITUTION DU CANADA

38. (1) La Constitution du Canada peut être modifiée par proclamation du gouverneur général sous le grand sceau du Canada, autorisée à la fois :
a) par des résolutions du Sénat et de la Chambre des communes ;
b) par des résolutions des assemblées législatives d'au moins deux tiers des provinces dont la population confondue représente, selon le recensement général le plus récent à l'époque, au moins cinquante pour cent de la population de toutes les provinces.

(2) Une modification faite conformément au paragraphe (1) mais dérogatoire à la compétence législative, aux droits de propriété ou à tous autres droits ou privilèges d'une législation ou d'un gouvernement provincial exige une résolution adoptée à la majorité des sénateurs, des députés fédéraux et des députés de chacune des assemblées législatives du nombre requis de provinces.

(3) La modification visée au paragraphe (2) est sans effet dans une province dont l'assemblée législative a, avant la prise de la proclamation, exprimé son désaccord par une résolution adoptée à la majorité des députés, sauf si cette assemblée, par résolution également adoptée à la majorité, revient sur son désaccord et autorise la modification.

(4) La résolution de désaccord visée au paragraphe (3) peut être révoquée à tout moment, indépendamment de la date de la proclamation à laquelle elle se rapporte.

39. (1) A proclamation shall not be issued under subsection 38 (1) before the expiration of one year from the adoption of the resolution initiating the amendment procedure thereunder, unless the legislative assembly of each province has previously adopted a resolution of assent by dissent.

(2) A proclamation shall not be issued under subsection 38 (1) after the expiration of three years from the adoption of the resolution initiating the amendment procedure thereunder.

39. (1) La proclamation visée au paragraphe 38 (1) ne peut être prise dans l'année suivant l'adoption de la résolution à l'origine de la procédure de modification que si l'assemblée législative de chaque province a préalablement adopté une résolution d'agrément ou de désaccord.

(2) La proclamation visée au paragraphe 38 (1) ne peut être prise que dans les trois ans suivant l'adoption de la résolution à l'origine de la procédure de modification.

Appendix J

Excerpts of the Manifesto of the Aboriginal and Quebec People's Equality Forum Issued in the Fall of 1993

1. Equality Forum

The Aboriginal and Québec Peoples' Equality Forum is a discussion group composed of spokespersons and representatives of Aboriginal and Québécois organizations, some of which include several thousand members. Some twenty people participate regularly in the Forum, which has held over fifteen formal meetings. For practical reasons, the Forum does not include all Aboriginal or Québécois organizations that could be interested in the debate; however, its goal is to widen this debate as its work progresses.

The Forum discusses fundamental aspects of the relations between Aboriginal and Québécois peoples: self-government, self-determination, relationship to the land, individual, collective and national rights, political framework, jurisdictions existing here and elsewhere in the world, conflict resolution, points of divergence and of convergence between Aboriginal and Québécois people, economic and social ties, cultural development, etc.

The Forum is a special meeting place where organizations and nations can exchange information on each other's concerns and share analyses of the situation in order to better understand each other and to draft the guidelines of a societal project which would include such concerns and analyses.

The Forum seeks to identify and eliminate prejudice; it also strives to improve the understanding by the participating groups of each other's circumstances.

The Forum should be seen as a place where the points of convergence between the various peoples can be identified and enhanced. In its concern to remain realistic, the Forum also wants to identify points of divergence and to clarify the means by which to overcome them.

Beyond the deadlock of the broad politico-legal debate on the place of Aboriginal peoples and of Québec within the Constitution, the Forum must be seen as a place where some "vital forces" of the Québécois and Aboriginal milieux are trying to fill the void that divides the population of Québec and Aboriginal peoples.

The Forum is neither an Aboriginal support group, nor a platform for a specific political option for Québec.

Some of the participating organizations promote sovereignty for Québec. The Forum considers this option to be plausible, not as an end in itself, but as a means to attain certain goals and to develop a viable vision of society.

In the opinion of the Forum, Québec sovereignty, if it is to be achieved, should be carried out in association with the Aboriginal peoples. It should constitute a means to become autonomous, to take control over their own affairs and to flourish at all levels — economic, political, social and cultural — according to the needs and interests of each people living on the territory. The Forum refuses to approach the debate on a theoretical basis which highlights only the legal difficulties. Sovereignty of the Aboriginal and Québec nations must be considered in a perspective of increasing autonomy with respect to decisions which affect them and, particularly in the case of Aboriginal peoples, of abolishing the present dependance so as to promote development at a pace which suits each nation.

In our opinion, sovereignty implies the power of a people to make its own laws, to collect its own taxes and to conclude treaties with other peoples.

The Forum is first and foremost a communication and a meeting place between Aboriginal and Québécois socio-economic forces.

2. Objectives
In the broader perspective of developing a true alliance between the Québec and Aboriginal nations, our efforts are geared towards five complementary objectives.

2.1 For Aboriginal and Québécois people to get to learn about each other and identify the major issues of coexistance.

2.2 To clearly articulate concepts which will allow us to come together around a joint plan of action (in matters such as: self-government, aboriginal rights, inclusion, etc.).

2.3 To agree on one or more proposals of components of a new alliance.

2.4 To aquire, within each group participating in the Forum, the means to inform, to raise awareness and to take positions on issues being studied.

2.5 To become an active voice in the public debate, in order to provide sound information and to objectively and positively influence the debate as well as any decisions which may be taken regarding the future relationships between Québécois and Aboriginal peoples.

3. Process
[...]

4. Principles
At the outset of its presentation, the Forum wants to state the principles, agreed to by all members, which guide its discussions and its positions.

4.1 The Forum recognizes the right to self-determination of the peoples living in Québec, that is the eleven Aboriginal peoples and the Québécois people. It also recognizes that the democratic exercise of this right could lead to their accession to political sovereignty. In such a case, the Forum maintains that geographical imperatives and political wisdom would imply a necessary association. The Forum is committed to the defense of this right to self-determination and of its exercise, and to promote this association, should the occasion arise.

4.2 The Forum considers that whether in the name of individual or collective rights, the mere legal protection of Aboriginal peoples on the Québec territory, even if they are in a minority position, would not in itself be sufficient. It recognizes that the aboriginal rights of these peoples include territorial rights yet to be defined and an inherent right to self-government.

4.3 The Forum recognizes the rights of the Québec people, which evolve from the fact that they have occupied and developed part of the territory over more than three centuries. [...]

The process of accession to political autonomy, or self-government, will imply the establishment of governments based on territory rather than on the racial or ethnic background of its subjects. However, these governments would be able to take special measures, inspired by international law and declarations of the United Nations, to protect the ethnic character of their components.

In addition, these governments must have the means to protect their language and national culture, as well as an independant economic base.

Non-Aboriginal people who live and work within territories under the jurisdiction of these governments will have the same rights and duties as the citizens of these territories.

4.4 The Forum recognizes that, should the political status of Québec be modified, the rights of Aboriginal peoples and of persons forming part thereof existing at the time will be fully maintained and all obligations previously borne by Canada towards them shall then be borne by Québec unless they are modified through agreements.

4.5 The Forum does not pretend to settle all contentious issues in the relationships between Aboriginal and Québec nations. However, it recommends the immediate creation, by the Québec nation and the Aboriginal nations, of a Québec-Aboriginal joint entity with the authority required to commence negotiations and the just and progressive application of agreements between the affected parties. [...]

5. Political Framework
Eleven Aboriginal nations have been recognized by the Québec National Assembly since 1985. These eleven nations have aboriginal rights that include territorial rights. [...]

6. Existing Economic and Social Ties
[...]

7. Cultural Development
[...]

The Forum does not believe that Québec should impose a second language on Aboriginal peoples. However, the Forum recommends the promotion of French as a language of exchange and that necessary steps be taken to develop the knowledge and use of Aboriginal languages, as well as steps to encourage the cultures of Aboriginal nations to flourish and become widely known in Québec society.

[...]

8. Individual, Collective and National Rights
The currently existing legal instruments are not adapted to the reality of the collective and national rights of the Québécois people and of Aboriginal peoples. The Forum believes that it is necessary to have a common charter based on the Universal Declaration of Human Rights, which will provide for the protection of fundamental individual rights as well as collective and national rights, and gender equality.

The Forum considers collective rights to mean among others, the right for everyone to work, freedom of association, the right to health and shelter, the right to the quality of the environment and to education; it considers national rights to include the right to self-government, the protection and promotion of language and culture, etc.

9. Conflict Resolution Between Nations
[...]

10. Conclusion
The approach of the Equality Forum comes within the process of developing a societal project which also aims to be a concrete formula of coexistence. The Forum seeks to envisage the future without forgetting the past.

At present, there are important political and legal tensions between the Aboriginal and Québec populations, and it has become urgent not only to improve communication at these levels but to establish it in other respects, in particular at the social and economic levels.

The initiative of the Forum represents only the beginning of an encounter, and the circle of common work shall have to expand so as to include other active participants in Aboriginal and Québec societies.

Differences will always exist with respect to culture, language, way of life and certain development priorities; we must learn to live with these differences and to respect them.

However, we have the common responsability to immediately do all that is within our power to reinforce our points of convergence. History and geography have summoned us to take up the challenge of living together, and identifying the basis for our mutual relations.

The historical meeting which took place in 1534 was compromised because it was based on a relationship of force; it must now be made real in a context of justice, equality and mutual respect. Our solitudes have become intolerable; Québécois and Aboriginal people must built the foundations of a social equilibrium on which a true alliance can be based.

The members of the Forum commit themselves to continue their work within their respective organizations and invite other organizations and persons who want to be positive agents of change to share in these reflections.

In order to promote equitable, harmonious, enriching and promising relationships between Québécois and Aboriginal peoples, the following persons have signed the present manifesto.

From the Assemblée des Évêques du Québec: Gérard Drainville

From the Québec Native Women Association: Jackie Kistabish

From the Centrale de l'enseignement du Québec: Lorraine Pagé, Daniel Lachance and Henri Laberge

From the Centre justice et foi: Julien Harvey

From the Confédération des caisses Desjardins: Michel Doray and Claude Têtu

From the Confédération des syndicats nationaux: Gérald Larose, co-chairman

From the Conseil des Atikamekw et des Montagnais: René Simon and Arthur Robertson

From the Grand conseil des Cris du Québec Co-chairman: Diom Roméo Saganash

From the Ligue des droits et libertés: Gérald McKenzie and Sylvie Paquerot

From the Regroupement des centres d'amitié autochtone du Québec: Édith Cloutier

Contact: Bernard Cleary

Animation and coordination: Pierre Bonnet and René Boudreault

Note: The present manifesto of the Aboriginal and Québec Peoples Equality Forum has obtained concensus among the signatories representing their respective organizations. The process of appropriation by these organizations' authorities is underway.

Appendix K

Excerpts of a Speech by George E. Sioui, Edmonton, March 17, 1995

Wendats in History: The *Sioui* Ruling

[...]

Our Nation, the Wendat, just like the Iroquois, had a very high gift for adopting people, assimilating them to our society.

[...]

Our [Wendat] ancestors were able to survive because they went on war expeditions to supposedly help the French fight the English, but their real agenda was to go and capture English children, English people, bring them back to their villages and raise them as Wendat people. The Iroquois did the same, many Amerindian peoples did the same, but we Wendat did this very systematically. And today there is not this notion that you are "part-Indian," that does not exist. I'm not part-Indian, even if I have this French accent; you all have an English accent, or a Spanish accent, it does not mean anything. I'm a Wendat. And I think that we're in a process of reclaiming our people that say that they are part-Indian, part-Cree, part-Cherokee, part-anything. They are going to come back and be First Nations people. And the door is also open to non-First Nations people: we were always able to transform non-Indians into Indian people, because we all come from the Circle. There is no such thing as distinct races and civilizations; there is only one civilization of the Circle. And the people who have chosen to become linear, who had to leave Europe because they had adopted this linear worldview, are not able to sustain their civilization much longer here, in our land, because it's not adapted to our land. Slowly, they will have to adopt our [worldview], because it's a circular worldview. So, we are going to eventually adopt and assimilate them, or as we said in our old Wendat language, "eat" them. The English word, "assimilate," carries the same meaning: to eat someone up, culturally. Even though we had very small numbers, we, Wendat, as well as many tribes in the East, were always able to "eat up" the dominant society. We never lost our distinct identity. We're not part-Indian. We're Wendat.

[...]

It's just coincidental that this Conference occurs in the city of Edmonton and that it will be fifteen years ago in two days that I met Eddie [Bellerose] and other Elders, Saulteaux and Assiniboine, Uncle Abe Burnstick, Peter Ochiese, and that they were able to liberate me and my friends from alcohol. My family, as most of our First Nations families, has suffered a lot from alcohol. We still do. But we were relieved and liberated through the teachings of our Elders. So, I very deeply respect Eddie Bellerose. Meeting Eddie Bellerose and the Elders that you have here in the West meant that then years after, I, and my brothers, were going to beat the Province of Quebec in the Supreme Court of Canada over a case of religious and territorial rights come to be known as the *Sioui* Case, because we learned with Eddie and the Elders. Eventually, we had wanted to take this learning back to our own home-territories in Ontario and Quebec. When we did take it back to Quebec, we fasted, in 1982, in Quebec, on some of our traditional hunting land. My stubborn family (that is how the Siouis are known since ever in Quebec) had always kept up the custom of going to those territories to hunt and fish, and collect plants. That time, we were not doing any of that, we were fasting, and that's why we won, eventually. It took eight years, we went to court four times and we eventually won in the Supreme Court. The *Sioui* Case started with this person [Elder Bellerose], and it meant a very great upheaval in Quebec politics and Canadian politics and world politics concerning Indigenous Peoples. And it started here in Alberta, on the Kootenay Plains with your Elders.

We were arrested for, they said, "mutilating the forest." We had made some fasting lodges, using willow saplings, and thus, had "mutilated the forest," while the rest of thousands of square kilometres of forest was clear-cut. The bush was all destroyed, but that is "forest exploitation" for linear-thinking people. We had mutilated the forest and so were prosecuted by Quebec. We finally pulled out from our archives an old document that we had, which was signed by the hand of the British Brigadier-General James Murray, in 1760, which said that under the new English regime, our Tribe would have the free exercise of our customs and our religion and our trade with the English. So, we looked at this as a Treaty because it talked about the customs and religion. They (Quebec) said it was only a safe-conduct to allow us to go back to our Settlements without being attacked by the British troops. So, we fought, and through the vision, through the tradition that the Elders gave us back, this understanding of our deeper identity, we were able to infuse a new meaning in that document, which was only a scrap of paper, 230 years old. We were able to put a new life into this dead piece of paper. And we eventually had it recognized by the Supreme Court of Canada that it actually was a Treaty. This had grave impli-cations for Quebec. By explaining about this case, I meant to stress the importance of Elders, the importance of spirituality, relating our own experience. We already had our pride and our counsciousness as Indian individuals belonging to this Eastern, very battered tribe, the Wendat, so-called Huron, but we lacked this deeper understanding of our spirituality, of our Indianness, a deeper sense of our being as Indian People, and the Elders, your Elders here, gave that back to us. That accorded with what our parents always told us about our Indian people: we are all one family. Wherever you go, South, North, East or West, approach your Indian people as your relatives, and treat them as relatives, and you'll be treated as relatives. So, the Elders gave us back what we had lost, the same way as today, as Indians, we have to give back to the non-Indian what they have lost. They have had to become linear, for some reason. It's none of their fault. That linear thinking can only produce destruction: there is only one word for what's been happening and what's still happening to our land and to us: des-truction. We have to give them back the Circle, their original circular vision, where we all come from, as human beings.

[...]

As a Wendat, I don't have very much left, but I have something very important left, which is my sense of history. And I receive all the time, continuously, I receive from everyone, and I really believe that together we are forming a very powerful people, a very powerful Nation. I have to congratulate Alberta. I don't know anything and am not interested in politics, but for the first time in the history of Canada, there is a "part-Indian" Prime Minister in one of the Provinces. I hope someday he says he is Indian, and not simply "part-Indian." And besides, his wife is Indian. So, this means that we're headed in the direction of Native leadership in this land. I very firmly believe that we are going to come back to a position of command in this land of ours. When I say "our land," I want to stress that when we say "our land," we mean that we come from the land, just as when I say my mother, my father: I come from them. I don't say: my mother is mine, she belongs to me: I belong to her. The non-Indians say: my land: it belongs to me. That's what we have to change all around. If we are able to give to them that feeling that they belong to this land, instead of this land belongs to them, we'll be OK. If we fail in meeting that challenge as First Nations people, what we can expect all of us is that great hunger in times ahead of which our Elder talked to us, this morning. I still think that we can hope together. But First Nations people have to get busy with the task of assimilating, Indianizing the non-Indian society and thereby, avoid what's coming our way if we keep on with this linear thinking, this path of destruction. We all know that. If we bring society back to seeing Life as a sacred Circle of Relations, we are going to achieve our goal and our responsibility as First Nations people, in relation to our White and Black and Yellow brothers and sisters, the great human family of which we are a part.

Thank you very much.

Sources

At the National Archives of Canada, I was able to count on Patricia Kennedy's usual helpfulness, as well as the efficiency of Carole Séguin and Claudette Larouche of the iconography section. At the National Library, Joyce M. Banks skilfully guided me through the collection of rare and old books.

At the Archives nationales du Québec, Reynald Lessard, Claude Boudreau, Christine Picard, Marjolaine Villeneuve, Jean-Paul de Beaumont, and Clermont Dupont facilitated my research and were always available.

It would be too long a list – and I would risk forgetting someone – to mention all those who welcomed me and guided me in the various documentation centres I visited. I am nevertheless deeply grateful to them.

TRANSLATOR'S NOTE:
The asterisk indicates
that quotations from
these sources in the text
are translations.

MANUSCRIPT SOURCES

National Archives of Canada

MG 10, vol. 1826 – Indian Records, vol. 7, Minutes of Indian Affairs, 1755–1790: Indian Conference, 26–02–1765.

MG 10, vol. 1828 – Indian Records, vol. 9, Superintendent's Office Correspondence, 1755–1830.

MG 11, C.O. 217, vol. 31 – Nova Scotia Papers, Treaty of 18–10–1752, Correspondence from Hopson to Holderness.

MG 11, W.O. 34, vols. 34, 38, 50 – Amherst Papers.

MG 18, L 2 – Letters written by James Murray, 1749–62.

MG 19, F1, vol. 1 – Daniel Claus's Papers.

MG 21, Add. MSS. 21631–21892 – Haldimand Papers.

MG 21, G II – Haldimand Papers, "papers left at Quebec . . ."

MG 23, I, 13, vol. 1 – Sharpe Papers, charges against James Murray, 1765–67.

MG 23, G II, 1: 1, 2, and 3: Letters by James Murray.

MG 24, B 1 – John Neilson Collection.

MG 24, G 45 – Reports and correspondence from Salaberry (1813) of the Department of Indian Affairs.

RG 4, A 1, vol. 1 – Redemption of Papers.

RG 4, A 1, vol. 2 – Murray Papers.

RG 10 – Indian Affairs: vols. 4–8, Minutes 1755–72; vol. 9, series 2, correspondence from William Johnson; vol. 14, series 2, Récla-mations, 1717–1842; vols. 625–627, Various, 1765–1843; vol. 715, Indian Claims, 1814–26; vol. 1822–1826, vol. 1829–1832, journals of W. Johnson and Guy Johnson, 1755–90; vol. 1840–1852, parts 1–2, treaties and concessions, 1725–1956.

RG 14, A 1 and A 3 – Lower Canada, Legislative Council, minutes, addresses, and petitions.

RPAC, 1904, app. B: 23–24 – Treaty of 18–07–1764.

National Archives of Quebec

3A19–2302A – Fonds Amherst.

3A19–3709A – Fonds *Halifax Gazette*.

3C30–4501A – Sessions de la Paix, 1823–1878.

4M00–2510A – Fonds John Neilson.

4M00–0575A – Biens des Jésuites.

4M00-2514A – Fonds Brown & =Gilmore, Gazette de Québec, account books, 1762–1912.

4M00–6328A – Seigneurie de Sillery.

IR 300298 – Fonds Barthélemy Faribault, fils.

IR 300939 – Fonds Georges-Barthélemi Faribault.

The collections of the following notaries: J.-B. Panet (Quarante Arpents, concessions by the Jesuits to the Hurons in 1792 and 1794); Dom Lefrançois (Charlesbourg), 1822 to 1826 (art. 8, 01–01–1822 to 30–03–1823 and art. 10, 01–11–1824 to 31–12–1826, are available for consultation, while art. 9, covering the laws enacted between 30–03–1823 and 31–12–1826, mention "originals permanently retained for consultation"); C.-D. Plante (1825–36); Archibald Campbell (1812–61); Errol Boyd Lindsay (1823–75); Louis Panet (1819–79); Pierre Paradis (1820–72).

New York Historical Society
The Journal of Jelles Fonda.

Archives des Colonies, France
Series $C^{11}E$. Boundaries and posts. Microfilms 1651–1818 and transcriptions 1651–1818.

Papers relating to the boundaries of the French colonies and various posts established in North America.

Volumes 1–9 – Setting of bounderies, 1685–1762.

Volume 10 – Rivalries between English and French colonies in North America, 1686–1764.

Volumes 13–16: French posts in North America, 1665, 1815.

Archives du ministère des Affaires étrangères, Paris
MG 5 B1

Volume 9 – Transcripts 1749–53. Boundaries of North American colonies. Taking possession of the Ohio Valley. Boundaries of the Abenaki territory. Treaty between Hopson and the Micmacs.

Volumes 21–22 – Transcripts, 1750–59. Boundaries of the colonies. Importance of Canada and Louisiana.

Volume 24 – Transcriptions 1750–59. Should Canada be abandoned? Plan to transfer Canadiens to Louisiana. Memo on the Ohio River.

Volume 25 – Transcripts 1760–63. Situation of English and French possessions. Boundaries of colonies. Opinions expressed on the abandonment or preservation of Canada.

Archives de la guerre, Service historique de l'Armée (France)

MG 4 B1 – Series of memoirs and acknowledgments. Microfilm 1699–1867. Article 247: Seven Years' War (analysis of the papers of Jean-Nicolas Desandrouins), 1755–83. Spool F-732.

Archives de la guerre, Comité technique du Génie (France)

MG 4 C2 – Ms in-folio 210d. Memos and plans: Canada and Ile Royale. Memo on the present state of Canada; names of the nations of savages living there, 1730. Fort at Detroit, 1752. Council held with different nations of savages at Fort Duquesne, signed by Contre-cœur, 1754.

MG 4 C1 – Ms in-folio 210e and 210f. Documents relating to Franquet. Article 14: foreign places. Transcriptions 1729–84. Northern America. The property rights of the French. A number of notes on savage peoples and their encouragement by the English to rise up against the French.

Printed sources

Gazette de Québec – 24–01–1765, 22–12–1766, 25–12–1766, 13–01–1785, 19–03–1818, 22–01–1819, 01–02–1819, 26–02–1821, 28–078–1823, 03–10–1823.

Boehm, Randolph (ed.) *Records of the British Colonial Office. Westward Expansion, 1760–1783; the Board of Trade, the French and Indian War.* 26 microfilm spools; guide written by Linda Womaski, ca. 1972.

*Bougainville, Louis-Antoine de. *Écrits sur le Canada.* Sillery: Pélican/ Klincksieck, 1993.

*Casgrain, H.-R. (ed.). *Collection de Manuscrits du maréchal de Lévis.* 12 vols. Quebec City and Montreal, 1889–95. Vol. 1, *Journal des campagnes du chevalier de Lévis en Canada de 1756 à 1760.* Montreal, 1889. Vol. 2, *Lettres du chevalier de Lévis concernant la guerre du Canada (1756–1760).* Montreal, 1889. Vol. 4, *Lettres et pièces militaires, instructions, ordres, mémoires, plans de campagne et de défense 1756–1760.* Quebec City, 1891. (Unsigned text titled "Suite de la campagne du Canada.") Vol. 5, *Lettres de M. de Bourlamaque* *au Chevalier de Lévis,* Quebec City, 1891. Vol. 10, *Lettres de divers particuliers au Chevalier de Lévis,* Quebec City, 1895.

Corey, Albert B., et al. (eds.). *The Papers of Sir William Johnson.* 14 vols. (including index volume). Albany, 1962. (See Sullivan, James.)

Doughty, Arthur G. (ed.). *Report of the Work of the Archives Branch for the Year 1910.* Ottawa, 1912.

———. *Report of the Work of the Archives Branch for the Year 1913.* Ottawa, 1915.

———. *An historical journal of the campaigns in North America, for the years 1757, 1758, 1759, and 1760.* [John Knox] Champlain Society, 1914–16.

———. *Report of the Work of the Archives Branch for the Year 1918.* Ottawa, 1920. In appendix B are orders, proclamations, and other documents issued by the military governor of Quebec City, Montreal, and Trois-Rivières from the surrender of Quebec City to the establishment of a civil government on August 10, 1764.

Doughty, A.G., and Short, Adam (eds.). *Documents Relating to the Constitutional History of Canada, 1759–1791.* Ottawa, 1921.

Drimmer, Frederick (ed.). *Captured by the Indians, 15 Firsthand Accounts, 1750–1870.* Dover, 1951.

Franquet, Louis. *Voyages et Mémoires sur le Canada.* Élysée, 1974.

[Fraser, Malcolm.] *Extract from a manuscript journal relating to the siege of Quebec in 1759 kept by Colonel Malcolm Fraser.* Published under the auspices of the Literary and Historical Society, Quebec City.

J.-C.-B. *Voyage au Canada fait depuis l'an 1751 jusqu'en l'an 1761.* Aubier Montaigne, 1978.

Jennings, Francis (ed.). *Iroquois Indians: A Documentary History of the Diplomacy of the Six Nations and Their League. Guide to the Microfilm Collection.* Woodridge: Research Publications, 1985.

Journal of the House of Assembly, Lower Canada, 1824. Fourth Session of Eleventh Provincial. Appendice R.

Knox, John. *The Siege of Quebec and the Campaigns in North America 1757–1760.* Ed. by Brian Connell. Mississauga: Pendragon House, 1980. (See also the edition prepared by Arthur G. Doughty for the Champlain Society.)

*Long, John. *Voyages chez différentes nations sauvages de l'Amérique septentrionale, 1768–1787.* Paris: A.M. Métailié, 1980.

*Malartic, Anne de Maurès de. *Journal des campagnes au Canada de 1755 à 1760 par le comte de Maurès de Malartic.* Ed. by Gabriel de Maurès de Malartic and Paul Gaffarel. Dijon: L. Damidot, 1890.

Mante, Thomas. *The History of the late war in North America and the Islands of the West-Indies including the campaigns of MDCCLXIII and MDCCCLXIV against His Majesty's Indian Enemies.* London, 1772.

[Murray, James.] *Governor Murray's Journal of Quebec – From 18th September, 1759, to 25th May, 1760.* Quebec City and Montreal: Literary and Historical Society of Quebec, 1871.

O'Callaghan, E.B., and Fernow, B. (eds.). *Documents relating to the Colonial History of the State of New York, procured in Holland, England and France.* 15 vols. Albany, 1853–87.

*Pouchot, Pierre. *Mémoires sur la dernière guerre de l'Amérique septentrionale entre la France et l'Angleterre, suivis d'observations, dont plusieurs sont relative au théâtre actuel de la guerre, et de nouveaux détails sur le mœurs et les usages des sauvages, avec des cartes topographiques.* 3 vols. Yverdon, 1781.

Roy, Pierre-Georges (ed.). *Rapport de l'archiviste de la Province de Québec pour 1923–1924.* Ls.-A. Proulx, Queen's Printer, 1924.

Sullivan, James, et al. (eds.). *The Papers of Sir William Johnson.* 14 vols. (including index volume). Albany, 1962. (See Corey, Albert C.)

Webster, J. Clarence (ed.) [Amherst, Jeffery]. *The Journal of Jeffery Amherst (1758–1764).* Toronto: Ryerson Press.

———. [Amherst, William]. *The Journal of William Amherst in America (1758–1760).* Toronto: Ryerson Press.

Ministère de la Justice, Quebec City

200-005-002-589-930 (Vault) – Request for an injunction by lawyer Pouliot in Superior Court of Quebec.

200-05-00520-945 – Action for a declaration by lawyer Larochelle in Superior Court of Quebec.

Mémoire du procureur général du Québec préparé en demande d'autorisation d'un appel auprès de la Cour suprême du Canada faisant suite au jugement de la Court d'appel du Québec, district de Montréal, le 17 mai 1983 (Côté v. Her Majesty).

Supreme Court of Canada, Ottawa

Simon ruling: 17006.

Sioui ruling: 20628. (Aside from the microfilm that contains the main documents related to the Supreme Court ruling, I consulted a collection of "documents of the attorney general of Quebec" also bearing on file 20628.)

*Supreme Court Records. Calder ruling. 1973.

VARIOUS LEGAL DOCUMENTS

Here are the main steps that led the Sioui brothers from their purification ritual of May 29, 1982, to the *Sioui* ruling of May 24, 1990.

1. Ruling by Judge André Bilodeau of the Court of Sessions of the Peace, 9 June 1983.
2. Notice of appeal (*de novo* process), 12 July 1832 by André C. Cartier.
3. Evidence presented by the Crown in Superior Court on 18 May 1984.
4. Evidence presented by the defendants in Superior Court on 18 May 1984, 24 May 1984, and 9 August 1984.
5. Ruling by Judge Gaston Desjardins of Superior Court (Criminal Court) on 6 September 1985.
6. Request for permission to appeal on 19 September 1985 by Michel Pouliot.
7. Permission to appeal to the Court of Appeal granted by Judge Yves Bernier, 19 October 1985.
8. Notice of appeal on 3 October 1985 by Pouliot.
9. Ruling of the Court of Appeal on 8 September 1987.
10. Permission to appeal to the Supreme Court on 25 February 1988.
11. Notice of petition of appeal before the Supreme Court on 8 March 1988.
12. Order of the Supreme Court on 23 March 1988.
13. Ruling of the Supreme Court on 24 May 1990.

Rulings leading to the Sioui ruling

*Court of the Sessions of the Peace, Quebec City district. Ruling rendered by Judge André Bilodeau, 9 June 1983.

*Superior Court, Quebec City district. *Sioui v. Procureur général du Québec*. Ruling rendered by Judge Gaston Desjardins, 6 September 1985. I was able to consult the court transcripts of 18 and 24 May 1984 and 9 August 1984.

Court of Appeal of Quebec, *Sioui v. Procureur général du Québec*. Ruling rendered by justices Paré, Bisson, and Jacques. Justice Paré was in accord with the opinion written by Justice Bisson, while Justice Jacques wrote a dissenting opinion. RJQ, 1982, pp. 1722–31.

Supreme Court of Canada, *Her Majesty v. Sioui*. Ruling rendered by Justice Antonio Lamer on 24 May 1990.

I have consulted the memorandum of the appellant, the attorney general of Quebec, presented by René Morin and Robert Décary; the transcript of the arguments made before the court by Jacques Larochelle, who represented the four Sioui brothers with Michel Pouliot; and the memorandum of the defendants signed by Jacques Larochelle on 4 October 1989.

Various rulings relating to Indian treaties of 1760

Supreme Court of Canada, *Simon v. Her Majesty*. Ruling rendered by Chief Justice Dickson in the presence of justices Beetz, Estey, McIntyre, Chouinard, Wilson, and Le Dain. SCR, 1985, pp. 387–416.

Superior Court of Quebec, *Decontie v. Her Majesty*. Ruling rendered by Justice Orville Frenette. RJQ, 1989, pp. 1893–1913.

Superior Court of Quebec, *Vincent v. Lanctôt.*, ruling rendered by Judge Robert Legris. RJQ, 1990, pp. 813–22.

Court of Justice of Ontario, *Her Majesty v. Vincent*. Ruling rendered orally by Justice R.G. Masse on 29 July 1991 in Cornwall, Ontario, and in written form on 16 August 1991 in Ottawa, Ontario. (Typed copy.)

Court of Quebec (Criminal and Penal Court). *Her Majesty v. Nicholas*. Ruling rendered in Saint-Jérôme by Judge Bruno Cyr, 26 February 1992. (Typed copy.)

Court of Appeal of Quebec, *Adams v. Her Majesty*. Ruling rendered by justices Beauregard, Proulx, and Rothman (diss.). RJQ, 1993, pp. 1011–43.

Court of Appeal of Quebec, *Côté v. Her Majesty*. Ruling rendered by judges Baudouin, Tyndale, and Delisle (diss.) on 17 May 1993. (Typed copy.)

Superior Court of Quebec, *Sioui v. Sous-ministre du revenu du Québec*. Ruling rendered by Judge France Thibault, 26 May 1995. (Typed copy.)

Studies written by historians for these trials

Beaulieu, Alain. *Les Hurons de Lorette, le "traité de Murray" et la liberté de commerce.* 25 April 1994. 104 pages including appendices and a bibliography. A slightly expanded version (112 pages) was produced for the trial of Gabriel Sioui in Superior Court, for which a ruling was rendered on 26 May 1995.

*Delâge, Denys. *Contexte historique du traité de 1760 entre les Hurons de Lorette et le général Murray.* 20 December 1988. 10 pages. (Typed document.)

*———. *Les Hurons de Lorette dans leur contexte historique de 1760.* March 1994. 41 pages. (Typed document.)

Eccles, William John. *The historical context surrounding the alleged document of September the 5th 1760 concerning the Hurons of Lorette.* February 1989. 17 pages. (Typed document.)

Graves, Donald E. *The Huron of Lorette, the General Murray Treaty of 1760, the Jay Treaty and the Treaty of Ghent. Historical Analysis and Opinion.* November 1990. 54 pages. (Typed document.)

MacLeod, Peter D. (1990). *The Huron of Lorette and the Murray Treaty of 1760. Historical Analysis and Opinion.* 1990. Also a 14-page "commentary" in reaction to Denis Delâge's study. (Typed document.)

*Parent, Raynald. *Les institutions et les fondements politiques des nations amérindiennes: 1760–1853.* n.d. 23 pages followed by 170 notes, mainly referring to the *Johnson Papers* and the RG 10 collection of the National Archives of Canada.

*Trudel, Marcel. *Mémoire sur un sauf-conduit accordé aux Hurons par le général Murray le 5 septembre 1760.* Ca. 1992. 15 pages. (Typed document; *Her Majesty v. Nicholas.)*

References

Assiniwi, Bernard. *Histoire des Indiens du Haut et du Bas-Canada.* 3 vols. Leméac, 1973–74.

*Audin, Marius. *Le Livre, son architecture, sa technique.* Robert Morel, 1969.

Axelrod, Alan. *Chronicle of the Indian Wars: From Colonial Times to Wounded Knee.* New York: Prentice Hall, 1993.

Axtell, James. *The European and the Indian: Essays in the Ethnohistory of Colonial North America.* Oxford University Press, 1981.

Baker, Charlotte Alice. *True Stories of New England Captives Carried to Canada during the Old French and Indian Wars.* Cambridge: Greenfield Press, 1897.

Bayefsky, Anne F. *Canada's Constitution Act 1982 & Amendments: A Documentary History.* McGraw-Hill Ryerson, 1989.

Beaulieu, Alain. *Les traités d'Oswegatchie et de Kahnawake (1760): contexte, acteurs et contenu.* Unpublished report, 23 Jan. 1995.

Beaulieu, Jacqueline, Christiane Cantin, and Maurice Ratelle. "La Proclamation royale de 1763: le droit refait l'histoire." *Revue du Barreau,* vol. 49, no. 3 (1989): 317–43.

Bellico, Russell P. *Sail and Steam in the Mountains: A Maritime and Military History of Lake George and Lake Champlain.* Purple Mountains Press, 1992.

Bennett, Paul A. (ed.). *Books and Printing: A Treasury for Typophiles.* Savannah: Frederic C. Beil, 1991.

TRANSLATOR'S NOTE:
The asterisk indicates that quotations from these sources in the text are translations.

Berger, Thomas R. *A Long and Terrible Shadow: White Values and Native Rights in the Americas Since 1492*. Vancouver: Douglas & McIntyre, 1991.

Blanchard, David. *Seven Generations: A History of the Kanienkehaka*. Kahnawake Survival School, 1980.

Blouin, Anne-Marie. *Histoire et iconographie des Hurons de Lorette du xviie au xixe siècle*. Doctoral dissertation, Université de Montréal, 1987.

Boisvert, Aurélien. *Une Vallée de la mort attendait les Français*. Éditions 101, 1993.

——. *Prisonniers des Agniers*. Éditions 101, 1994.

Boiteau, Georges. *Les Chasseurs hurons de Lorette*. Master's thesis, Université Laval, 1954.

Boudreau, René. "Réflexions sur une réalité moderne à incarner: le traité préconfédératif de la nation huronne-wendat." *Recherches amérindiennes au Québec*, vol. 32, no. 1 (1993): 5–15.

Brown, George, and Ron Maguire. *Historique des traités avec les Indiens*. Ottawa: Research Division, Department of Indian and Northern Affairs, 1979.

Charbonneau, André. *Les fortifications de l'Ile aux Noix*. Méridien, 1994.

Clark, Bruce. *Native Liberty, Crown Sovereignty: The Existing Aboriginal Right of Self-Government in Canada*. Montreal: McGill-Queen's University Press, 1990.

Clarkson, Stephen, and Christina McCall. *Trudeau and our Times*. Vol. 1, The Magnificient Obsession. Toronto: McClelland and Stewart, 1990.

Clifton, James A. (ed.). *The Invented Indian: Cultural Fiction and Government Policies*. Transaction Publishers, 1994.

Coleman, Emma Lewis. *New England Captives Carried to Canada between 1677 and 1760 during the French and Indian Wars*. 2 vols. Portland, ME: Southworth Press, 1925.

Commission royale sur les peuples autochtones. *Partenaires au sein de la Confédération*. Introductions by the co-chairs, René Dusseault and George Erasmus. 1993.

*Côté, Louise, Louis Tardivel, and Denis Vaugeois. *L'Indien généreux. Ce que le monde doit aux Amériques*. Boréal and Septentrion, 1992.

Delâge, Denys. *Les pays renversé. Amériendiens et Européens en Amérique du nord-est 1600–1664*. Boréal Express, 1985.

———. "L'Alliance franco-amériendienne, 1660–1701." *Recherches amérindiennes au Québec*, vol. 21, no. 1 (1991): 3–15.

———. "Les Iroquois chrétiens des 'réductions', 1667–1770." *Recherches amériendiennes au Québec*, vol. 21, no. 1–2 (1991): 59–70, and no. 3 (1991): 39–50.

———. "L'influence des Amérindiens sur les Canadiens et les Français au temps de la Nouvelle-France." *Lekton*, no. 2 (1992): 103.

Deloria, Vine, Jr., and M. Lytle Clifford. *American Indians, American Justice.* University of Texas Press, 1983.

Desbiens, Jean-Paul. *Comment peut-on être Autochtone?* Secrétariat aux Affaires autochtones, Gouvernement du Québec, 1993.

Dickason, Olive P. *Canada's First Nations: A History of Founding Peoples from Earliest Times.* McClelland & Stewart, 1992.

———. *Le mythe du sauvage.* Septentrion, 1993.

Dickerson, Oliver Morton. *American Colonial Government, 1696–1765: A Study of the British Board of Trade in Its Relation to the American Colonies, Political, Industrial, Administrative.* Arthur H. Clark Col, 1912.

Dion-McKinnon, Danielle. *Sillery. Au carrefour de l'histoire.* Boréal, 1987.

*Dupuis, Renée. *La Question indienne au Canada.* Boréal, 1991.

Eccles, William John. *The Canadian Frontier, 1534–1760.* University of New Mexico Press, 1974.

Falardeau, Jean-Charles. *Ce qu'il est advenu d'une ancienne tribu de Sauvages canadiens: préhistoire, histoire et description contemporaine de la réserve des Hurons de Lorette.* Bachelor's thesis, Université Laval, 1939.

Fauteux, Aegidius. *The Introduction of Printing into Canada.* Montreal: Rolland Paper Co., 1929.

Filteau, Gérard. *Par la bouche de mes canons.* Sillery, QC: Septentrion, 1990.

Flexner, James Thomas. *Mohawk Baronet: Sir William Johnson of New York.* Harper & Brothers, 1959.

Forum paritaire—Québécois–autochtones. Manifesto of the Aboriginal and Québec Peoples' Equality Forum, 1993.

Fournier, Marcel. *De la Nouvelle-Angleterre à la Nouvelle-France. L'histoire des captifs anglo-américains au Canada entre 1675 et 1760.* Montreal: Société généalogique canadienne-française, 1992.

Fredrickson, N. Jaye, and Sandra Gibb. *The Covenant Chain: Indian Ceremonial and Trade Silver.* National Museums of Canada, 1980.

*Frégault, Guy. *La guerre de la Conquête.* Fides, 1955.

*——. *La Société canadienne sous le régime français.* La Société historique du Canada, 3 (1969).

Gaumond, Michel. "Premiers résultats de l'exploration d'un site archéologique à Sillery." *Cahiers de géographie de Québec,* no. 9 (Oct. 1960–Mar. 1961): 63–72.

——. "Une découverte spectaculaire." *Journal des armes, vol. 2, no. 1 (1980): 2–7.*

*Gérin, Léon. *La Seigneurie de Sillery et les Hurons de Lorette.* Mémoires de la Société royale du Canada, 2nd series, vol. 6 (1900): pp. 73–115.

——. *The Hurons of Lorette.* Transactions of Ottawa Literary and Scientific Society (June, 1900): pp. 69–92.

*——. "Le Huron de Lorette." *La science sociale suivant la méthode d'observation.* Paris: Librairie de Firmin-Didot. Vol. 32 (1901): pp. 334–60; vol. 33 (1902): pp. 312–42.

Grégoire, Pierre. "L'arrêt Le Procureur général du Québec c. Régent Sioui et al." *Recherches amérindiennes au Québec,* 20 (1990): 73–75.

Gros-Louis, Max, and Marcel Bellier. *Le "premier" des Hurons.* Montreal: Jour, 1971.

Hamilton, Milton W. *Sir William Johnson, Colonial American, 1715–1763.* Kinnikat Press, National University Publications, 1976.

Hubbard, R.H. *Thomas Davies in Early Canada.* Toronto: Oberon, 1972.

Jaenen, Cornelius J. *Friend and Foe. Aspects of French-Amerindian Cultural Contact in the Sixteenth and Seventeenth Centuries.* New York: Columbia University Press, 1976.

——. *Rapport historique sur la nation huronne-wendat.* Document submitted by Jacques Larochelle in Superior Court on 7 June 1994 to support a request by the Conseil de la Nation huronne-wendat, as applicant-claimant.

Jennings, Francis. *The Invasion of America: Indians, Colonialism and the Cant of Conquest.* Norton, 1976.

——. *The Ambiguous Iroquois Empire: The Covenant Chain Confederation of Indian Tribes with English Colonies.* Norton, 1984.

——. *The Founders of America: How Indians Discovered the Land, Pioneered in It, and Created Great Classical Civilizations; How They*

Were Plunged into a Dark Age by Invasion and Conquest; and How They Are Now Reviving. Norton, 1993.

Jennings, Francis, et al. (ed.). *The History and Culture of Iroquois Diplomacy: An Interdisciplinary Guide to the Treaties of the Six Nations and Their League.* Syracuse University Press, 1985.

Jetten, Marc. *Enclaves amériendiennes: les "réductions" du Canada 1637–1701.* Sillery: Septentrion, 1994.

Johansen, Bruce E. *Forgotten Founders: How the American Indians Helped Shape Democracy.* Harvard Common Press, 1982.

Josephy, Alvin M., Jr. *500 Nations: An Illustrated History of North American Indians.* New York: Alfred A. Knopf, 1994.

Kennedy, Patricia. "En quête des traités originaux. *L'Archiviste*, vol. 16, no. 6 (1989): 12–13.

——. "Des voix dans l'ombre." *L'Archiviste*, vol. 20, no. 1 (1992): 2–4.

——. "Treaty Texts: When Can We Trust the Written Word" *SSHARE–ERASSH*, vol. 3, no. 1 (1995).

Lacoursière, Jacques. "The Battlefield." In Jacques Mathieu and Eugen Kedl (eds.), *The Plains of Abraham: The Search for the Ideal,* pp. 75–105. Sillery, QC: Septentrion, 1993.

Le Moine, James MacPherson. "Le premier gouverneur anglais de Québec, James Murray." *Mémoires de la Société royale du Canada,* Section 1 (1890): 73–90.

Lightall, W.D. *La Corne St-Luc: The General of the Indians.* Montreal, 1908.

Lindsay, Lionel Saint-George. *Notre-Dame de la Jeune-Lorette en Nouvelle-France.* Montreal, 1900.

MacLeod, Peter. *The French Campaign of 1756 in the Lake Ontario Theatre and the Siege and Capture of Chouaguen.* Thesis, University of Saskatchewan, 1985.

Mahon, Reginal Henry. *Life of General the Hon. James Murray, a Builder of Canada.* London, 1921.

Major, Marothy, Eva. "Images historiques des premières nations du Canada." *L'Archiviste*, vol. 20, no. 1 (1993): 5–7.

Meinig, D.W. *The Shaping of America.* Vol. 1, *Atlantic America, 1492–1800.* New Haven: Yale University Press, 1986.

Miller, J.R. (ed.). *Sweet Promises: A Reader on Indian–White Relations in Canada.* Toronto: University of Toronto Press, 1991.

Ministère des Affaires indiennes et du Nord canadien. *Vous voulez savoir. Quelques réponses aux questions les plus souvent posées au sujet des programmes et des services destinés aux Indiens inscrit du Canada.* Approvisionnement et Services du gouvernment du Canada, 1991.

Morgan, Lewis Henry. *League of the Iroquois.* 1851. Rpt. Carol Publishing Group, 1993.

Morissette, Rodolphe. *Les juges, quand éclatent les mythes. Une radiographie de la crise.* VLB, 1994.

Morissonneau, Christian. "Huron of Lorette." In Bruce G. Trigger (ed.), *Northeast.* Vol. 15 of *Handbook of North American Indians.* Washington, DC: Smithsonian Institute, 1978.

Musée de la civilisation, *Rencontre de deux mondes.* Quebec City, 1992.

Patterson, Lisa. "À la recherche d'un traité de paix." *L'Archiviste*, vol. 16, no. 6 (1992): 14–15.

Philpot, Robin. *Oka: dernier alibi du Canada anglais.* VLB, 1991.

Proux, Jean-René, and Rémi Savard. *Canada: derrière l'épopée, les Autochotones.* Montreal: L'Hexagone, 1982.

Rapport de la Commission d'étude sur le contrôle parlementaire de la législation déléguée. Richard French and Denis Vaugeois, co-chairs. Assemblée nationale du Québec, July 1983.

*Ratelle, Maurice. *Étude sur la présence des Mohawks au Québec méridional de 1534 à nos jours.* Quebec City: Ministère de l'Énergie et des Ressources, 1991.

———. *Le "Two Row Wampum" ou les voies parallèles.* Quebec City: Ministère de l'Énergie et des Ressources, 1992.

Reid, W. Max. *The Mohawk Valley: Its Legends and Its History.* Rpt. Harbour Hill Books, 1979.

Richter, Daniel K. *The Ordeal of the Long House: The Peoples of the Iroquois League in the Era of European Colonization.* University of North Carolina Press, 1992.

*Sawaya, Jean-Pierre. *Les Sept Nations du Canada: Tradition d'alliance dans le nord-est.* Paper presented to the Royal Commission on Aboriginal Peoples, September, 1993.

Sévigny, P.-André. *Les Abénaquis: habitat et migrations.* Bellarmin, 1976.

Sioui, Georges E. (1989). *Pour une autohistoire amérindienne.* Quebec City: Presses de l'Université Laval, 1989.

———. *For an Amerindian Autohistory: An Essay on the Foundations of a Social Ethic.* Montreal and Kingston: McGill-Queen's University Press, 1992.

*———. *Les Wendats. Une civilisation méconnue.* Quebec City: Presses de l'Université Laval, 1994.

Snow, Dean R. *The Iroquois.* Cambridge, MA: Blackwell, 1994.

Stagg, Jack. *Anglo-Indian Relations in North America to 1763 and an Analysis of the Royal Proclamation of 7 October 1763.* Ottawa: Indian and Northern Affairs Canada, 1981.

Steele, Ian K. *Warpaths: Invasions of North America.* Oxford University Press, 1994.

Stone, William L. *Life and Times of Sir William Johnson.* 2 vol. Albany, 1865.

Sylvain, Philip. "Sauvegarde des traités conclus avec les Amérindiens." *L'Archiviste*, vol. 20, no. 1 (1992): 10–11.

Tanner, Helen Hornbeck (ed.). *Atlas of Great Lakes Indian History.* University of Oklahoma Press, 1987.

Toupin, Robert S.J. *Arpents de neige et Robes noires. Brève relation sur le passage des Jésuites en Nouvelle-France aux XVIIe et XVIIIe siècles.* Bellarmin, 1991.

Trigger, Bruce G. *Les enfants d'Aataentsic. L'histoire du peuple huron.* Montreal: Libre Expression, 1991.

Trigger, Bruce G. (ed.). *Northeast.* Vol. 15 of *Handbook of North American Indians.* Washington, DC: Smithsonian Institute, 1978.

Updike, Daniel Berkeley. *Printing Types: Their History, Forms, and Use: A Study in Survival.* Cambridge, MA: Belknap Press of Harvard University Press, 1966.

Vaugeois, Denis. "Le Québec, un creuset méconnu. *Mémoires de la Société généalogique canadienne-française*, vol. 39, no. 4 (1988): 277–90.

———. *Québec 1792. Les acteurs, les institutions et les frontières.* Montreal: Fides, 1992.

———. "Les Indiens et la Conquête." *Cap-aux-Diamants*, no. 41 (1995): 22–26.

Vincent, Sylvie, and Jean-René Proux. *Bilan des recherches ethno-historiques concernant les groupes autochtones du Québec.* 5 vols. Ministère des Affaires culturelles du Québec, 1984.

Vincent-Tehariolina, Marguerite. *La Nation huronne—Son histoire, sa culture, son esprit.* Pélican, 1984.

Viola, Herman J. *After Columbus: The Smithsonian Chronicle of the North American Indians.* New York: Orion, 1990.

Viola, Herman Jl., and Carolyn Margolis. *Seeds of Change.* Smithsonian Institute Press, 1991.

Waldman, Carl. *Atlas of the North American Indians.* New York: Facts on File, 1985.

White, Richard. *The Middle Ground: Indians, Empires and Republics in the Great Lakes Region, 1650–1815.* Cambridge University Press, 1991.

Winn, Fred. "General Jeffrey Amherst's Expedition: From Oswego against Montreal in 1760." *Eleventh Publication of the Oswego Historical Society* (1947): 19–24.

Wright, Ronald. *Stolen Continents: The "New World" through Indian Eyes.* Houghton Mifflin, 1992.

Recent works of interest

Anderson, Fred. *Crucible of War. The Seven Year's War and the Fate of Empire in British North America, 1754–1766.* New York: Alfred A. Knopf, 2000.

Delâge, Denis and Jean-Pierre Sawaya. *Les Traités des Sept-Feux avec les Britanniques. Droits et pièges d'un héritage colonial au Québec.* Sillery: Septentrion, 2001.

Münch, André. *L'expertise en écritures et en signatures.* Sillery: Septentrion, 2000.

Vaugeois, Denis. (ed.). *Les Hurons de Lorette.* Sillery: Septentrion, 1996.

Illustration Sources

Introduction
p. 10: National Archives of Canada [NAC], C-138082.

Part I
pp. 16–17: NAC, C-12248; p. 20: made from E. Raisz, State Education Department, Albany, NY; p. 22: D.W. Meinig, *The Shaping of America*, p. 209; p. 23: made from John A. Dickinson and Brian Young, *Diverse Pasts* (Toronto: Copp Clarke, 1995), p. 105; p. 24: NAC, C-874; p. 25: BNC, rare books collection; p. 26: NAC, PA 23376; p. 27: NAC, C-561; p. 28: Musée du Séminaire de Québec; p. 30: NAC, C-6217; p. 31: NAC, C-10547; p. 32: author's collection; p. 33: top: Library of Congress; bottom left: Joy Hakim, *From Colonies to Country* (Oxford: Oxford University Press, 1993), p. 24; bottom right: NAC, C-7220; p. 35: NAC, C-100609; p. 37: NAC, C-2433; p. 38: author's collection; p. 39: top left: State Library at Albany; right: New York Historical Society [NYHS]; bottom: *Johnson Papers*, vol. 6, frontispiece; p. 40: top: New York State Museum; bottom: D. W. Meinig, *The Shaping of America*, p. 127; p. 41: New York State Library; p. 42: top: *Nos Racines*, vol. 27, p. 536; bottom: *Johnson Papers*, vol. 3, p. vii; p. 43: brochure published by the State of New York, Office of Parks, Recreation and Historical Preservation; inset: Canada Post Corporation, 1986; p. 44: BNC, F 5065, P 68, v. 1; p. 45: top: BNC, F 5065, P 68, v. 3; bottom: ANQ-Q, 971.018, P 872, v. 2; p. 46: top: NAC, C-13319; bottom: author's collection; p. 51: NAC, C-34215; p. 54: MBAC 6271; p. 55: NAC, C-577; pp. 56–7: MACQ; p. 59: NAC, C-142422; p. 61: NAC, C-100375; p. 65: *Johnson Papers*, vol. 4, p. 222.

Part II

p. 68: top: Supreme Court of Canada brochure, 1993, p. 10; bottom: idem, title page; p. 69: Supreme Court of Canada brochure, 1988, cover; p. 72: top: NAC, C-113480; bottom: Bibliothèque de la Ville de Montréal, Gagnon Collection; p. 73: top: Collection Yves Beauregard; bottom left: Helen Hornbeck Tanner, *Atlas of Great Lakes Indian History* (Norman, OK: University of Oklahoma Press, 1987), p. 31; bottom right: Karlis Karklins, *Les parures de traité chez les peuples autochtones du Canada* (Ottawa, 1992), p. 67; p. 75: detail of a seventh-century document preserved at the Archives nationales de France with the title "Dessin iroquois, 1666," Série C^{11}E; p. 76: NAC, C-6975, detail; p. 78: idem; p. 79: *Cap-aux-Diamants*, no. 41, p. 26; p. 80: NAC, C-2726; p. 82: NAC, C-37828; p. 83: NAC, C-51653; p. 85: top: NAC, C-40367; bottom: Helen Hornbeck Tanner, *Atlas of Great Lakes Indian History,* p. 30; p. 86: NAC, C-6975, detail; p. 87: author's collection; p. 92: idem; p. 93: NAC, PA-32442; p. 95: top: author's collection; bottom: idem; p. 96: Archives du Séminaire de Québec; p. 100: author's collection; p. 106: top: Archives nationales de France, Fonds des Colonies, Série C^{11}A, vol. 9, fol. 43; bottom: *Johnson Papers*, vol. 6, p. 694; p. 107: top: NAC, C-135290; centre: NAC, C-135291; bottom: Alvin M. Josephy Jr, *500 Nations* (New York: Alfred A. Knopf, 1994), p. 279; p. 112: Supreme Court of Canada brochure, 1993, p. 11; p. 113: Supreme Court of Canada brochure, 1988, p. 23.

Part III

p. 128: top: Daniel B. Updike *Printing types. Their history, forms and use. A study in survivals* (Cambridge: The Belknap Press of Harvard University Press, 1966); bottom: *Cap-aux-Diamants*, no. 42, p. 23; p. 129: *Cap-aux-Diamants*, no. 41, p. 26; p. 131: author's collection; p. 135: author's collection; p. 137: NYHS; p. 139: University of Winnipeg, Western Canada Pictorial Index; p. 140: Library of Congress; p. 142: author's collection; p. 150: NAC, C-95525 p. 153: Marius Audin, *Le livre: son architecture, sa technique* (Forcalquier, Robert Morel Éditeur, 1969), title page; p. 155: Fournier, le jeune, *Manuel de typographie, utile aux gens de lettres...* (Paris, 1764), title page; p. 156: top: Audin, *Le livre: son architecture, sa technique...* p. 66; bottom left: Joseph-François Lafitau, *Mœurs des sauvages ameriquains...* (1724), vol. 4, p. 1; bottom right: Audin, *Le livre: son architecture, sa technique...* p. 67; p. 157: Arthur Davies, *Printed Jewish Canadiana 1685–1900* (Montreal, 1955), p. 47; p. 161: NAC, C-28211; p. 162: NAC, C-6042; p. 163: NAC, C-38948; p. 168: NYHS.

Epilogue

p. 170: *Johnson Papers*, vol. 9, p. 940; p. 171: top: *Nos Racines*, no. 28, p. 549; centre: MBAC; bottom: MBAC 6271, detail; p. 178: *Johnson Papers*, vol. 5, p. 30; p. 179: top: NAC, C-83514; bottom: NAC, C-83498; p. 181: Library of Congress; p. 182: idem.

Appendices

p. 194: top: NAC, C-135294; bottom: *Johnson Papers*, vol. 1, p. 260; p. 195: top: *Johnson Papers*, vol. 12, frontispiece; bottom: author's collection; p. 199: Joseph-François Lafitau, *Mœurs des sauvages ameriquains...* (1724); p. 201: Musée du Séminaire de Québec; p. 202: NAC; p. 207: E. J. Devine, *Historic Caughnawaga*, p. 207; p. 208: author's collection.

Original Document Discovered, 1996

The Murray "treaty" was found in the collection of notary B. Faribault, Jr., at the Archives nationales du Québec in 1996 during a search made for the lawyer David Schulze.

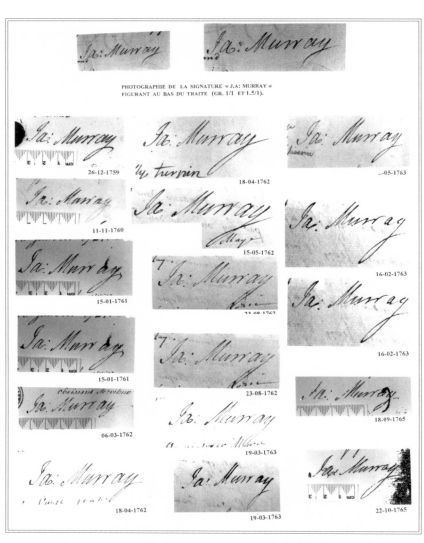

Specimens of J.A. Murray's signature appearing on documents dated between 1759 and 1765. See André Münch, *L'Expertise en écritures et en signatures* (Sillery, QC: Septentrion, 2000), pp. 137–49.

Photograph of the torn
upper-left corner.

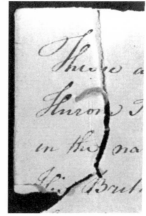

The match between
the torn corner and the rest
of the document.

The word "Garrisons" is spelled "Ganisons."

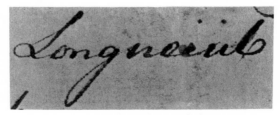

A word partially crossed out and replaced by "kindly."

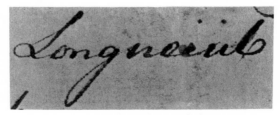

The second period is not inked
and the name is spelled "Longueiul."

On May 24, 1990, the Supreme Court of Canada gave the value of a treaty to the safe-conduct that Murray had issued to the Hurons on September 5, 1760. Curiously, the court neglected to verify the authenticity of the document that was submitted to it, and a modified version was accepted. Now, one question must be ask: in 1760, did the Hurons obtain "the liberty of trading with the English," or "the liberty of trading with the English Garrisons" in conformity with the original, or with Doughty's version, to which the court in fact had access?

Index